THE Education of a Typographer

Edited by Steven Heller

ALLWORTH PRESS
NEW YORK

School of
VISUAL ARTS

This book is dedicated to Louise Fili,
the most elegant typographer I know.

08   07   06   05   04   5   4   3   2   1

Published by Allworth Press
An imprint of Allworth Communications, Inc.
10 East 23rd Street, New York, NY 10010

Cover design by James Victore Inc.

Page composition/typography by SR Desktop Services, Ridge, NY

Library of Congress Cataloging-in-Publication Data
    The education of a typographer/edited by Steven Heller.
        p.   cm.
    ISBN 1-58115-348-1 (pbk.)
    1. Type and type-founding—Study and teaching.   2. Graphic design (Typography)—Study and teaching.   I. Heller, Steven.

Z250.E295   2004
686.2'2—dc22

                                                        2004002396

Printed in Canada

Contents

vi **Acknowledgments**

vii **Introduction: Teaching Typographic Fluency** Steven Heller

1 **Section One: Teaching Type**

2 **An Introduction to Typography for Students of Graphic Design**
Chuck Byrne

8 **Unlearned Typography** Allan Haley

10 **Teaching the Parameters** Paul Shaw

14 **The Pressure to Be *Branché*** Leslie Becker

17 **What I Have Learned about Typography. What I Teach.**
Denise Gonzales Crisp

19 **Typography: The Complete Education** Laura Chessin

27 **Voice** Hank Richardson

30 **Just Looking** Laurie Szujewska

35 **With Thanks to Leonard Jay: A Typographic Education** Caroline Archer

38 **The List** Geoffry Fried

42 **Teaching Typography: Integrating the Old and the New**
Introduced and compiled by Claire Hartten

52 **True Knowledge Derives from Knowing How to See** Huub Koch

55 **Concerns for Education in Today's Typographic Universe**
Michael Schmidt

77 **Section Two: Traditions and Conventions**

78 **What Is a Letter?** Johanna Drucker

91 **Fine Typography: Is It Relevant? How Can It Be Taught?** Terry Irwin

98 **The "Crystal Goblet" as a Teaching Tool** Shelley Gruendler

101 **Convention and Creativity in Typography** David Jury

108 **Back to Basics: Stopping Sloppy Typography** John D. Berry

111 **The Language of Letters** Max Kisman

116 **Type Casting** Steven Brower

123 **My Backward Step to Lettering** Art Chantry

125 **Section Three: Typographic Narratives**

126 **The Value of the Narrative in the Education of a Typographer**
Chris Myers

134 **The Letter as Such: Aleksei Kruchenykh as Closet Typographer**
Jared Ash

142 **Alef-Beit: A Typographic Journey** Martin Mendelsberg

146 **Charting a Course for Arabic Typography** Tarek Atrissi

151 **Section Four: Digital Literacy**

152 **Digital Type Decade** Emily King

160 **Learning Curves: Teaching Typography with the Computer**
Katherine McCoy

165 **The Newness in the New Typography** Teal Triggs

173 **Hearing Type** Frank Armstrong

179 **Section Five: Type Dialogues**

180 **How to See** Doyald Young

183 **If It's Good It Touches Me** Stefan Sagmeister

184 **Kerning at Twenty Paces** Michael Johnson

187 **Type Is for Reading** Jeffrey Keedy

191 **Negative Space** Keith Godard

193 **Attention to Detail** Nick Bell

195 **The Stroke of a Pen** Jonathan Barnbrook

201 **Using and Abusing** Ed Fella

203 **Section Six: Syllabi and Projects**

204 **Introduction to Typography** Instructor: James Craig

206 **Type One** Instructors: Martha Scotford and Tony Brock

230 **Type and Graphic Design** Instructor: Joseph Coates

239 **Experimental Typography** Instructor: Pablo A. Medina

242 **Visual Literacy** Instructor: Audrey Bennett

247 **Contributors**

255 **Index**

Acknowledgments

I am first and foremost indebted to all the contributors to this book for their dedication to design education.

Thanks also to my editors at Allworth Press for their hard work on behalf of this and my other books: Nicole Potter, senior editor, and Monica Rodriguez and Jessica Rozler, editorial assistants. Also, thanks to Gebrina Roberts for looking after the contributors, and to Tad Crawford for his continued and appreciated support.

Much gratitude goes to James Victore for this and other designs in the *Education of . . .* series.

Thanks to David Rhodes, president of the School of Visual Arts, for his continued cosponsorship of this series.

Finally, a warm embrace for my type mentor, Brad Holland, who, years ago, introduced me to the work of Herb Lubalin, my typographic hero.

Teaching Typographic Fluency *Steven Heller*

Teaching a student graphic design before teaching her type and typography is like teaching a baby to walk before she crawls. More to the point, it is like allowing a student the freedom to make Web sites before she scrawls—on paper. Type is the formal expression of writing, and writing is the physical representation of language. Type *is* the *lingua franca* of graphic design—a vessel that holds the codes that represent ideas that convey meanings that trigger understanding. Type is the single most important graphic design element, and typography is the most consequential course (or set of courses) a student can take as an undergraduate. Yet, recent evidence reveals—if portfolios are an accurate measure—that typography is simply not taught rigorously enough to achieve the necessary high level of linguistic fluency.

The reason is similar to when, during the 1950s, drawing lost favor in many American art schools with the advent of abstract expressionism. Academic curricula, rooted in the Greek concept that art is the vivid recreation of nature, required that drawing be taught as a foundation upon which painting and sculpture are built. Modernism, however, put more emphasis on interpretation, so that expressionism, cubism, and abstraction radically veered away from slavish recreation, thus demanding that art be taught as a process of inner discovery or rational analysis. Drawing from life was pushed to the sidelines, and has only recently returned. Likewise, in the age of the computer, learning to actually draw letters or compose type on a page by hand was deemed unnecessary, so students bypassed basic typographic apprenticeships, where they would have learned the subtleties of composition, and went directly to setting their own type, using programs like PageMaker, Quark, or InDesign. Yet, as everyone knows, even with automatic kerning functions, the computer does not allow for the nuances that can be accomplished with handset, or even machine-set, type—this comes from experience, not algorithms.

That so-called obsolete handcraft, acquired by setting type the "old-fashioned" way, actually taught students the idioms and vocabularies of type. Therefore, most students who lack such experience do not know why certain letterforms are harmonious with different weights or families, or why others are not. Today, rather than spec type based on an understanding of intricate formal attributes, students are routinely given an unlimited selection of classical and novelty fonts, then simply told to design with them as if they were putting together a jigsaw puzzle. While allowing students to play or experiment (and learn from their own mistakes) is not inherently wrong, without the proper foundation (indeed, without knowing the time-honored tenets), busting rules is problematic and, undoubtedly, redundant. A student must learn to follow rules "to the letter" (pun intended) before finding exceptions.

Of course, not every school is negligent in matters of typography, and not every student lacks typographic skill. Moreover, not everyone is expected to be a Jedi type-master. Even those students who receive the best education possess varying degrees of genetic typographic acuity. Some are simply born with the ability to make type "speak," while others, no matter how hard they try, do not possess the talent. Nonetheless, with current high enrollments in design schools, a decidedly larger pool of typographically substandard students is sent out into the world. A key reason is the increased burden on the typical design curricula to teach advanced software programs and new media, which, in some instances, has nudged out necessary type classes. These days, the typical graphic design student leaves school with a well-stocked portfolio and a résumé revealing a long list of computer skills, but very little understanding of the fundamental language and how to make it work.

Since graphic designers do not have to take a licensing exam before they enter professional practice, typographic proficiency is rarely tested before one leaves school. The senior portfolio is the only evidence of prowess. While a prospective employer at a design firm or art department can doubtless ascertain whether the student is *not* typographically fluent from this sampling, the converse is not always true, since the provenance of portfolio pieces is sometimes questionable (i.e., they could have been done by another or in collaboration with a better typographer).

On the Masters of Fine Arts (MFA) level, unless the student comes directly from a solid undergraduate school, typographic proficiency usually is surprisingly poor. If students do not receive rigorous instruction before they earn their undergraduate diploma, rarely will they improve on the job except when placed under the tutelage of a real type maven—which is rare. Although all designers give lip service to "loving" or "being passionate for" type, the bar of typographic fluency has been critically lowered ever since the computer made it easy to "choose" a typographic template. The word "choose", as opposed to "compose", may be semantic nit-picking, but it is key. The former means the designer selects from a palette of pre-digested options, while the latter indicates a greater degree of artful consideration.

The basic class critique theoretically should be the best way to weed out "default" typographers—those who allow the parameters of the software to dictate their aesthetic decisions—but even these teacher-student evaluations sometimes suffer from lowered expectations. When teachers reduce their demands and students produce less in the way of rigorous typography, the practice itself becomes devalued. This regenerative devolution of standards often rises to the level of professional status quo and simply perpetuates itself. Nonetheless, tough, frequent crits, built on a real knowledge of typographic tradition, yet broad enough to accept new approaches, are important in addressing deficiencies and encouraging students to spend hard time developing typographic expertise.

Arguably, the seeds of less rigorous typography were planted in the early nineties, when the desktop computer encouraged both serious and voguish experimentation (or what could be termed the "*New* New Typography"). In addition to the demand for digitized classical types, the very standard of legibility and readability was being challenged—on one hand, inspired by linguistic theories; on the other, encouraged by quirks and errors brought about by software glitches. Graphic design, in general, was in a predictable state of generational flux. While the resulting concoctions were not all bad—because skilled designers produced the most challenging typographic forms—those with less ability created faddish monstrosities. Of course, it was axiomatic that, in the short term, fads were more popular than worthwhile experiments, but by the end of the decade, things began to level out, and the centrality of fine typography was reestablished.

In addition to the new styles of typography, the computer gave graphic designers, as opposed to otherwise-trained typeface designers, the opportunity to create customized alphabets, often for use in their own magazine, poster, and book layouts. These faces were also distributed through "digital foundries" for others to use. Some foundries were serious hothouses, while others issued a few novelties before ceasing business. The longest-running and greatest contributor to late twentieth-century type was Rudy Vanderlans and Zuzana Licko's Emigre Fonts, the leading proponent of the new digital typography. It was followed by David Carson's type direction of *Ray Gun*, which established a visual code based on "distressed" typography. Both publications had incalculable impact on impressionable students by underscoring self-expression and rebellion. While many classically trained teachers continued to teach venerable standards, younger teachers proposed alternatives. And this was not all negative, either. But the new pedagogy did promote the typographic equivalent of teaching abstract expressionist art, because it rejected any method that seemed antiquated, including the valuable aspects of tradition.

All art forms, typography included, must go through an "anything goes" phase, leading to a winnowing phase, before old and new are incorporated into a "settled down" phase. By the end of the nineties, typographic excesses were receding in favor of reapplied modernist minimalism and neoclassicism. Type designers with deep roots, including Matthew Carter, Jonathan Hoefler, and Tobias Frere-Jones, issued smart revivals and contemporary iterations of faces with heritage. Even some of the more wildly radical experimenters returned to more traditional methods. The proverbial separation of the wheat from the chaff occurred in recent years, and currently, fine type design and typography are experiencing a renaissance—the most valuable by-product of which is a renewed appreciation for the nuances of type that can only be attained through rigorous education.

The Education of a Typographer, like other books in this series, is a detailed anthology of viable proposals and working concepts by various educators for current and future pedagogy. Unlike the broad strokes of *The Education of a Graphic Designer* (Allworth, 1998), this book takes a dedicated look at the most primal need of every designer: typographic fluency. The essays in "Teaching Type" address core concerns; there is a review of rules and regulations in "Traditions and Conventions"; lore and the legacy of type is the focus of "Typographic Narratives"; while "Digital Literacy" discusses new techniques and defines present and future requirements and options. Each *Education of . . .* book includes a generous sampling of syllabi and projects to be used as models for teachers and students, and to advise on possibilities related to their courses. But, most of all, this book is about teaching and learning formal, yet continually evolving, language(s). The efficient study of type and typography is an ongoing process that involves much more than knowing the names of a few typefaces. Fluency means having the confidence to make instantaneous responses. Yet, good typography does not happen with the flick of a switch. Fluency means having the ability to draw from a reservoir of knowledge and experience in order to make considered choices, which is the paramount result of a good education.

Teaching Type

An Introduction to Typography for Students of Graphic Design
Chuck Byrne

What Is Typography?
Typography is the considered arrangement of letters and words that conveys information and meaning.

The Purpose of Typography
Typographic communication can inform, document, persuade, entertain, or elicit a response.

The visual form typography takes can help gain attention, make an impression, and signal intent.

Where Type Is Found
Typography is associated with all forms of traditional print media, including books and other publications, advertising, forms, instructions, and packaging.

Type plays an important part in corporate branding, as well as in television, movies, and signage.

New forms of interactive design, such as multimedia, electronic games, and the Internet, also require typography.

How We See Type
Type is perceived through a complex physiological process: the brain processes information that is absorbed through our eyes.

The process of reading is a learned, flexible activity that changes over time and reflects the reader's culture.

The Evolution of Typography
History, culture, technology, and aesthetics all influenced the development of type and its use.

4000 B.C.
Early man draws and carves images on rocks and cave walls, and begins visual communication.

These marks are primarily pictographs, but are sometimes ideograms.

3000 B.C.–1500 B.C.

The need for record keeping precipitates the evolution of the first writing systems.

Marks made by Sumerians, using a wedge-shaped stylus on clay tablets, establish the visual character of *cuneiform*.

Both the Sumerians and the Egyptians begin *rebus* writing by using pictographs to create phonograms, which indicate sounds in spoken language.

Hieroglyphics is one of three writing systems used by the Egyptians, and is considered the first complete writing system.

Lines of hieroglyphs can be oriented in different directions, be quite decorative, be organized with grids, and be combined with illustrations.

The Egyptians not only carve their characters in stone, but also write with brushes and rush pens on papyrus (which they invented) and other materials.

The Phoenicians develop a true alphabetical system of writing, in which only sounds are represented by characters.

1800 B.C.–A.D. 1400

In Asia, the Chinese develop calligraphy, paper, printing, and moveable type.

1000 B.C.–A.D. 500

The Greeks adopt the Phoenician alphabet, which is the basis of what we use today.

In the hands of the Greeks, the visual character of the letterforms used in Western civilization evolves, and the direction of reading changes from *boustrophedon* to left-to-right.

The Greeks' use of hard reed pens leads to the appearance of *uncial-style* characters.

The Etruscan alphabet, which is based on the Greek, is adopted by Rome for use with Latin.

Serifs on characters are an outgrowth of the Roman process of carving stone inscriptions.

The selection of one of three kinds of Roman capital letters depends on the material used and its purpose.

The *codex* format, anticipating the modern signature of paper and made from parchment and vellum, begins to replace papyrus scrolls.

To accommodate changes in the language, letters are added to the Latin alphabet until the twelfth century, when the present twenty-six characters are reached.

500 B.C.–A.D. 1450

During the Dark Ages, monks in monastery scriptoriums produce thousands of beautiful illuminated manuscripts for the Church. Each manuscript takes about a year to create.

The characteristics of quill and reed pens, and the need for increased writing speed, precipitate the development of the *half-uncial* letter, leading to improved legibility and, ultimately, lowercase letters.

Manuscript pages often contain elaborate illuminated letters, and sometimes, calligraphy and illustrations combine to create images.

Carolingian minuscule script, with ascenders and descenders, is introduced and serves as the basis for our lowercase letters, but is soon combined with Roman capitals.

Secular illuminators and scribes form guilds and begin to work for the emerging merchant class.

A Gothic style of lettering, emphasizing the vertical stroke of letters and multiple columns, emerges. Illustration comes into greater use.

A.D. 1400–1800

The availability of paper, advances in metal technology and block printing, and demand for books sets the stage for the invention of moveable type.

Johannes Gutenberg develops the basic process for casting moveable type, and produces the first typographic books.

The production of printing rapidly spreads, and independent craftsmen prepare page-layout structures and illustrations for pages, as well as design typefaces.

The Italian Renaissance produces the first pocket-size book and italic type, along with elegantly crafted, legible typefaces.

While type is largely organized as a centrally located rectangle on a page, more elaborate schemes, such as the golden section, are sometimes used.

French type designers develop typefaces that continue to increase clarity and efficiency, and attempt rational typeface designs based on pure geometry.

Improvements in metallurgy, engraving tools, printing presses, and paper and ink make it possible to create typefaces with extreme stroke contrast that produce brilliant, clear pages.

Different versions of the points system of measurement come into general use.

A.D. 1800–1900

The birth of modern advertising leads to the use of large decorative wood display type. Sans serif and condensed typefaces come into use.

The Industrial Revolution brings automation and color to printing presses, photography is invented, and complex mechanical typesetting machines begin to replace handset type.

Several art and cultural movements lead to elaborate letterforms and dense, highly ornate pages.

A.D. 1900–2000

European artists and poets undertake free-form type experiments, and designers begin to take a rational, systematic approach to typographic layout.

Revolutionary Dutch and Russian aesthetic movements cause a shift towards an animated two-dimensional page space. Photography and typography are integrated.

In Germany, the new page space is combined with the quest for rational organization of information and typographic clarity, and new geometric typefaces are developed.

European designers emigrate and radically influence American design and type aesthetics, as well as design education.

Exploiting the freedom provided by photomechanical printing and type technology, designers combine the new page space with expressive typefaces and type compositions, and integrate type with illustrations and photography.

Rationalized, modular, gridded page space and ordered type families from Switzerland and Germany influence typography and design internationally, and provide the foundation for what becomes known as "information design."

Inexpensive desktop computers, combined with new digital type and page software, move typographic production from trade shops into the studio and become the vehicle for radical new typefaces and graphic design.

Interface and interactive design, and the World Wide Web, emerge as major new media, based primarily on typographic communications.

Type Terminology

A *typeface* is a specific design or drawing of the alphabet and various other associated characters in a series of standard variations.

The possible variations, or styles, and weights of a typeface are: Roman (or regular), italic, bold, demi, heavy, condensed, extended, and various combinations of these.

Type families are more elaborate hierarchical collections of variations of a typeface.

The basic typeface categories are: serif, sans serif, script, outline, shadow, text, and display.

Typefaces generally belong to loose historical and stylistic classifications, such as: Old Style, Italic, Transitional, Modern, Egyptian, and Sans Serif.

The various parts of an individual type character include: baseline, capline, meanline, x-height, apex, arm, ascender, bowl, counter, crossbar, descender, ear, fillet, hairline, leg, link, loop, serif, shoulder, spine, spur, stem, stroke, tail, and terminal.

Type characters can be: capitals or uppercase, lowercase, small caps, lining figures, old style figures, superior figures, inferior figures, fractions, ligatures, digraphs, mathematical signs, punctuation, accented characters, dingbats, and monetary symbols.

Other characters besides letters are used in typography: rules, dashes, boxes, dingbats, underscore, leader, bullets, ornaments, and borders.

In addition to serving as another term for a typeface, the word *font* also refers to an assortment of pieces of type in metal, the digital code, or outlines of a typeface for use with computers.

A standard font, of a single weight, of a typeface consists of a character set that includes an upper and lowercase alphabet along, with numerals, punctuation, and some special characters, symbols, and accents.

Expert fonts can contain items such as old style figures, small caps, fractions, and other special characters.

Many different measurement systems and terms are used with type, including: inches, points and picas, agate, didot, units, en, and em.

Different kinds of spacing in typography include: leading or line spacing, letter spacing, word spacing, tracking, kerning, line length, and column depth.

Type can be aligned in several ways: flush left/rag right, rag left/flush right, justified, or flush right and left, centered, asymmetrical, runarounds, contours, and tabular.

Paragraphs can be indicated in many ways: indention, paragraph spacing, hanging indent, and paragraph marks.

Marking how type is to be set and what corrections are to be made to proofed type is done using various proofreading marks and terms.

Using Type

Selection of a typeface depends on the purpose of the communication, its utility, and visual appropriateness.

Basic criteria for using type include the typeface, style, size, line length or column width, leading, alignment, and letter spacing.

The arrangement of type on a page can create a visual composition that can help communicate a message.

The arrangement of type on a page can provide an underlying visual structure or order to a page.

Contrasting typeface, style, size, and placement can establish a visual order, or hierarchy, that aids in communicating information.

The legibility of type involves the character and style of the typeface, the color and contrast of the letters in their surroundings, the size, letter spacing, line length, and leading of the type, and the distance and angle from which it is viewed.

Aesthetics of Type and Design

Type can be used as the sole means of communication in graphic design, be compositionally integrated with photography and illustration, or serve as an accompaniment to other media.

Graphic designers approach the use of type with different philosophies, history, training, and attitudes.

Different typefaces can imply various messages and reinforce various aesthetic approaches.

The arrangement of type can communicate different meanings, as well as control the way one reads.

While most typography is executed using precision tools and techniques, optical corrections are necessary to every aspect of type and typography.

Craftsmanship and attention to detail are an important part of typography.

Unlearned Typography *Allan Haley*

Perhaps typography doesn't have to be taught. Just maybe, all those courses that attempt to instill the canons of typographic design aren't necessary.

If you think about it, the craft of typography is little more than the combination of three very simple things: attention to detail, common sense, and visual acuity. Sure, there are typographic rules and guidelines, but they are, for the most part, just based on what is sensible and pleasing to the eye. Learning to identify the parts of a character may increase a designer's business vocabulary, and knowing the lineage of modern Garamond designs may aid in the choosing of a good modern revival of the face, but the real key to typographic success is basically "sweating the details" and a simple coordination of mind and eye.

Take, for instance, the typographic rule of avoiding all-cap headlines. It's one of the first typographic rules on an educator's hit lists. It's also one of the first rules professional graphic designers break. The tenet about not setting all capitals, however, is really based on little more than simple logic. Capital letters take up more space than lowercase letters—up to 30 percent more space. Headlines, subheads, and pull-quotes are about setting brief blocks of copy in a relatively small space. It's only common sense to use the most space-efficient letters: lowercase. Sure, there's all that stuff about how "word shapes" (made from ascending, descending, and x-height lowercase letters) help us read faster and how all capitals only create rectangles as visual identifiers, but just the fact that the little letters can pack more information than capitals into a given piece of design real estate ought to be enough reason to rely on them.

Correcting typographic widows and orphans is also just about making things look right, as is the rule about not cluttering the right edge of a column with a bunch of hyphens. Keeping word spacing tight and even is simply creating an inviting block of copy that does not have visually disrupting white-space gaps that also slow down the reading process.

Common sense and what looks good even apply to the basic issue of choosing the correct typeface. Some typefaces are better in one size than in another. One may be bad for lengthy text in a book or brochure, but good for short blocks of promotional copy. The best typeface for a particular occasion can depend upon its size, weight, or its position on the page. The best typefaces, however, are always those that are appropriate for the time, the reader, and the situation. Rules don't provide the answers here. All one has to do to make the correct choice is look at the design and think about how it will be used. If it looks right, it probably is.

Oh, it helps to know when to use an em-dash instead of an en-dash, or that "smart quotes" are preferable to foot and inch marks, but so much of what it takes to create good typography is just paying attention to the type.

Look at the headline after it has been set. Does it space well? Is it easy to read? Does it lead naturally into the text copy that follows? If there are more than two lines of copy, does the line spacing look even? Is the message enhanced by the typeface? Is the text copy inviting? Is it an even texture? If columns are set rag-right, do all the lines end in about the same place? If they are set justified, is the copy block free from ribbons of white running through it? Are the lines short enough, and is there enough line spacing so the reader won't read the same line twice? All are simple questions to answer—if the designer looks at the type, uses a little common sense, and sweats the details.

Okay. Typography probably should continue to be taught. An appreciation and understanding of the basis of good typography is a strong foundation to build on. But all the typographic education in the world is of little value if designers do not use a little common sense and look at the work they produce. The job is not done when the headline is dropped into the layout or the text copy is poured into a column. It is only complete when the designer has looked at the finished product—really looked at it—and made sure the type looks correct, is handled consistently, and makes visual sense.

Points, picas, line spacing, and kerning are only the mechanics. Software applications are just tools. It takes a concentrated effort to create typography. It takes common sense and a careful eye to create communication that is inviting, makes an impact, focuses attention, organizes information, and creates a mood—ultimately, giving life and personality to the printed word. It also takes the time and attention necessary to ensure that the job is done right—really right. That is what typography is all about. And that is what must also be part of any typographic curriculum.

Teaching the Parameters *Paul Shaw*

I am a self-taught calligrapher, lettering artist, typographer, and graphic designer—and a professionally trained historian. Since 1991, I have been teaching typography at Parsons School of Design, principally in the continuing education division, but also in the certificate degree program. Initially, I taught Type I, but for the past seven or so years, I have taught Type II (currently renamed Intermediate Typography) and, occasionally, Type III (or Advanced Typography). My Type II classes—running thirty hours in ten weeks—usually consist of students with varied and unpredictable backgrounds, such as those in the certificate degree program, foreigners who have graduated from design schools in Europe or South America, and professionals working in advertising agencies, graphic design and Web design studios, and newspapers.

My approach to the class has always been to intertwine practice, history, and theory—in that order. I put practice first, not only because it is what students in a part-time schooling situation desire the most, but also because I believe history and theory must play supportive roles. I use history to place current typographic practice in a continuum that extends back to the invention of the codex. Finally, theory is introduced as a means of better understanding the practices of the past and their continued relevance today.

By "practice," I mean analyzing the nuts and bolts of text typography, what I have come to refer to as its parameters: type style, case, type size, leading, line length, paragraphing, alignment, details, rules, ornaments, etc. I focus on text typography for several reasons: 1) it makes up the bulk of all typography done today; 2) it is often overlooked in graphic design programs in favor of display typography; 3) the advent of the personal computer, combined with page software programs and affordable fonts, have made teaching it practicable in a way that was not possible during the days of phototypesetting; and 4) my background as a historian and calligrapher have instilled in me a deep reverence not only for letters, but also for words and writing itself. My three typographic commandments are: respect the text; respect the reader; and respect the type.

I initially derived the idea to structure my class around the parameters of text typography, from Erik Spiekermann's "novel" about typography,

Rhyme and Reason. At the heart of my approach are Spiekermann's notions that the various aspects of text typography are all interrelated, and that "rules" about typography are not immutably fixed, but depend upon the situation. In class, we attempt to isolate the various parameters of text typography in order to see what role they play in readability (as opposed to legibility), and to what extent any traditional "rules" governing them— whether from Stanley Morison or Karl Gerstner—are valid. As we progress through the list of parameters, students discover Spiekermann's truth for themselves, as well as gain an understanding of the experiential roots of typographic "rules." At the same time, they learn how, when, and why the "rules" must sometimes be flaunted.

In juggling the parameters of text typography, students are forced to respond to the contents of a text, as well as its purpose and context. I provide them with a wide range of often mundane but real-life texts. They are often complicated texts that involve notes, glosses or commentaries, translations, bibliographies, and indices. These have included: a guide to insects, a dual-language cookbook recipe, a dictionary of saints, a foreign language bookseller's catalogue, a bus timetable, a law book, a science experiment, a health insurance application, instructions for defendants placed on probation, and a scholarly history of slavery. Texts about design, art, music, film, or other creative endeavors are studiously avoided to insure that the students do not treat the projects as excuses for self-expression.

My class also includes an exploration of display typography, whose parameters are, in reality, fundamental design precepts in a new guise: position, orientation, scale, negative space, balance, etc. It is here that the students are allowed more freedom for self-expression, as they realize that the traditional "rules" of typography have been formulated for text situations, and, thus, can be successfully challenged when they deal with display type. The projects assigned for this portion of the course tend to combine both text and display type needs: a hardware catalogue with an order form, a mail-order music company brochure, a museum exhibition poster, a calendar exploring different ways of visualizing time, etc. Imagery and color, downplayed in the text typography assignments, are essential components of these projects.

As the students explore the parameters of text typography, they are simultaneously introduced to the history of texts from manuscripts to printed books. History is used to show the evolution of current ideas about ways to structure and arrange texts through the increasing divergence of visual language from oral language over the past two millennia. Historical examples of typographic design are presented in context, so the technical limitations and achievements of the past, as well as cultural, political, and religious factors, are understood. The origins of many of the "rules" of typography are discovered alongside alternative practices that are no longer in favor. Past practice is not presented as a series of models to be copied, but as examples to be analyzed, learned from, and improved upon.

The historical component of the course also includes an examination of the development of the Roman alphabet from ancient Rome to the Baroque and the evolution of type styles from Gutenberg to Emigre. The calligraphic roots of Latin typefaces are stressed, as are the changing technological influences as type migrated from metal to wood to light to data. Although properly belonging to a Type I class, I devote considerable time to the discussion of typeface identification and classification (since many students require it). Various systems of classification are presented, but more emphasis is placed upon methods of identification than upon a particular system. Classification is viewed as a means of aiding identification by organizing and grouping features. Once again, I use history to support practice, because the examination of typefaces of the past provides a foundation upon which to choose and use typefaces today.

Theory is discussed as a means of more fully understanding historical practice, whether it is the allusive typography of Bruce Rogers or the new typography of Jan Tschichold. Current and older theories of typographical practice are tested as part of an exploration of how the various parameters of typography function. It is in this context that we discuss issues of legibility and readability, and confront the functional/informational purposes of typography versus the expressive/persuasive ones.

My approach to typography is principally nuts and bolts because I believe typography is, first and foremost, a craft. It is still something that needs to be learned, not just intuited.

Addendum

As a response to the drawbacks of cramming practice, history, and theory into a single-semester course, I have created a utopian, four-semester course in typography. Stretching out the teaching of typography for an additional three semesters allows for more reflection in discussions, sufficient time for completion of complex projects, and the addition of calligraphic and hand-lettering training as a basis for understanding the fundamental structures of typefaces. The presence of calligraphy in a course on typography is intended to familiarize students with the physical nature of letterforms and, equally as important, with the physical aspect of space in lettering (as counter, letterspace, word space, and line space). The goal is not to train calligraphers but to provide typographers and graphic designers with a deeper sensitivity to the nuances of letterforms, whether machine-made or handmade. A multi-semester course in typography also provides the necessary time required for an exploration of alternative traditions in Western typography, such as that of blackletter in German-language countries. Examining the blackletter tradition provides an opportunity to discuss the roles of culture, language, religion, and politics in typographic design and, ideally, offers new insights into the hidden assumptions and biases underlying our dominant Roman-based approach to typography.

The Pressure to Be *Branché* *Leslie Becker*

The French have a word they use to acknowledge stylishness, referring to an aura of being *au courant* in dress or appearance. The word *branché* translates, literally, to being "plugged in" or "connected." Teaching typography and designing typography courses have become increasingly complex as pressure to be *branché* increases. This has been especially true since typography "plugged in" (literally, to the computer), often needing a design choreographer to fashion its behavior over time. Text has become subject to previously unknown fancy and whim, resulting in the creation of images far more literal (though not necessarily legible) and far less vivid on the page than anything summoned to the imagination by a well-set passage from Proust. As a result, the camps have been divided.

Design programs continue to evaluate the place occupied by typographic studies and the content of those studies inside a graphic design curriculum. Pedagogical writings—too often doctrinaire—fail to acknowledge differences among institutional emphasis, programmatic emphasis, faculty talents, and historical and geographical positioning. There is no overarching curricular answer, but, rather, a series of questions regarding the teaching of typography, that have potentially large and complex answers. Nevertheless, the following questions can be addressed by most institutions and programs engaged in the education of graphic designers:

• What does your program do well?
• What kind(s) of designers are you trying to educate?
• Do you have the faculty to support pedagogical goals?
• Does your institution have a tight turning radius? If you determine changes in course content or structure are necessary, how quickly can changes be implemented?
• Do you view typography as an autonomous course of study?
• How much time do you have to teach the subject?
• Most importantly, but within your institutional context, what does it mean to be typographically educated? (Not *branché*, but educated. This means the ability to think and act well in a variety of currently unknown typographic circumstances.)

As a program explicitly defines what it does well, the faculty should project this question of focus into its future. Design programs inside large research universities often support a scientific approach to design. This might include emphasis on subjects like cognition and information design. Typographic problems within this context might be subject to usability testing. A private art and design college does not have a central, scientific mission and is more likely to approach typography in an intuitive, experimental way. At either of these two extremes, or anywhere between them, typographic relevance is typically addressed within a specific curricular context. It presumes that an institution is asking and defining what it can do well in a finite period of time. Answering the broader philosophical question about program emphasis clarifies the best use of limited time to teach typography.

The construction of typography as a course of study separate from graphic design raises questions about whether the ongoing separation is an artificial one. If graphic design is mostly characterized by the concurrent use of word and image in forming a communication, current technologies used to produce design may point to a time for typography to be subsumed by graphic design. Typography has remained apart from image for hundreds of years due to the original distinction between the process used to print type compared with the process used to reproduce images. As a result of the historical means of production, the study of typography was required to be separated from graphic design. This separation aided the focus required to master the details of typesetting. Additionally, it respected the separateness of place (the type shop) in which type was assembled and printed.

Though type and image are created now in mostly electronic forms using a single technology, this pedagogical separation lingers on. Some consider typography wholly different from graphic design as a major area of study. In fact, with current means of production, we might do well to revisit the separation. This requires the creation of a curriculum that, while not artificially separating graphic design from typography, provides a strong, detailed focus that denotes a thorough and competent knowledge of typography.

Typographic competency means understanding and mastering typographic behaviors. Different programs could prioritize or further customize the content list, according to their particular programmatic vision, whether or not typography was subsumed by courses called "graphic design." At least, the following genres of typographic behaviors would be addressed:

- Type as text: Type primarily conveys the thought and craft of the writer. It is invisible, seamlessly set, and optically even. Legibility is critical to this behavior.
- Type as information delivery: Type conveys detailed information, labels, identifies, and directs. Legibility is critical to this behavior.
- Type as image: Type conveys point of view and attitude. Legibility lives on the periphery of this behavior.

Typographic history also remains an important component of design education because it provides the soon-to-be practitioner with a way to think about the artifacts she or he will make in relation to the larger culture. Historical awareness reinforces the currently accepted practice of training a thoroughly engaged, reflective designer. What may be missing from most contemporary typographic histories, however, is the meta-history that evaluates cyclical behaviors of typographic invention and reinvention, rather than simply presenting a linear storytelling of who created what, and when. Understanding the life cycle of typographic preference helps designers put into context both the meaning and meaninglessness of styles and their reincarnations. A meta-history needs to assess patterns of bringing back into vogue something that has long gone out of style, and to assess how something reappears in design culture, influencing the tastes and choices of students. This is not about bending to student wants. It is about understanding faculty prejudices, formal knowledge domains, and typographic fashion.

Each program needs to routinely revisit its own typographic history in relation to what its typographic present is and what its future could be. Because styles collapse into history, being stylish does not equate with being educated. How much more *branché* could a designer be than to have the competence to influence the unknowns of the future?

What I Have Learned about Typography. What I Teach.

Denise Gonzales Crisp

As an illustration student in 1980, I observed my design peers as they carefully arranged rigid blocks of text amidst rectangles of flat color or photographic images. Compared with the paint I was learning to manipulate, the materials of design held little appeal.

Before art school, I was a type worker. I had done pasteup, and had mastered an IBM compositor and a photo headliner. After graduation, I took production jobs to help support my fledgling illustration career. I figured out how to spec type, mark up galley proofs, and even input code and text on the non-WYSIWYG screen of a massive typesetter that then issued near-complete layouts. The machines and systems proved mysterious and complex. The output did not.

Hoping to have the intricacies (and attractions) of typography revealed, I studied with a tutor who himself had learned under a master named Müller-Brockmann. On eight-by-eight squares, I did exercises in a methodology that led to precision and rational beauty (I suppose), yet failed to entice.

I didn't connect viscerally with type until 1985, when I sat before the tiny screen of a Macintosh computer. Having control over typographic minutiae and seeing words shift almost instantly on a virtual page was akin to wielding a juicy paintbrush.

I caught my first glimpse of *Emigre* magazine, which assembled pixels into surprising letterforms and playful visual statements. I was introduced to April Greiman's digitally generated experiments. Those bricks of text with which I had built pages on the Varityper promised now, on the Mac, to billow into clouds.

I learned that typography is light, incrementally malleable, and that letters can be liquid stitches.

In 1992, I had access to a letterpress shop, where I meticulously constructed lead words on a composing stick. If the Macintosh led me to infatuation with typography, setting galleys letter by letter awakened affinity. Designing pages constrained to ancient agates and coppers linked my process and product to that of every type composer, printer, and graphic designer before me.

I learned that typography is heavy, as heavy as thick volumes inked on iron letterpresses.

I went on to design nearly every kind of typography: magazines, annual reports, stationary systems, books, signage, pamphlets, and packages. For years, my approach to each was burdened by the fear that I was unwittingly transgressing immutable laws. Though I had been teaching typography since 1991, I somehow had not been able to identify the so-called rules. They loomed vaguely overhead.

Working under a few skilled designers, I discovered that these laws that so eluded me were just the slippery nature of taste. The laws were, in fact, secret passwords and salutations handed down through centuries of apprenticeship. Like choosing the correct fork or knowing when brown doesn't work with black, this taste is acquired only by immersion. It is pointed out by people who know, and who slyly fix the fine line between restraint and tedium by example and signal.

I learned that typography is discrimination, and that such sensitivity to refinement determines one's position in the professional, if not social, pecking order.

In graduate school, I looked to typography to enlarge design—not for self-expression, but for extra (!) other (...) expression. I manipulated the form of my own words, and designed my own writing instead of that of copywriters or journalists. I confess that I got confused, and was not sure when my words should dominate or when the form I gave them should hold sway. I was smitten by both, so I determined that any attempt to separate them would be cruel.

I learned that typography is word love.

Are lightness and heaviness and tastefulness and tenderness the essence of good typography? Yes, and not quite. Typography is the form of words, and words cannot be present without form, and form is never not present. This interdependence predisposes all typographic form to meaning.

Typography's myriad functions and attributes can only be placed within this inescapable context: the forms of all words always transmit meaning (and do so in spite of us). All typographic forms tell past, present, regional, technological, or doctrinaire stories. To glibly toss off any line of type is to be cynical about the designer's role in the manufacture of meaning.

In this light, the typography of casino coupons might be as important as the typography of books on Greco-Roman history. Pragmatically, of course, we have to distinguish between what matters less and what matters more. To the lesser concerns, a good typographer responds with the sensitivity of a master craftsman. To the greater ones, she responds with the invention and conviction of a performer crafting a tale.

Typography: The Complete Education *Laura Chessin*

In the late 1970s, the beginning of what I thought would be a five-year course in architecture at Cornell included a one-credit Intro to Architecture lecture class, a sort of orientation to the next five years of our academic life. The entire freshman class crowded into an aging lecture hall, a steep amphitheater with wooden seats worn smooth by generations of art, architecture, and planning students. Hinged to the seats were book rests, scratched and scarred by decades of scribbles and note making. A massive plaster cast of Zeus stared vacantly out from a front corner of the room.

Two pronouncements from the first few days stand out clearly. The first was that we could expect one of the highest attrition rates of any program in the university. The second was that the academic discipline of architecture—regardless of our ultimate career path—provided among the most rigorous and complete foundations in creative problem solving, integrating arts with technology, history, sociology, philosophy, and psychology.

As much as I was ready to purchase whole the latter statement, I didn't make it past the first year in the program, as I quickly began to spend less time in Rand Hall, the architecture studio, and more time in Franklin Hall, the fine arts building. At eighteen, I was less interested in conceptual possibility than I was in the tangible—the smell of paint and turpentine, the application of color on paper, the marking of tools on a page, or a metal printing plate.

As luck would have it, I was drawing in my dorm room one evening with my door open, when another resident in the hall poked his head in, peered over my shoulder, and invited me to join the production team on a start-up tabloid weekend alternative to the local Gannett-owned daily. On my first day of work, I learned how to shoot photostats and run the headliner for 36-, 42-, 60-, and 72-point type. This required the operator to exercise some finesse in visual judgment by placing one character of the headline at a time in the viewfinder before exposing that letterform onto the film. Kerning was a matter of guesswork and luck, but inconsistencies could be corrected in the pasteup. Along with the IBM Selectric Composer, setting galleys of news articles with a metal golf ball, stamping characters in Univers and Times Roman in 10- and 12-point type, this was my introduction to typography.

Later that year, I heard rumors of a metal type shop in the basement of my dormitory. After searching in vain for the key to the padlock, the resident assistant led me down through the dank subbasement of the building, and proceeded to break open the padlock with a hacksaw. The shop had been abandoned for at least a decade, but there was still a decent bank of type cases, with assorted tools for composition, and a usable Vandercook press. I was struck in much the same way one might experience infatuation in the early stages of true love. I was fascinated by the remarkable recognition of the cool physical object cast in lead in the palm of my hand—the sharp edges of the letterform against my skin—as a facsimile of the same two-dimensional character I might set from a filmstrip image, exposed onto photo paper, later that night at the newspaper.

While completing a degree in photography, I continued to help pay my way through school as a production artist, first for *The Ithaca Post*, then for the university administration's newspaper, and, later, a local weekly arts tabloid, *The Grapevine*. After graduation, I maintained my position in the production department of *The Grapevine*, and recognized that I was not only satisfying my creative itch, but I was also learning a marketable skill that would allow me entrance to anywhere the printed word was produced. To this recent college grad with a BFA, this was the ticket to anywhere I wanted to go.

Had it been just the craft of drawing out a sketch, and the game of marking up copy to fit the comp as accurately as possible, or the mar-ketability of the skill, I would probably have been compelled to stick to my original plan and pursue a career as a photojournalist or filmmaker. The physicality of type would not have sustained my excitement if I hadn't been able to draw a connection to the intellectual stimulation a career the published word would provide. In typography, I saw the perfect marriage of the beautifully crafted physical object with the limitless world of ideas. I suspected my choice to abandon a career in architecture had inadvertently led me to another discipline that promised an equally rich core education: one that would provide a lifetime of exploration into the connections between art and technology, and the role of the humanities in modern life.

The following two decades provided continued opportunities to refine my craft: from a freelance career in Boston to the completion of a master's in graphic design at RISD to a successful design practice in western Massachusetts. Gratitude to my teachers continued to deepen through my own professional practice, sustained by a solid formal and analytical foundation and the confidence to think for myself and develop my own aesthetic. Recognizing the continued role mentors played in my ongoing professional development, I was drawn to consider a career in teaching as a way to "give back" to the profession I found so rewarding, as well as to honor my own teachers.

In Defense of Craft

The courses I teach include all levels of type, from introductory classes for sophomores to intermediate and advanced classes for juniors and seniors, publication design for juniors, thesis development for grad students, and a general creative problem-solving class for sophomores called Visual Fundamentals. In a recent Visual Fundamentals class, students were cramming for a Type I class with homemade flashcards displaying a set of characters on one side and the name of the font on the other. I heard from across the room, "New Baskerville," and my antennae shot up. "Oh no," I thought, "not that." When I asked if this was the "cut" of Baskerville they had been studying, they looked confused. "Cut?" "Is there some other Baskerville?" At the risk of making either myself appear to be a tyrant or the other instructor—an adjunct, and recent MFA—look bad, I offered a brief lecture on type design and history.

Later, I wrote the following letter to the instructor:

> *A note on something I've observed in speaking to Type I students: I've noticed students referring to "New Baskerville," as if this were THE "correct" name for Baskerville. Please be advised that this face was a "redesign" of the more classic and elegant cuts that remain true to the nature of John Baskerville's original drawings. ITC's New Baskerville may not be the best example of transitional style of type for beginning students. Compare this with Monotype's design. One thing you might want to consider in selecting fonts for study is avoiding as examples the odd "redesigns" of the '70s and '80s, when beautiful classic fonts were redesigned to look "new" and "modern." This was an unfortunate (or unusual, in any case) period in the history of type design. Compare this with the big, big hair of the '80s or the super-wide bell-bottoms and bubble graphics of Peter Max in the '60s.*

Please understand that this is not a criticism of your teaching. I tend
toward the belief that teaching good visual judgment to a designer begins
with such small details as the counter of a letterform, or the proportion of
x-height to character width.

I mailed this wondering if I had just alienated a new educator, hoping he
would take it in the spirit in which it was sent.

In every type and publication design class, I find myself several
times throughout the semester repeating lectures on type design and selection. With so much to think about, from mastering the software to the real
conceptual problem solving, students learning this language of typography
need to be reminded that a vital part of the design is making informed
choices: Bembo, Minion, or even Palatino over Times Roman; Futura, if
they are attracted to the geometry, over Avant Garde, pointing out how the
excessively open counters and exaggerated x-height of the latter create an
undesirable flicker, like a lightbulb with a short circuit. Sometimes
teaching is less pedagogy, and more the opportunity to share my passion
for enjoying the beauty of a single letterform, and to see the sublime complexity of the system: an entire alphabet. My pedagogical style is based on
the intention that they learn to appreciate the study of typography as an
education in discernment and judgment, and a discipline that exercises
both intuitive and analytical parts of our being—an integration of both
right brain and left brain.

I often draw an analogy from type design to the design of a violin
because I live with a violin maker, and I have struggled with my own
attempts at proficiency as a player. (I teach by analogy—more from intuition than conscious effort—given that I find great pleasure in how one
experience of my life informs or gives meaning to another, and I hope to
promote this attitude of learning with my students.) The violin is an
instrument that reached its most highly refined state by the mid- to late-
seventeenth century. Current violin makers still hold the Cremonese
makers up as the models upon which their own instruments are built.
Modern makers have created radically new shapes, both electronic and
acoustic, but the acoustics and craftsmanship of a Stradivarius or Guarneri
are unrivaled. It is an easy comparison to make with the elegant cuts two
centuries earlier by Nicolas Jenson or Francesco Griffo.

This makes for delightful storytelling about the development of various forms and styles throughout history. Still, an integral aspect of the

beauty of a typeface is how well it functions: how it appears on the page in terms of color and visual activity, and how well we are able to read it in terms of legibility. Teaching a student to recognize the difference between an ITC Garamond with compromised legibility and Slimbach's cut for Adobe is an excellent exercise in legibility, style, system design, and aesthetic theory. I include these previous examples in side-by-side comparisons with Stempel Garamond, Simoncini Garamond, Garamond 3, and Sabon, and suggest to my students that they never again choose indiscriminately whenever Garamond happens to appear in their drop-down font style sheet.

In the art of violin making, beauty and function are equally interlocked. A precious instrument not only displays a luminescent varnish and sensuous outline; it rings with warmth, clarity, and a complex blend of overtones. A well-crafted instrument should exhibit a consistency of tonal qualities from the lowest to the highest string. But, equally important in the performance of an instrument is the player. A fine musician can make even a mediocre instrument sing with richness and subtlety in the same way a great typographer can make even a marginally tasteful face appear lovely and entirely appropriate on the printed page.

The education of a typographer has much in common with the formal training of a musician. I willingly discuss my own attempts at formal education with the violin after years of playing Irish and Old Time fiddle tunes, learning almost exclusively by ear. I use formal training in an instrument as a tangible metaphor for an academic study of typography. Both require that the student bring strong intuition—a gift we're born with—and both demand a focus, a solid base of knowledge of history and style, and a careful attention to exercises and studies that build technical proficiency.

Reading music requires us to learn a new language of key, patterns, time, and rhythm. For an adult fiddle player who relies almost solely on intuition, it can be laborious and exhausting to ask the brain to override old habits and apply conscious attention to so many details: bowing patterns, time, physical posture, and the notes as written. Intonation—one of the crucial skills of a violinist—is the ability to play in tune. This requires both the facility to discern if a note is flat or sharp, and the physical hand memory of exactly where the finger should be on the fingerboard to create that note. Very few are born with perfect pitch. For all of the rest of us, it requires daily practice and a good teacher to "develop the ear."

By the time I see most students as sophomores or juniors, they have already developed an intuitive sense, as well as a proven skill in visual mark making. Drawing skills are required for admittance into the program. So, when it comes to asking students—based on examples provided—to accurately render certain letterforms, like a Bembo and Caslon capital *A*, I ask them to be able to discern the subtleties. I ask them to carefully represent proportion (height to width, or placement of crossbar) and accurately reproduce the thick/thin relationship and serif structure. Drawing, for the beginning student, is not so much a test of one's ability to render as the ability to look closely, judge, then accurately present on paper their assessment. Drawing letterforms and drawing out their names in capitals with optically even letterspacing is the visual equivalent of "developing one's ear."

Focus attention to the parts as they relate to the whole—the proportion of the page—of a poster. All of the more complex problem solving is based on a very sound and refined sense of visual judgment. I owe it to my students to help them understand that attentive study of form and history is more than just an archaic academic rite of passage—especially now, when setting type is so easy and designers have more control than ever in how we are able to arrange type on the page. A music student practices scales not solely for the love of the exercises but in order to be able to play music, to bring a personal and heartfelt interpretation to the performance of a written piece, or to creatively and spontaneously improvise on an idea or theme. I try to impress that, ultimately, it is to produce more original and creative expression that we need command of our craft—to have more freedom, not less.

If I've lost them with my comparison to music—some may have never picked up an instrument in their life—I draw from any number of analogies in an effort to breathe life and energy into the foundations of typography. Learning to drive is an excellent example of how judgment is the product of careful observation and experience. Skiing can work as a metaphor in talking about counterintuitive responses.

In the end, whether or not they've been able to respond to the comparison with high Renaissance achievement in the arts, the ground has been prepared before they begin to address more advanced typography issues of content development, research, and personal expression. They've been exposed to the idea that type is not only a highly refined (and transcendent) craft, but also a discipline in the realm of a much greater study of the advances and the history of the Western world, especially in today's world, with the violent clash of Western culture and Islamic culture. It is crucial that our students recognize that the very alphabet with which they have learned to be literate beings has its formal and philosophical foundations in the Roman Empire, and that Islam has roots in a very different language system and set of beliefs and laws. Along with the rules of society and government by which we live, this legacy of the Roman alphabet is but one institution of language, culture, and philosophy. Language, the means by which we communicate, is a key to recognizing these differences.

Breaking Silence

I have a friend, a novelist, who claims that she finds the mere appearance of text on the page to be one of the most pure and beautiful visual expressions. I asked her if it was the color and texture of the printed matter, or the actual words, with the promise of the rhythms and nuances of human speech, and the ideas and experiences behind the language. She said it was both.

Teaching typography at all levels allows me to incorporate an appreciation for all of these things: the pure formal beauty of a letterform, and the system of letterforms we refer to as a font, and the precision and depth to which we can express our ideas, opinions, experiences, and feelings. More than once, I've sat with a student and discussed a solution to a project, and listened to an idea or opinion expressed verbally but missing in the solution to the assigned problem. When I've asked them why they haven't said with their project what they've just said to me informally, I've heard, "I didn't know I could do that."

Ultimately, typography education teaches us how to use language: Not just how to form a message, but to form an idea. In more advanced classes, as much as I continue to emphasize the development and understanding of craft as an activity that continues throughout professional life, I introduce research as the means by which we make the connection between who we are as individuals and who we are as professionals.

An assignment for my spring Type III class asks students to create a poster raising public awareness of an issue of social justice. I created this project to coincide with the university's school for social work's Social Justice Week celebration, which includes lectures and public events, including an art exhibition open to all students and faculty. The project not only continues to provide an opportunity for personal expression, but opens the classroom to discussions ranging from how to define social justice to how our "voice" or the "tone of our voice" affects how the message is received. The project requires the student to present not only a historical perspective of the issue, but also an appreciation of how this issue is commonly received and what the barriers to greater understanding might be. For many, this project gives them—some for the first time in their educational experience—permission to express an opinion in a way that may be controversial and most certainly will expose some piece of who they are outside the classroom.

As an educator, I often think about a statement I heard when I was a student: that architecture provides a complete foundation for any profession demanding creative problem solving. I've since come to realize that this can be easily applied to any number of disciplines, and that the responsibility lies as much with the teacher as with the subject. I've heard a friend who teaches circuit design in an engineering program speak of the aesthetics and beauty of good design. A biologist I know is credited with an innovative and creative approach to science that has produced breakthroughs in the understanding of how insects can be the source of data collection for air quality and potential environmental hazards.

A typographic problem can provide an entrée into almost any conceivable discipline, with the goal of translating complex ideas into a clear and appropriate form of communication, whether sequential and special (as with a geological diagram or a map), conceptual or literary (a poster for a play or political statement), or purely informational (a transportation schedule). All disciplines have an extremely specific language and a range of methodologies. Typography is no exception. If a student leaves the classroom with the confidence to control the formal composition on the page, the insight to look deeply into a problem, and the courage to speak out and think for herself (or himself) then we've done our job as educators.

Voice *Hank Richardson*

I use the term *play*, but I mean coping with the problem of form and content, weighing relationships, and establishing priorities. Every problem of form and content is different, which dictates that the rules of the game are different, too.
—Paul Rand, "The Play Instinct," *Graphic Wit*, 1991

Years ago, when I was a college student, I couldn't fathom how I could hate my art history class so much, considering my love for art history. As I struggled to stay awake while memorizing slide after slide, I thought, "There's got to be a better way." And I vowed then that if I ever had the opportunity to teach—which was not, incidentally, in my plan—I'd find one.

Fast-forward thirty years, past careers in advertising and design and, later as (yep), an instructor in those areas. I'm president of Portfolio Center, and still teaching a few courses I refuse to hand over to anyone else, even if it means holding classes at 5 A.M. I teach the classes students are afraid of, the subjects that sound boring and overwhelming all at once— like Modernism, History and Criticism, and Publication and Editorial Design. Both employ, to an enormous extent, the study of typography.

I've been teaching those classes for over ten years, and I challenge anyone to find a single student who would say he was ever bored in my class— tired, perhaps, but never bored. In my classes, the students are the teachers. They teach each other. They must be fully engaged with the assigned material because they're charged with imparting that information to their classmates.

It becomes a kind of competition, really, as the students attempt to one-up each other with visuals, activities, or (sometimes shocking) performances. Plays, videos, finger painting, yoga—the things they come up with! Once, a student did a parody of the Larry King show. As a result of this infectious interaction, students remember what they learn, and, at the same time, gain invaluable presentation skills and confidence.

In the publication class, I have an exercise I dreamed up to illustrate the impact created by choices in typography. I use as the text an old annual report considered revolutionary for its dynamics of color, impacting scale, and, most importantly, its ability to use typography to tell a story in its best sense. Over the years, we've had many visitors drift in and out of this class who like to recount what they witnessed. One such guest was my friend, designer John Bielenberg, who described the experience this way:

I was instructed to arrive at the class by 6 A.M. (Made even worse for me because I was still on West Coast time.) I'd never seen this "boot-camp" technique used in a design program before.

I arrived about a half hour late. The class, in the Portfolio Center "basement" near Hank's lair, was already sitting at a big table covered by books, papers, bagels, and cups of coffee.

About 6:45 A.M., in the middle of a discussion about Marshall McLuhan, Hank got up quickly from his chair and swept all the stuff off the table, including bagels and coffee, with his arm. He then pointed at three sleepy students and barked, "You, you, and you—up on the table!" and handed a copy of the 1993 Chicago Board of Trade annual report, designed by Dana Arnett at VSA Partners, to one of the guys on the table.

"Read the cover," said Hank. It was tabloid sized, all white, with one word centered in the middle. Annual report as theater?

"Open," said the student.

"Is that really how it looks?" asked Hank.

"Open," said the student, slightly louder.

"Louder," said Hank.

"Open!"

"LOUDER!"

"OPEN!"

"Good," said Hank, as he grabbed the annual report and handed it to the next student on the table.

This went on for a dozen spreads as each student read the text like they would at a casting for a play, pushed along by Hank acting as the demanding director.

This is all happening before 7 A.M. on a Friday morning.

I'd bet none of the designers present will ever forget typography has a "physical" voice, not just a position on a page.

Type has volume and pacing, depending on how it is set and composed by the designer.

Thin,

thick,

big,

small,

caps,

lowercase,

serif,

sans serif,

black,

colored,

reversed,

letterspaced,

leaded,

pushed to the top of the page or centered.

> *Each decision plays a role.*

> *It was certainly the most dramatic type lesson I'd experienced, even if it was perhaps staged for my benefit.*

Well, John should ask my assistant, Claire, whose office adjoins our class space, and who's had to endure for many a quarter the moans and groans elicited by this exercise; it was not staged. Countless students, long before John's visit and long since, have been traumatized and illuminated by such theater classes.

Or, he could talk to a later student, Eleanor Dickinson, who might have been the most reluctant individual I've ever tossed onto that table. In one of those ironic twists of fate, Eleanor, a designer, now works for VSA Partners, where Dana Arnett is a principal. She remembers the morning of her performance this way:

> *I was totally embarrassed. I would have avoided the exercise if I could have—"My throat hurts . . . I have a headache . . . I can't read." It was a way to get the shy ones noticed. It was also a way to get the "party" started—and kind of like* Dead Poets Society, *when Robin Williams makes Ethan Hawke recite a poem in front of the class, and then says, "Don't you forget this." (For the record, I don't personally like that comparison, but, as the architect Philip Johnson once suggested, "Originality comes from something that looks like something else.")*
>
> *And that's the great thing about the exercise—that I will never forget it. It is one of those events that carries more meaning than meets the eye and the ear. Whether the person standing on the table turns to the quietest page or the noisiest, she will be heard, and the page will be realized.*

Finally, I'd like to note that because it's the primary tool for communicating a message, a thorough grasp of typography is the most crucial thing a designer can acquire. As an educator, I believe it's my duty to get this idea across to my students in a way that is meaningful, memorable, and moving. After all, imagination comes from things that move you.

Just Looking *Laurie Szujewska*

The study of typography begins with looking: Looking at words, looking at type used to set words, looking at the interactions of letter shapes in words, and looking at the arrangements of words in space. To put it another way, the study of typography relies upon seeing the visual and rhetorical relationships of shapes in space.

How does one learn to look in this way?

For me, it began while I worked in a bookstore after graduation from college, when I came across a little book called *About Alphabets*, by Hermann Zapf. Here was a more elaborate investigation of looking at letterforms than I had experienced in my journalism undergraduate studies. I also found a paperback copy of *Manuale Typographicum* by Zapf that helped me look at letters for the sheer joy of their forms and patterns. After that initiation, I began a lifelong hunt for books on typography and design, frequenting new and used bookstores, and, soon, discovered two compendiums of typographic works by Joseph Blumenthal—*The Printed Book in America* (Godine, 1977) and *The Art of the Printed Book* (Godine, 1973). I also stumbled upon *Pioneers of Modern Typography*, by Herbert Spencer (Lund Humphries, 1969) and *Jan Tschichold: Typographer*, by Ruari McLean (Godine, 1975).

If, like me, you like to touch things, the images of typography in these compendiums will make you eager to get your hands on original works. In my case, I went to the Newberry Library in Chicago and, later, to the rare book rooms of the New York Public Library and the Beineke Library at Yale University. While these collections are among the best, you should be able to find collections of rare books in most urban public libraries, where even the smallest selections will often yield extraordinary typographic works. My method was then, and still is now, to simply look up in the card catalog whoever I was in admiration of at the moment. Shortly afterward, a stack of wonderful books was placed before me.

Typography's history is intertwined with that of printing and imaging. Whether the medium is a piece of paper, the computer screen, a celluloid or digital film sequence, a billboard, or a museum exhibition wall, each has a set of limitations that enhance or degrade a particular typeface. Many typefaces are constructed specifically for use in a particular medium.

My early passion for typography initially led me to a job in the printing industry as a print broker. This gave me an opportunity to work with plate makers, silk screeners, die cutters, Web- and sheet-fed printers, engravers, and typesetters—all provided invaluable exposure to the limitations and advantages of working with type in the print medium.

I also began a study of the history of writing and printing. There is no better way to understand why typefaces look the way they do, and how they have evolved with innovations in the printing process. For example, in the 1490s, the great printer and scholar Aldus Manutius based some of his typeface designs on the chancery cursive writing of the time. Later, in the 1750s, John Baskerville derived his typeface from his own handwriting and skill as an English roundhand writing master. He invented wove paper and special printing ink to accommodate the contrast in the thick and thin elements of his design.

Because I take an experiential approach to learning, I began studying chancery script writing with calligrapher Jeanyee Wong. Learning a writing hand aids in understanding how letterforms are created with a writing instrument and how letter shapes interact. I came to, see also, that many typeface designs are extensions of contemporary handwriting styles, as was the case with Manutius and Baskerville. This knowledge helps in choosing and using the many calligraphic typefaces now available as digital typefaces.

The most important thing a typographer must understand is how the visual and rhetorical relationships of type are changed through its location within a space. For me, that meant buying a letterpress machine to get the hands-on freedom of working with metal letterforms. I found an old Vandercook press and began purchasing old foundry and wood types at auctions or from print shops that were happy to get rid of obsolete type. Working with the press introduced me to the idiosyncrasies of hot typesetting, as well as to the origins of typesetting terminology. Most importantly, it provided me with a visceral experience of letterforms as shapes and sculpture moving in space. Today, the personal computer—the printing press and typesetting machine of our time—provides a good laboratory for playing with type at little cost, but it will not help you understand the origins of printing and typefaces. If you are so inclined, get your hands on an old letterpress, or find a public letterpress facility, such as the Center for Book Arts in New York, or San Francisco's Center for the Book. Many universities have letterpresses in their art departments.

One of the challenges of working with type today is the sheer number of digital type choices available. To be a good typographer, you don't need a lot of typefaces; you just need to choose wisely. The fonts you choose should work for myriad projects. Jack Stauffacher, a distinguished typographer in San Francisco, has used one typeface—Kis-Janson—to set almost everything for more than fifty years. To make good choices, study the comprehensive typeface families available from reputable, high-quality type sources. Compare serif and sans serif font families, and notice the differences. The typeface family should include text, display, small caps, old style and lining figures, fraction fonts, and all their bold, semi-bold, and italic counterparts. Study specimen books, if available. Examine books and other ephemera typeset using these fonts. A good typeface family is like a classic black dress: well made, simple yet stylish, and works for any occasion—it is, in other words, timeless.

Early in my career, I was fortunate to work as a graphic designer at Adobe Systems for type designers Sumner Stone, Carol Twombly, and Robert Slimbach. They taught me to look at type through their eyes, pointing out subtleties in the structure of letterforms—counters, serifs, stems, thicks and thins, x-heights, baselines, ascenders, descenders, character widths, kerning, and tracking—and to observe how these elements can differ depending upon point size.

The art of typography often depends on knowing how to work with the idiosyncrasies of a typeface family. The character set of a family reveals such secrets. Some typeface families have characters in their sets that you won't find in any other family, such as swashes and ornaments. Other characters, like ampersands or question marks, may be strikingly individual, making the font exactly the right choice for a particular design. The German typographer Max Caflisch never misses an opportunity to appropriately exploit a unique character from a typeface, and he is a master at working with ornaments. His book, *Max Caflisch: Typographia Practica* (Maximilian-Gesellschaft, Hamburg, 1988), is a treasure to look through, especially for his inventive work with ornaments and swash characters.

Much as John Cage demonstrated in music, the space between letters and words is as important as the letterforms. While in graduate school at Yale, I was fortunate to study typographic space with master teachers. Alvin Eisenman required that we spend hours setting paragraphs of type in different point sizes, at different line lengths, and with different line spacing, so we would understand how these three elements of typography worked together. It was a valuable and, yes, tedious exercise. Wolfgang Weingart had us take a small paragraph of a hundred words and, using one typeface at one text size, investigate how many ways we could set the type to indicate the start of a paragraph. In doing so, we were forced to explore inventive ways of working with word spacing, letterspacing, and line spacing, disregarding traditional approaches. Inge Druckrey had us set type for display headlines and finesse the spaces between the words and letters to accommodate changes as the type increased in size. Dorotea and Armin Hofmann had us draw and play with large letterforms as abstract forms in space.

The need to understand space also led me to the study of grid systems, symmetry, asymmetry, and the power of the center as ways of developing visual strategies for working in space. The strategy games that can be devised for working with or against such systems are endless. Some good books on this topic include *Grid Systems*, by Josef Müller-Brockmann (Hastings House, 1981), and *The Power of the Center*, by Rudolph Arnheim (University of California Press, 1982).

Aside from the formal aspects of design and typography, I found it helpful in my education to study drawing and painting. Drawing trains your eye to decipher details, and your hand to reproduce what your eye sees. It allows your hand the freedom to make what you want or need, rather than simply manipulate given forms. If you want to customize letterforms for design solutions, you need to know how to draw on both paper and on a computer. Painting utilizes many aspects of visual form and demands that you work the whole space, a lesson that has always kept me out of trouble when designing.

Fresh approaches to typographic problems often result from bending or breaking the rules. But to break the rules you first have to devote some time to learning and mastering them. A book on the principles and details of classical typography is *The Finer Points in the Spacing and Arranging of Type*, by Geoffrey Dowding (Hartley & Marks, 1998). A very entertaining book on the basics is *Stop Stealing Sheep and Find Out How Type Works*, by E. M. Ginger and Erik Spiekermann (Adobe Press, 2003).

Lastly, and most importantly, set as much type as possible. Typeset whatever anyone around you needs or wants. I began my career designing posters for musician friends at an avant-garde venue in New York called Roulette. Inspired by Kurt Schwitters and the Russian constructivists, I started setting type in as many styles as I could mimic. Experiment as much as possible and, as my graphic design teacher, Paul Rand, used to tell me, make a lot of mistakes.

Typography is an exacting art. Typographers may start out as calligraphers, printers, architects, artists, or, as in my case, graphic designers, but no matter how you come to typography, your mastery of it will be a synthesis of how you have learned to look. I am still looking, arranging, and endlessly rearranging these curious shapes in space. Keep setting type. In time, you will look and know you are a typographer, too.

With Thanks to Leonard Jay: A Typographic Education

Caroline Archer

I was never taught how to be a typographer. I never went to design school. However, I was fortunate to have been brought up in a household where metal type filled drawers that should have housed cutlery; where printers' ink was kept in the spare bedroom; where paper was stored where clothes should have hung; and where printing presses lived where a car might have been garaged. My earliest remembrances were of the smell of letterpress printing ink and the clatter of a vertical Meihle; old issues of the *Penrose Annual* were favorite childhood picture books. In such an environment, it was difficult to avoid being schooled in typography.

My education came partly through osmosis, and partly from natural inquisitiveness. But, to a large degree, it was the result of the patient but enthusiastic tuition of a father who loved his work as a compositor. With him, I learned how to draw letters, analyze text, produce layouts, compose type, and print—not as classroom exercises, but as real jobs for real people. Concomitant with practical experience came *ad hoc* lessons in printing history. It was a typographic education that emphasized the wholeness of the subject and the interdependence of its departmental aspects, where the mechanics were inseparable from the aesthetics. It was a rather recherché approach to typography at a time (the 1970s and 1980s) when formal education was specialized, not comprehensive: designers were taught to design and printers to print, and never the twain should meet.

But typographic education has not always been so compartmentalized. My father was fortunate to have been a pre-apprentice under Leonard Jay at the Birmingham School of Printing in the 1930s. Here, he received a strong, wide-ranging, and inclusive typographic education, from which I benefited nearly a half century later. Jay, head of the Birmingham School of Printing, was a teacher par excellence, who influenced and transformed the outlook of a whole generation of printers, thereby making a significant contribution to British printing education in the first half of the twentieth century. He made the Birmingham School without equal in Britain, or, possibly, in any other country, and exercised a worldwide influence on printing education policy.

Jay first became known in 1913, when he began teaching at the Central School of Arts and Crafts in London as an assistant to J. H. Mason.

In 1925, after twelve years at "The Central," Jay moved to Birmingham, where he worked until his retirement in 1953. When he began, he was the only full-time teacher on the staff, and there were only two half-day classes a week. At his retirement, 537 students attended the school; there were seventy-four classes, of which forty were in the day and thirty-four in the evening.

Leonard Jay was instilled with the principles of the "Private Press" movement, and was an admirer of Morris. However, he was more egalitarian in his work than Morris, and he strove to link the aesthetic principles of the Arts and Crafts movement with the typographical renaissance of the 1920s and 1930s, and bridged the early twentieth-century chasm between book and jobbing printing.

Jay was also a pioneering teacher, who advocated the application of fine printing standards in commercial jobbing work. He was rare in having the perspicacity and courage in 1925 to practice and teach the new idea that mechanical composition could be used to produce excellence in printing as effectively as hand composition. His instruction was directed by the belief that nothing worth printing was too small, humble, or inconsequential to be well designed, and that every job deserved the highest possible standards of composition and presswork. In order to achieve superlative levels of work, Jay saw it was necessary to understand and experience all areas of the printing process. Although the machinery of printing was important, the mechanics were of little service without the human element of experience and brains, and if the human element that controlled the machines had acquired all of the artistic qualities necessary in good printing, it was possible to produce work of exceptional quality and achieve commercial success.

Jay was a superlative craftsman, and made craftsmen out of others by teaching them to discriminate and to reject whatever was substandard in design or execution. He also taught that, if there was no end to the making and issuing of good books, there was certainly no end to the education of a typographer, as Updike had written:

> *[Printing is] a broad and humanizing employment which can indeed be followed merely as a trade, but which if perfected into an art, or even broadened into a profession, will perpetually open new horizons to our eyes and new opportunities to our hands.*

There are influential men in every generation, but few whose influence transforms the outlook of a whole generation and leaves an indelible record on the history of their times. Leonard Jay made a major contribution to the development of technical education. His combination of idealism and practical vision transformed not only the work of the Birmingham School but, in due course, the prevailing landscape of typography in one of the largest and most important centers of printing in Britain, and in Europe.

Under Jay, the Birmingham School of Printing produced over 150 publications that won worldwide praise for their high quality of design and production. They are his indelible record on printing history. However, Jay's most important legacy consists of those boys who trained under him and took their learning into printing businesses throughout the country and, thereby, helped raise standards in the industry. But his bequest does not stop with the cohorts he trained: that generation educated the next, and I, for one, am a grateful beneficiary of the holistic teachings of Leonard Jay.

The List *Geoffry Fried*

The best teaching comes from a distinctly personal perspective, using knowledge and understanding of a subject developed over years of study and practice. For a good teacher of typography, as for a teacher in any area, this personal approach becomes a guide through a thicket of complex material. A member of our faculty speaks constantly about the need to develop a "typographic voice," while another emphasizes the value of experimenting with an infinite variety of typographic choices and manipulations. One speaks passionately about typographic structures, while another never lets content slip away, always asking: "What is it you are trying to say?"

While each teacher develops his or her own personal perspective, one of the tricks of good teaching is to remember that this approach, or organizing principle for a course, is not the whole story. It is merely a compass in the wilderness. Along with a compass, one needs a good map and a thorough knowledge of the territory. Even the best typographers and teachers need a guide to the broad range of typographic knowledge that makes up a complete curriculum.

In the mid-1990s, a group of us at the Art Institute of Boston sat down to discuss guidelines for our typography program.[1] While we believed in and supported each other in our separate personal approaches to teaching, we felt the program itself would benefit from some common understanding of the breadth of the subject we were trying to teach. At the time, we were also concerned about a lack of differentiation between what was taught in typography classes versus what was taught in graphic design classes. We felt both areas of the curriculum could be strengthened by trying to understand and articulate their individual qualities.

The result of that discussion was a list of typographic subjects. We organized it as the "Preliminary Type Curriculum Outline," reproduced below.

Preliminary Type Curriculum Outline
I.   The Mechanics of Typography
     A. Manipulation
        1. Moving and changing physical parameters (size, spacing, placement, angle, alignment, etc.)

2. Using tools (hand and computer)

3. Craft skills; seeing and working in smaller increments

B. Measurement and Structure
   1. Typographic measurement
      a. points and picas
      b. leading and line spacing
      c. line lengths
      d. letter and word spacing
      e. type sizes
   2. Grids and structures
   3. Grouping and alignment

C. Detail and Refinement (finer points)
   1. Usage
      a. traditions and history
      b. rules and traditions: punctuation, small caps, old style figures, hyphenation, spacing conventions, etc.
      c. ornamentation: rules, dingbats, etc.
   2. Visual details and craft
      a. kerning
      b. letter and line relationships (length to leading, line endings, etc.)

D. Navigation and Reading
   1. Legibility
   2. Readability
   3. Hierarchy and editorial structure
   4. Pacing and sequence

E. Applied Usage (special knowledge or traditions for books, magazines, schedules, exhibits, Web, etc.)

II. Interpretation and Critical Thinking
   A. Understanding and Interpreting Content (in its broadest sense)
      1. Differing kinds of content: levels, types, uses
      2. Connecting with and understanding audiences

3. Developing your own content
    a. writing/designing
    b. self-expression
    c. self-authorship
4. Determining appropriateness

B. Critical Thinking
    1. Analysis (good, bad, ugly)
    2. Reading, looking, interpreting
    3. Presentation
        a. spoken
        b. written
        c. visual

C. Visual Ideas
    1. Conceptual and symbolic
    2. Concrete
    3. Puns and visual/verbal language

III.   Learning to See
    A. Appreciation and Comprehension
        1. Connecting different kinds of work (art and media)
           to typography
        2. Connecting human and physical experience to typography
           (perception)
        3. Developing aesthetic tastes and distinctions
           a. seeing and knowing the differences between things
           b. being able to describe the differences between things

    B. Understanding and Using Visual Relationships
        1. Foundation issues (form, counterform, balance, gesture, etc.)
        2. Typographic relationships (contrast, scale, hierarchy,
           typographic palettes, etc.)
        3. Spatial, structural, and proportional relationships (borders,
           columns, forms and voids, layering, etc.)

    C. Understanding Letterforms
        1. Structure
        2. Style

3. Fonts and families
4. Classifications and groupings
5. Uses and abuses

IV.   Type History (Context for Use)
    A. From Writing to Typography
    B. Tools and Media, and Their Effect on Letterforms
    C. Cultural Connections
    D. Type Design and Designers
    E. Classifications (historical connections)
    F. Connecting Type History with Art History and General History
       (styles, movements, technologies, etc.)

This very basic outline was not intended to be a curriculum by itself. Rather, it was intended to serve as an organized list of typographic subjects we all needed to be aware of. Regardless of the level you were teaching at, you could look at the list and gauge how broadly or how narrowly you were covering the field. And, by picking and choosing from different areas of the list—by drawing from this common well of understanding—you could enhance or enrich your own particular approach.

The list also was not meant to be presented in any specific order of importance, nor with each section being a guide to a particular class. The individual elements mix and reinforce one another. For example, our Typography 1 course focuses heavily on understanding letterforms (III, C), and the beginning mechanics of typography (I, A, and B). Learning letterforms not only involves craft skills (I, A, 3), but also enhances seeing and making distinctions (III, A, 3), while presenting historical material (IV, A, B, and E), as well.

Several years later, we still find the list to be a valuable reference tool. We now use a few more detailed curriculum guidelines (such as class goals and objectives, lists of appropriate levels of projects, and technology competencies) to keep multiple course sections on track. But the list reminds us of shared values and knowledge, as we each develop our own personal way of teaching and communicating what is important to us.

Notes
1. Participants in the discussion were: Geoffry Fried, Lucinda Hitchcock, Jim Hood, John Kane, and Mary Ann Frye.

Teaching Typography: Integrating the Old and the New

Introduced and compiled by Claire Hartten

What do typography instructors say about teaching? The following comments indicate that they are increasingly integrating digital typography with historical and cultural inquiry in their classrooms. Many of them teach traditional methods, such as setting type by hand and printing by letterpress, whereas others ask their students to draw letterforms, classify type styles, or analyze type designs in a cultural context. All of these instructors encourage students' curiosity and knowledge of type history in order to engage more confidently in contemporary practice.

Peter Bain, Pratt Institute, Brooklyn, United States

One first-semester assignment is the creation of a personal logotype or monogram. Before exploration with the letters themselves, each student has to locate and present six examples from multiple designers or typographers, credit the originators and the year, give full citations for their sources, and include at least two items that are over thirty years old. The results are highly individual, splitting into tight stylistic choices or broad-ranging surveys. I use the classroom critique to discuss the periods of typographic fashion represented, formal design strategies, and context and purpose of the originals, and I highlight key names in these groupings. This way, students can see the many links between typographic history and their own design process.

James Craig, The Cooper Union, New York, United States

Why teach comping? Before the introduction of computers, a designer would never think of setting type before getting the job approved by the client, and the only means of knowing what a job would look like in advance was to create a comprehensive of the design, more commonly referred to as a "comp." A simple comp was generally created with pencil and paper, while a more elaborate comp included color. Once approved, the comp was sent along with the typewritten copy to the typographer. Usually, the type specifications were indicated on both the copy and comp, so any error could be spotted in advance.

In order for a comp to be effective, the display type had to be accurate and the specific typeface recognizable. The text type was usually indicated by either parallel lines, a single line made with a chisel-point pencil, or a series of wavy lines. The text area also had to be accurate, and this was determined by "copyfitting"—that is, by calculating how much space type-written copy would occupy when set in a specific typeface. A mistake in calculation could be disastrous and require resetting the type, which was time-consuming and expensive—and the cost could not be passed along to the client.

Until recently, comping type was an essential skill. Today, this has been replaced with the creation of a text box and flowing in the type. If you don't like the results, or the type doesn't fit, no problem; hit a few keys and keep experimenting until you see something you like—every designer's dream come true.

Having said that, you may well ask if there is any reason to continue teaching comping type. I believe there is. At the Cooper Union, where I teach Typo 1: An Introduction to Typography, I spend the first two weeks of a sixteen-week semester using comping as a method of introducing five typefaces (Garamond, Baskerville, Bodoni, Century Expanded, and Helvetica) and five typographic arrangements (justified, unjustified, flush left and flush right, centered, and random). While all this could be accomplished on the computer, the students would not appreciate the subtle characteristics that make one typeface different from another, any more than a photograph could ever take the place of a detailed drawing of the same subject.

Furthermore, if our goal is to produce well-rounded students, I believe it is important that they understand and are familiar with our typographic traditions. It is for that reason that one of the projects I give the students involves setting type by hand and pulling proofs on a Vandercook press.

Will the students ever have an occasion to use comping? Will they ever have the opportunity to set a job on letterpress? It's most unlikely in both cases, but will they be richer for the experience? Well, according to my students, the answer is a resounding YES.

David Dabner, Jamie Hobson, and Tony Pritchard, London College of Printing, London, United Kingdom

In the School of Graphic Design at the London College of Printing, we take a forward-looking perspective on design thinking. This view does not imply that we reject the lessons from the past. We adopt a holistic approach that places emphasis on an investigation of process, in terms of research and development, preceding the production of a final artifact.

We regard old and new technologies as ones that can coexist, as opposed to one necessarily replacing the other. It is often the interface between technologies that provides the richest source for exploration. In terms of exposure to letterpress, students in undergraduate and postgraduate courses study hot metal setting. Students report that engaging in the physical process of composing type 1) aids in their understanding of the derivation of typographic terminology; 2) develops their appreciation of typographic form; and 3) helps them learn the system of spacing inherent in traditional and digital forms of setting. This system of spacing introduces them to the notion of grid structures, which has currency within the digital domain.

Students develop an understanding of the key influences on the development of letterforms by understanding the technical restrictions and production constraints associated with each period in type design. Students are encouraged to consider the generic forms within each classification. They are introduced to the basic forms first—for example, serif and sans serif. They are required to perform exercises in the structuring of typographic compositions utilizing the elements of typographic hierarchy, such as weight and size. The exercises allow for an exploration of type families and their associated variants.

Students are initially involved in letterform drawing exercises. This helps them develop an appreciation of form and acts as training for a more judicial selection of typefaces. The ability to draw letterforms reinforces the necessary visualizing skills that assist in their visual research and development of ideas through sketchbooks.

Catherine Dixon and Phil Baines, Central Saint Martins College of Art and Design, London, United Kingdom

In our studio at college, we house the Central Lettering Record (CLR). This is a teaching collection begun by Nicholas Biddulph in 1963 as a way of supplementing the inadequate amount of visual material then available for teaching about the diversity of lettering practice. Biddulph's efforts were later encouraged when the lettering historian Nicolete Gray also began teaching. Between them, they amassed a collection comprising some 10,000 black-and-white photographs, 3,000 slides, several hundred type specimens, books, rare printed and manuscript material, information about lettering, typography, and type design practice and manufacture, as well as actual three-dimensional examples of signs and lettering practice.

As we came to know more about its content, we began to understand how it might be better integrated into the life of the course. An opportunity for that arose when BA (honors) graphic design moved in 1999 to the college's Lethaby Building, and we suggested a studio exclusively for teaching typography (regardless of year), with the collection housed in an adjacent secure office. This is how it is now, with the teaching and managing of the collection as a joint responsibility.

As far as the history of type is concerned, we run two main teaching programs: the first with Year 1 students and the second with Year 2 students (ours is a three-year course). We each take responsibility for a different year and join in with each other's teaching when the timetable allows.

Catherine Dixon: For first-year typeform teaching, I spend a week with students in their introductory term—that is, the period when they try a bit of everything (e.g., illustration, advertising, photography, etc.)—to help them gain some greater understanding of the breadth of graphic design. Time is short, so I focus on equipping them with a framework for making sense of the diversity of typeforms that surround them. At that point, they can lack confidence in choosing fonts and often feel overwhelmed by an awareness of their own ignorance.

We begin by writing letterforms—uncials, gothic (textura), and humanist miniscules—then move on to drawing typeforms. This sets the scene, if you like, for explaining how basic formal aspects of types, such as modeling, have evolved. It is important, I think, that students understand that many types owe much to the pen and writing traditions, and yet have also achieved a degree of formal independence.

We then embark upon an analysis exercise, in which students are asked to compare and contrast six fonts: Dante, Baskerville, Ionic, Grotesque 215, Futura, and Gill Sans. They are asked to visually document their analysis process, considering in detail how these six types differ from each other in form. They are also asked to consider which of the different types they like best and why, and which they like the least and why. I use the student's own ideas and feedback as an introduction to a broader discussion of the six key trends in type design represented in the forms of these six fonts. Therefore, we cover a huge part of the history of typeface design here: Roman sources and the key trends of old and modern faces, nineteenth-century vernacular sources and mechanical influences, and the twentieth century's increased formal flexibility in design, as demonstrated by the reinterpretation of the idea of the grotesque sans serif through geometry and Roman inscriptional models. But, while history plays a part here, I am keen throughout to stress that the fonts we are discussing are all digital and could very much be considered part of a contemporary typographer's basic font repertoire.

A slide-lecture ties up all these various formal, historical, and contextual threads. This presentation is necessarily broad in outlook—from Gutenberg to Letterror—but it is not so much about detail as it is about providing some sense of the bigger picture of type design as it has evolved over 550 years. Too many books on this subject stop in the mid-twentieth century, so the student has no real sense of how what is happening now relates to practices of the past. Students are then encouraged to use this very broad overview as a starting point from which to embark upon an individual learning program, adding detail to it through their own reading (a recommended book list is provided). The presentation is also not strictly chronological—it is too misleading, in terms of explaining developments that were actually more concurrent than sequential. The presentation is accordingly structured using several of the key identified concurrent themes, such as handwriting, Roman ideals, and nineteenth-century vernacular influences.

These workshops conclude with a project for two main reasons: (1) to ensure that the handouts provided are actually read (!), and (2) to lighten up a subject that can all too easily appear to be about following rules and learning a seemingly intimidating amount of "stuff." So, in small groups, students are allocated a typeform idea (old face roman, modern face roman, slab serif, sans serif), and are asked to present information about that formal idea (historical, technological, contextual, etc.) to the rest of the main group in the most engaging, entertaining way they can think of. We are usually rewarded with a summary teaching session of very good humor. To give you some examples of student responses, we have had a "Gladiator"-style dramatic enactment of the battle of the Romans, complete with togas, letterform shields, and swords; a serif sheriff knocking a sans into slab serif shape; serif hairdressing and general typeform makeovers; a typographic wedding; a sock-puppet theater; typo cookie baking; and any number of game shows, as well as many film and animation pieces.

In addition to this main teaching program, Year 1 students take part in a half-day introductory letterpress workshop. We see this not as an exercise in nostalgia or even craft, but as an essential part of teaching contemporary designers about contemporary design practice. The physical manipulation of type cast on a physical body and the experience of controlling type and space on the block facilitates an understanding of the way type can be seen to similarly (though not precisely) operate on-screen in programs such as QuarkXPress, and helps those who may go on to use the type design programs. It also fits well with the rest of the course, which has retained all the old printmaking media alongside the new. Having done the induction, students can then use letterpress when they need it for other projects throughout the course.

When scheduling allows, I also ask students to draw a series of contrasting individual typeforms in large sizes (A1 or A0) in charcoal, so they trace the curves with their whole bodies. This experience can help students really begin to see and feel just how different typeforms can be. It is also a very un-typy kind of activity. Students' preconceptions about typography often involve the idea that all one does is sit in front of the computer working on a microscale designing fonts. So, any activity that can help shake them out of such preconceptions and encourage them to define typographic practice on their own terms is helpful.

Phil Baines: To begin the second year, I take students on a lettering walk that crosses central London and takes in a wide variety of public lettering, including carved English letters, road signs, street names, and shop fascias. The object is to get students looking at their surroundings and seeing things. It also reinforces the history of typeforms by discussing the relationship between lettering and type, as well as showing some of the cultural and historical contexts of different letterforms.

In addition to the above reasons, the walk also informs project work. One project involved designing a piece of lettering for a specific building and place. Designing a street name legible from fifty yards away was another. The latter has proved especially useful in alerting students to the fact that typography is at the same time very easy and very hard. The success of work for this project often relies upon attention to the details, especially spacing, and students quickly learn that the defaults of type designers and program makers do not in themselves make good typography.

The walk, which I started doing in 1995 or thereabouts, has since been made into a Web site—*www.publiclettering.org.uk*—by three ex-students, Jack Schulze, Matt Hyde, and George Agnelli. The subject matter also forms the basis for a book we have written, *Signs: Lettering in the Environment*, published by Laurence King.

For the second-year typeform project, students are each given a particular font to research: who designed it, for whom, when, why, etc. The fonts (e.g., Bembo, Plantin, Playbill, Helvetica, Bitstream Charter, OCR-A) are chosen to represent major formal groupings. In discussing history, our teaching now uses Catherine's type description framework, which also forms the basis for historical discussion in *Type & Typography*. To reiterate, we see history not as an exercise in learning about the past for the sake of it, but, rather, as a way of informing and better understanding aspects of current practice. All the fonts used in this project, therefore, are digitally available to the students on the college networks. We have both the Monotype Classic Library and the complete Bitstream Library, plus a few others bought as separate families.

At the next session, they present their findings to me and the group, so they all learn from each other. Their information is then supplemented and qualified by me, using material from the CLR. (One problem we've become aware of in recent years is that students find it easier to go to the Internet for research instead of our library, but for well-published subject areas, the Internet is actually a poor substitute for books.)

The collection literally comes alive in these teaching sessions as specimens, prints, photographs, and examples are laid out on the table for students to look through. Having gained some greater understanding of the ideas behind their allocated typefaces, each student is asked to design an A2 portrait format poster about their respective typeface. The second-year book-design project is designed to introduce the students to the issues of editorial design, and is set up to be realistic. They are given a target number of pages to fill, real (unformatted) text to work with, and lo-res scans. They must attend to all aspects of the job. The project is introduced by a group discussion about book design. They are each given a book to study—chosen by me to represent both historical changes in production over the last century or so and good practice in design. The general design, as well as the treatment of different kinds of text and minutiae of detailing, is discussed. This session is followed up with a visit to the college's museum and study collection, which has examples of incunabula and early printed books.

The teaching of this project is (at present) based around QuarkXPress, and I give instruction in using the program. There is a significant difference between learning a program from a non-designer whose approach is, "this is what the program can do," and a designer whose approach is, "I want to do this." The arrangement of the first part of Chapter V, and all of Chapter VI, in *Type & Typography* is based on this project, as taught over the last few years.

In terms of teaching and practice—a general point—neither Catherine nor I is full-time. The rest of our week is spent on our own freelance designing or writing work. This gives us a unique combination of experiences to bring to our teaching. We know about history because we write about it; we know about the editorial and authorial roles from first-hand experience; and we are using programs like QuarkXPress on a daily basis. And, it is always our intention to teach in a nondirective manner. We let students know what is good and bad practice, when relevant (in detailing work and in the legibility of running text, for example), but do not let our personal taste affect marks. What matters is whether a solution works rather than whether we like it or not.

Jerry Kelly, Pratt Institute, New York, United States

I believe that typography must be taught with a historical and factual basis. Students cannot be thrown into aesthetic projects right away and expect to succeed if they do not know (i.e., have not been taught) anything about type as a tool. Therefore, I devote the entire first term to the history and technology of type. I start with historical development (From Gutenberg, type mold, and type body through linotype, monotype, and phototype, and up to digital typography). Through this historical discussion, we cover nomenclature and use. Leading, point size, x-height, characters in a font, etc., are all covered through the historical context. This takes up about one third of the term. The next third is devoted to typeface classification, which helps students learn about letterforms and identify various characteristics of typefaces. The final third of the term is devoted to practical application, applying all they have learned to application on the computer. No design projects are done in the first term, and there is no hand lettering. I am a firm believer in the importance of hand lettering and calligraphy, but we are teaching typography, not lettering. By definition, typography is not hand lettering. I believe both hand lettering and calligraphy should definitely be part of a design school's curriculum, but as separate courses. I also feel calligraphy should be required—preferably, taken before typography. I would like to have letterpress taught, also, and, again, it would be nice if it were required. An ideal program would include (in this order):

1. Calligraphy

2. Letterpress typography

3. Typography 1 (as outlined above)

4. Typography 2 (beginning of design projects)

5. Typography 3 and 4 (further design projects)

Also required: history of design courses, and design procedures (i.e., learning computer graphics applications), taken concurrently with above.

Elective courses: hand lettering; book design; advanced letterpress printing; type design; and advanced Quark tips.

Gerry Leonidas and Gerard Unger, University of Reading, Reading, United Kingdom

Gerry Leonidas: One thing that has remained a constant in the years I have been at Reading is the emphasis on approaching each design project as something informed by history, theory, and technology, as well as the design brief. In quotidian terms, these generalities translate to an appreciation of context, the potential for critical evaluation, and a thorough understanding of production potential and limitations. For example, in the master's program to type design, we include hand-setting sessions, a demo of a fully operational monotype caster, sessions on calligraphy, and a period of obligatory sketching on paper. These happen alongside lectures on the history of letterforms, seminars on theoretical approaches, and technical issues, as well as sessions with a wide range of world-class visitors. We're also very keen on student feedback, and review the specs every year accordingly.

Gerard Unger: In terms of presenting old and new technologies, if I do not introduce "old" technologies and styles to the students, they will do so themselves. It is much better to head them off. Theoretically, they get as broad an overview as possible. As far as technologies are concerned, "old" is a tricky word. Hot metal, and everything connected to it, is definitely old, but large parts of it are of immediate interest to students. Drawing by hand is not old at all. I would not say learning to do letterpress is vital, but it certainly helps students understand a lot. Look at Phil Baines's and Andrew Haslam's recent book, with all the rectangles around the letterforms. If students can handle some metal type, they understand ideas like that immediately. We do introduce students to setting lead type by hand for letterpress, so they might understand digital typesetting as a process that evolved from three-dimensional forms. Our students gain an appreciation for the evolution of type styles, including typefaces being developed for specific purposes today, through lots of theory and discussions. We enable our students to cultivate an eye and vocabulary for type classification and for choosing a typeface for a project, again, by giving them as much information, advice, and theory—and some decidedly biased views—as possible so they are stimulated to form their own opinions.

Ina Saltz, The City College of New York, New York, United States

By mid-semester, my students have been exposed to the names of some of the most famous type designers through the initial study of type classification, but they have yet to feel that these type designers were (and, in some cases are) type-passionate artists whose creations are still relevant and useful today. Every method of interactivity is encouraged, so I place the names of twenty type designers, ranging from John Baskerville and Firmin Didot to Jan Tschichold and Eric Gill, to some great living designers, such as Hermann Zapf, Matthew Carter, Jonathan Hoefler, and Carol Twombly. The students choose from the hat, then write and deliver an oral report to the class. They must include samples of his or her most significant fonts and examples of contemporary usage of those fonts. Each student becomes a mini-expert on one designer, and, also, feels the responsibility of communicating that bit of typographic history to the rest of the class.

True Knowledge Derives from Knowing How to See *Huub Koch*

Typography is a craft with its own set of rules, limits, and values that belong to tradition, to the present, and . . . to the future.

Typography is not art, but it certainly is *an art*. Once you understand the difference, you are ready to practice the discipline as a philosophy in action.

A knowledge of good design principles, history, and its implications contributes to your appetite. Such knowledge serves as a starter, not as the main menu.

True knowledge is derived from knowing how to see, learn, love, play, act, and share. It can transform serious business into joyous business.

Typography is used to communicate with others, but in order to do so, we first have to learn to communicate with ourselves. This ability becomes an attitude by learning how to ask questions. If such questions are absent, there will be no progression.

Being an all-around human being is more important than being a designer, but, sometimes, it helps.

As long as your client asks you, "What does this seduction scene on the cover have to do with the fine art of fondue cooking?" you might have missed the point, or need another client.

Graphic design is a path that unfolds through making decisions on a white sheet of paper. Don't think too much; it's all about gut feeling.

We need exercise as an experience, because it teaches us in a natural way. We do things, make mistakes, and improve by adjusting to reality and its demands. Please, relax and take your time. The deadline is only twenty minutes ahead.

It will take you three weeks to learn the art of optical letterspacing and get THE QUICK BROWN FOX JUMPS OVER THE LAZY DOG just right. Tough lessons are always blessings in disguise. When the going gets tough, the tough get going, and ready for surprise!

Practice does not leave much room for illusions.

Desktop publishing made designers aware that they need a basic understanding of typography . . . and . . . of project management, the use of technology, collaboration, and doing business with real clients. Hmmm, you thought design was art?

New media gives you power over all the tools of production. Designers had an advantage until now because they are visually and typographically literate. But the language of new media is rapidly becoming the territory of architects, artists, gamers, filmmakers, musicians, and scientists. While growing out of its infancy, it will become a whole new language. So, where is the dictionary?

Education has its limits. It can never give you all the tools you need. Be open-minded! Read books, meet people that seem to matter to you, go practice, and take your chances!

The most mysterious part of design is "the interesting." The interesting is hard to describe, but we know that if something has meaning for us, it will also have meaning for others. That is why only the best is good enough, but what is best depends on goals and budget.

Styling is the use of a tone of voice that relates to people of today, in their language, which does not mean a designer should be fashionable or make *l'art pour l'art.*

Respect is the basic ingredient of collaboration, but it needs to be shared. In print, you have to rely on the craftsmen you work with. Without a relationship, they will only do "exactly" what you want. That's where most things go wrong. If they like you, and notice a mistake you made, they will help you out. Make friends by being one.

All disciplines of typography hold a challenge and their own rewards. Every challenge makes you perceive yourself and your expertise in a new way. It is better to regret having taken a chance than to regret having let the opportunity go by.

Ninety-eight percent of graphic design is trash. The other 2 percent is sanctioned into designer's heaven. Have ever talked about trash with your local trash collector? There is much more value in trash than you ever imagined. Trash is our natural environment. Be aware of that, and once in awhile, go out and collect some trash! Get rich by becoming inspired and humane!

Nothing is fixed, and everything must change; such is life. To be honest, there are no rules or prescriptions. The secret of typography is a question of manners—a way to behave yourself, and to act proper and decent. Once learned, it gives you access to all areas.

Duke Ellington was once asked if he rejected certain types of music. His response was: *Oh no . . . it's all music.* I guess the same counts for type.

We all have strengths and weaknesses. If you cannot improve the latter, take up the first. Some people are specialists, while others are generalists. If you can join these forces, nothing will stop you! If you can't, nothing can stop you, either! Just be who you are until the end.

Teaching typographic literacy is not an end in itself. There will always be a difference between theory and practice. In theory, you develop a method; in practice, you go beyond.

Concerns for Education in Today's Typographic Universe
Michael Schmidt

I'm a Ford Truck man
That's what I am
I ain't got no boundaries
I don't compromise.[1]

Astronomers now believe the universe is expanding with ever-increasing speed: the distance between celestial bodies is becoming mind-numbingly vast. It's only a matter of a few ticks on the cosmic clock before oblivion engulfs the elements of light and matter.[2] No boundaries. No compromises. Space—the empty surround—will become a homogeneous black void, rendering any object within it an anomaly: a token of a once-diverse cosmos. Warn the folks in Crawford; science just discovered a force more hegemonic than capitalism and Big Oil put together.

The typographic plenum appears little threatened by the obliterating force of homogeneity. Yet, despite the continued discovery of new galaxies, new stars, and the celestial appearance of unending diversity, all is not well in the twinkling typographic firmament. A critical need to challenge the dominant assumptions regarding the nature of our present typographic universe exists now with its own exponential urgency. The principle aim of this call to question is to expose issues of critical concern for typographic instruction today.

Type instruction[3] is based on an amalgam of influences—from traditionalism to the Bauhaus and Die Neue Typographie to the International Typographic Style to the New York School and American eclecticism to Dan Friedman's codification of Wolfgang Weingart's New Typography, and to the myriad of individual design and teaching approaches that fueled the debates and diversity of postmodernist and deconstructionist pedagogy. So, how should those of us faced with the challenge of teaching typography question, select, and sequence this subject's most vital aspects for students today? Many of us rely on the lessons we learned as students. Yet, for all the supposed "timeless principles" of this particular discipline, we'd have to be very stubborn and dogmatic not to acknowledge the subject's breadth and the clear fact that it *does* change.

Many philosophies of "good" typographic form and purpose can be classified as static, serving the ideological agendas of a specific moment. Other convictions regarding the nature and use of type are fluid, accommodating change while providing a lasting benchmark. The words of Peter Behrens, avant-garde German artist, architect, and product and graphic designer, achieve the latter goal. He maintained that, second to architecture, typography embodies "the most characteristic picture of a period, and the strongest testimonial of the spiritual progress" and "development of a people."[4]

Behrens's time-honored adage provides obvious guidance: type instruction must relate to its period. The difficulties, of course, are to understand the forces affecting the present moment, then translate that knowledge into a pertinent typography curriculum—no mean feat. The growing rift between interpretations of our present reality further complicates this challenge; Behrens's adage is now bifurcated. Modernists clung to this axiom, and postmodernists used it to defend their innovations as relevant to the changing times. Presently, however, there are two main paths affecting design and typography instruction that diverge from this maxim.

On the one hand, there are designers and teachers who grasp the implication of this terse statement: To proactively and effectively meet your responsibilities to students, clients, and society, you first need to investigate the social, political, ideological, and economic forces surrounding design education and practice. Yet, on the other hand, there's the vastly more trafficked route of corporate synergy: If we *see* clients want services like localization, narrowcasting, and "tailorable" products and media, the world is obviously becoming more diverse, or—at the very least, thank God—diversity is finally embraced at boardroom level. Educate your students about diversity, then. They need to be more ready than ever to work as typographic ventriloquists and vernacular chameleons, or so this line of reasoning goes. For ease of conversation, let's call this latter group—concerned largely with brand implementation, brand sustainability, and corporate design needs in general—"the Diversity School."

Right now, the Diversity School holds the dominant position in the graphic design field due to its heavy involvement in the ubiquitous realm of brands: the mainstream of design practice and typographic implementation. From globalization to frenzied mergers and acquisitions, corporate and brand identities—and all their myriad implementations—are in high demand. As corporations compete in global trade, they find it more vital than ever to establish strong market presence for their products and services. Type is the designer's meal ticket, though it is but one component of the complex methodology behind brand sustainability. The brand gurus of graphic design are hot commodities at conferences, and their work fills the pages of awards annuals and design magazines. These brand practitioners, influential design personalities winning all those big awards, may very well affect design and type education for years to come.

The precocious typography student will insist that corporate design, branding, and advertising are only a few instances of "real world" typographic design. What about publication design? Movie titles? Typeface design? Theater posters? Signage? Information graphics? Web sites? Motion graphics? Interaction design? Etc., etc. Well, like most precocious students, this one is right. All these things exist, and it's everything design faculties can do to cover the basics, let alone the near infinite applications of type. Yet, as Rick Poyner aptly points out, "The vast majority of design projects—and certainly the most lavishly funded and widely disseminated—address corporate needs, a massive overemphasis on the commercial sector of society, which consumes most of graphic designers' time, skills, and creativity."[5]

We could say, then, that the overwhelming majority of designers understand brands and their conveyance through global trade to be the most characteristic typographic picture of this period. And, in cursory overview, these brands do indeed seem to be all about diversity.

Diversity is clearly a laudatory concept. Who could argue with the fair recognition of individual choice and taste, ethnic traditions, and regional practices? But is this really what the Diversity School supports? Kathy McCoy, longtime design educator and now, also, brand-experience advocate, points to the impending evisceration of "consumer monoculture" by the praiseworthy advance of audience-centered design, "de-massification," and an "economy of choice."[6]

McCoy and her husband, Michael, run a series of seminars for design professionals under the general program heading of "High Ground" (a title appropriate to the sessions' location atop a Rocky Mountain vista). The McCoys invite prominent field practitioners to conduct "master" sessions in topics such as "Designing the Brand Experience" and "Designing the Product Experience." Their workshops are popular and influential, once drawing Sony's entire U.S. design staff.[7] When they're not running workshops or their own design business, the McCoys instruct graduates and postgraduates in human centered design at Illinois Institute of Technology's Institute of Design.

During an AIGA Chicago conference, titled "FutureHistory," Kathy McCoy traced her trajectory from the modernism of Unimark to the typographic deconstruction of Cranbrook to her present status as experience-design guru for professionals and students alike. She praised the distance design theory and practice have traveled since the early days of standardization. McCoy's lecture presented a new era characterized by "narrowcasting," "tailorable" products and media, and a giddy enthusiasm for the unending supply of diverse graphic communications—to serve diverse audiences and needs—now required by clients, corporate or otherwise. At last, the postmodern designer's land of milk and honey—or is it?

The Diversity School is undergirded by a massive corporate interest in "localization": the process of tailoring transnational corporate brands, communications, and products to specific regional constituencies. McCoy's efforts, however, go beyond geography and tailoring to cover the shifting habits and tastes of individuals as they move from one context to another. This is a very sophisticated form of specialization, eschewing crude demographic data for the techniques of cultural anthropology—specifically, ethnography—and creating and documenting stories of user experiences with products and communications.

From localization to specific-user specialization, the Diversity School celebrates the visible evidence of heterogeneity. Yet, this vision is akin to the telescopic single-sightedness of a stargazing astronomer whose view blinds him to the invisible structures of celestial expansion and homogenization. Diversity—as practiced by corporations and the design establishment—is not insuring "cultural sustainability," as McCoy contends. Instead, this mere appearance of diversity surrounds and conceals the very real forces of hegemony, homogenization, and the increasing U.S. corporate-governmental impatience with different points of view at home and abroad.

Localization will not sustain culture, individuality, or custom in the face of expanding capital, service, media, and trade conglomerates. Localization is, in fact, a *tool* of exploitive globalization in the hands of free and unchecked markets. In other words, localization is necessary because globalization is advancing. Heterogeneity *appears* more prevalent because the homogeneity of trade, intellectual property law, and transnational corporate interest *is* more prevalent. In the case of Web localization, the company site will appear one way in Malaysia and quite another way in the U.K. That very information, however, is coming from, and flowing back to, one central source: it is channeled through various servers and routers to a central body of decision makers. Diversified structure does not equal diversified power or shared wealth.

Typography students learn from current textbooks that, "These days, people need better ways to communicate to more diverse audiences. We know from experience that what we have to say is much easier for others to understand if we put it in the right voice; type is that voice, the visible language linking writer and reader."[8]

Throughout her conference presentation, titled "Speaking in Tongues: Audience-Centered Communication and Cultural Sustainability," Kathy McCoy enthused that we can now communicate to specific groups, such as ethnic minorities, like never before. Maybe we should stop to ask ourselves how necessary it would be for a national giant like Wal-Mart to target small communities had it not destroyed local businesses. Or, would our transnational corporations be striving to meet specific needs within developing nations had they not used the coercive forces of the World Trade Organization, International Monetary Fund, World Bank, and corporate and intellectual property lobbyists to sentence the indigenous workforce to sweat labor and to bury the gross national products of indigent nations under insurmountable debt? Increasingly, the common denominator in all this apparent diversity is poverty.[9]

Native Americans, such as author and anthropologist D'Arcy McNickle, cogently portray a particularly harsh set of nineteenth- and twentieth-century encounters between First Nationers and the forces of expansion and homogenization. In his novel, *The Surrounded*, McNickle explicates the processes of land dispossession, further Euro-American encroachment on reservation lands, the loss of natural resources, and the oppressive dominant legal system. Appropriately titled, McNickle's 1936 publication characterizes how difference is surrounded by dominant structures and, subsequently, strangled by, or assimilated into, the dominant social, legal, and economic systems.[10] Furthermore, these systems operate as a network of interrelated concerns and agendas, facilitating expansion and engulfment.

While more recent literature focuses on the resistance and perseverance of indigenous peoples, the processes described by McNickle tightly correspond to current trade agendas—largely manipulated by U.S. corporate influence—that force similar consequences upon millions of citizens in developing nations.[11] Knowing this, can we ask our students to embrace a false version of diversity whose repercussions warrant serious criticism? If the Diversity School model is suspect, as I contend, what other exemplars might we use to aid education?

Any worthy example would have to demonstrate its potential to successfully operate without the momentum of the Diversity School. In doing so, this counter-model could offer a more equitable definition of diversity that responds to the moment in a manner unique to our networked world. While modernism and postmodernism both possessed strategies that responded to the crises of their times, these theories are insufficient resources for practice and education today, due to significant changes in commerce, technology, design practice, and academic thought. Given that type education has always been predicated on current convictions operating in concert with, or in opposition to, past theories, educators face new quandaries: What ideas, what theories, and what notions of the present will undergird the set of exemplars we seek once we understand more about the nature of our present circumstances?

Astronomers searching for structural relationships between different celestial bodies had to shift their focus from an analysis of these objects to the space between them. Jack H. Williamson provides much the same service to typography in his essay, *The Grid: History, Use, and Meaning*. Williamson charts the implicit structure between objects of visual communication as he follows the transformation of the grid from the Middle Ages to the Renaissance to modernism and, finally, to postmodernism. Just as the shape of space changes in relation to gravitational forces, the shape of the grid changes in relation to historical precedents. Long a standard in type education, the grid serves as a tool for compositional arrangement of words and images. But, as Williamson explains, the grid is more than a tool: it is the expression of an age.[12] Behrens's classic dictum is renewed once again.

Williamson's discussion adroitly illustrates the grid's expansion over time. Importantly, he includes typography in this journey as an elemental structure wedded to the history of the grid. The grid, as we know, is as much theory as substance: it is an ontological marker as well as a graphic device. Like the firmament engulfing our universe, the metaphysical grid is spreading, carrying with it the solar winds of typography to new reaches and expanses, surrounding the globe.

A Quick Summary of the Grid, Courtesy of Your Author

IN THE BEGINNING, there was the point and the line: a coordinate system that referenced the God above and the terra firma below. With the rise of secularism and the expansion of the known world, there formed a grid, the expanse of the earthly plane: longitude and latitude and, later, the modernist mysticism of universal principles.

THEN CAME NIGHT: The postmodernist simulacrum—the untrustworthy surface of even the grid—and the murky underworld of the "below."

Pardon my creative license with Williamson's highly respectable scholarship, but that's pretty much the history of the grid, in a nutshell. Conveniently, my ridiculously concise summary concludes right before the Diversity School's latest iteration, when postmodern designers rejected modernism, its theories of universalism, rationalism, and legibility, and its belief in societal reinvention through design.

Emphasis on individual innovation, rather than grand systematic programs, characterized this period in typographic thought and teaching from 1970 to, roughly, 1995, when postmodernism finally lost momentum in graphic design. As Williamson cogently indicates through examples of popular films and scholarly insights, postmodernist work possessed a keen mistrust of surfaces, bearing, as they did, little resemblance to the contents and messages within.[13] This postmodern concern with the surface was, of course, part of a broader initiative of social, political, and ideological criticism. Though opposed to the idea of social engineering, certain designers and design educators of this period sought to set the record straight on social disenfranchisement, the cultural "other," neocolonialism, imperialism, and the hidden, largely decentralized mechanisms of power and control, following more the path of post-structuralism's tenets than postmodern pastiche.

Postmodernists were accused of nihilism because of their heavy reliance on contextual relativism, their evisceration of fixed truths, and their disavowal of independent genius. *Pluralism* is also a term used to characterize the movement, though some of its proponents would disagree with this assessment. Nonetheless, advocates of postmodern design, many of whom were design educators, dramatically qualified and modified typographic instruction. Type, as in previous "isms," was the logical vessel for the thoughts of the period and a likely tool in classroom discussions that emphasized critical thinking skills. Critical thinking, however, was fostered more by the growing academic interest in deconstruction—a form of literary and linguistic analysis popularized by philosopher Jacques Derrida—than postmodernism per se. Deconstruction offered a more complex and detailed look at the operation of language, again embodying serious implications regarding the construction of reality.

Once again, the grid changed; multiplied, overlapped, and repeatedly mutated variants reconfigured its constituent parts into new relationships and networks of association and dissociation. This iteration of the grid is still in flux. And, if Derrida is correct, its ontological relevance will never cease.[14]

Postmodernism's investigation of contextual specificity is co-opted by the Diversity School, in whose hands the postmodern emphasis on context is retooled to facilitate the construction of *networks* of contexts: experiences that move with the user. Critical postmodern commentary of the design establishment is replaced with, of all things, a new establishment. We stand upon the absurd ends of Aristotelian logic so often predicted: the experience is reality. The actual location of truth is moot in this networked world without surfaces. This state of manufactured experience hardly seems conducive to "cultural sustainability."

The Diversity School's branding philosophy, described by McCoy in her presentation, maintains that the ability to speak a constituency's language somehow insures the longevity of that language, and, thereby, the culture itself. If colonialists had possessed the ability to speak the five hundred native languages dispersed between the oceans, Euro-America would have hastened, not altered, its agenda of Manifest Destiny. The motivation behind the typography, spoken words, images, and experiences depends on who's selling the new "reality."

The Diversity School is now both the design establishment and the dominant force in graphic design, due to its reach in both education and transnational corporate business (globalization, to be precise). Typographic expertise applied to branding is the main visible means the graphic design establishment employs to play its role—and establish its marketability—in the globalization race. Chris Riley, chief strategic officer with branding and advertising giant Wieden & Kennedy, explains: "The cultural role of brands is to respond to the spirit of the times."[15] Sound familiar? Behrens linked *type* to the Zeitgeist, and Williamson linked it to the grid. Now, however, the eminent cultural domain of type—where the big bucks and true graphic hegemony await—is *branding*. The cultural nature of type lives in the brand, which is not a new condition, just incredibly more pervasive, thanks to transnational corporations.

Because implicit structures—trade and global commerce—are expanding like the void of space, typography's value through global branding stands to dwarf the importance of its other cultural roles. The networks presently dominating typographic usage were initiated in trade agreements, not design schools, agencies, or firms. More specifically, these implicit structures were, and still are, shaped and refined by powerful corporate lobbying groups, such as the International Trademark Association (INTA) and the U.N.'s World Intellectual Property Organization (WIPO), of which the International Council of Graphic Design Associations (ICOGRADA) is affiliated. INTA's influence over the Free Trade Agreement of the Americas (FTAA), for example, jeopardizes the right of New Zealand's Maori to trademark, or otherwise legally protect, their own ideograms, often found tattooed to their bodies. INTA's rationale is twofold. First, Maori iconography is composed of forms that have likely been used for brands already. Second, Maori iconography is rife with forms that may yet prove useful to brand design.[16]

Type, just like Maori symbolism, is treated as a natural resource for brand design. This is why the U.S. Copyright Office will never allow copyright protection for typeface designs, despite the best efforts of luminaries in our field, like Rudy Vanderlans and Zuzana Licko.[17]

Concern regarding the dominant activities of graphic design— advertising, branding, globalization, and localization—is building. Practitioners and educators alike are voicing their hesitations as they search for alternatives. The republication in 1999 of Ken Garland's "First Things First Manifesto" (1964)—"FTF2000", as it is called—continues to generate debate. The last installment of the *Looking Closer* anthologies, *Looking Closer 4: Critical Writings on Graphic Design*, is replete with essays debating the risks and merits of "FTF2000", branding, and globalization. A general feeling of displacement—a renewed banishment to the periphery for critical thought, humanist ideals, and alternative viewpoints—pervades the collection. This may account, as Véronique Vienne's writing suggests, for the current design- and critical press interest in the 1957–1972 Situationist International movement, and its opposition to the society of the spectacle: an important precedent for our current critique of "designed" brand and product experience.[18]

Kenneth Fitzgerald's curatorial venture, *Adversary*, amassed and continues to showcase alternative definitions and uses of graphic design and typography from many of our field's top practitioners and several new voices. And Victor Margolin recently pointed out to me the growing debate on globalization voiced among members of the international Design Research Society, at international design conferences such as *Common Ground* (September 2002), and within resources posted on Illinois Institute of Technology's Institute of Design Ph.D. student-run Web site.[19]

Looking Closer contributor, and former editor of *Eye* magazine, Max Bruinsma, accounts for this growing critique of the corporate design establishment. Culturally speaking, in spite of the growing forces of corporate convergence and globalization, the world has become a network of peripheries. These peripheries may be called lifestyles, subcultures, pressure organizations, lobby groups, themed communities, special interests, activists, or what have you, but, regardless of their tag, they interlink, communicate, interact, and overlap. Linking these peripheries with each other and with what remains of the centers of cultural identity and power is a design commission of the greatest importance.[20]

I have come across, been informed of, and all out searched for what I feel are useful exemplars that take full advantage of the network paradigm Bruinsma summarized. What follows, however, is not a list of principles, tactics, or strategies. Methodological specificities are the purview of the individual instructor, in my opinion. Instead, I offer examples that cut a different path through our present universe: that other side of Behrens's bifurcated maxim.

The advertising and design firm Johnson & Wolverton donates its services to a host of social causes. Their work for Amnesty International is particularly poignant in its ability to involve a network of people in the communication process. One poster they created for Amnesty members was perforated into postcard-sized sections. A somewhat distressed image of an abuser and his abused prisoner covered the front of the poster (Figure 1). The image on the back was indecipherable, appearing more like a puzzle with its pieces out of order. The poster was then pulled apart into postcards, and mailed to members with the simple request that they write short messages on the cards and send them back. Once all the cards were returned, the staff reconfigured the poster following the proper structure of the previously indecipherable backside image—now the visage of a woman personifying peace (Figure 2). This time, the front image was indecipherable (Figure 3); the abuse was metaphorically quashed and supplanted by the resolve of the membership.[21]

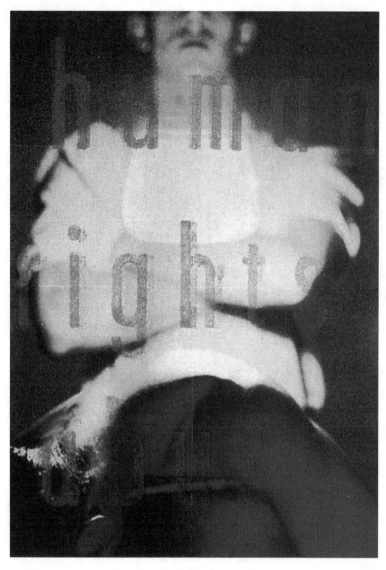

Figure 1

Figure 2

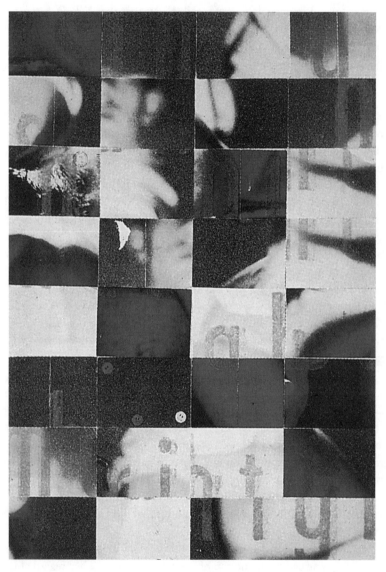

Figure 3

Johnson & Wolverton's Amnesty poster is powerful because it connects people—showing, in a very tangible way, that they belong to a network of like-minded peers. This connection stands in contradistinction to the "white noise" around them. It is a path through the general surround—the day-to-day asphyxia—that would otherwise muffle their agency and hopes.[22] Even for those interested in building and supporting digital community networks, this poster and its "snail" mailing serve as a very useful example of interactivity. And, through this interactive, collaborative involvement, Johnson & Wolverton succeeded in using the same talents they apply to Nike accounts to reinforce the motivations of a very different constituency.

To bring this discussion closer to typography per se, take the work of Open, a design studio recently established in New York City. Open colleagues Susan Barber and Scott Stowell collaborated with socially conscious Yale design educator Sheila Levrant de Bretteville on a campaign for Not In Our Name (NION). Prominent U.S. scholars, authors, filmmakers, and entertainment celebrities established NION in response to the tragedies of September 11, 2001. More specifically, NION opposes the U.S. government's responses to September 11, e.g., the War on Terrorism.[23] Through a series of full-page newspaper ads, the collaborators used the media to further establish a network of concerned citizens: a network partly rendered by the dozens of names appearing in the ads (Figure 4). The typographic representation of these individuals attests to fellow U.S. policy dissidents that their concerns are shared. In these quiet, typographically elegant ads, ironically, peripheral voices invade the mainstream.

Open and Levrant de Bretteville's campaign for NION is reminiscent of *Right On!*, a text for political and civil rights activists first published in 1970. Michael Worthington recently brought this book back to the fore in *Eye* magazine, where he enthusiastically explains: "*Right On!* is a reminder of the ability of graphic design to communicate and document points of view and create design that can inspire and collaborate in changing the world for the better."[24]

Postmodernists, for all the crucial issues they brought to bear, never completely warmed to the notion of "bettering society." They regarded this concept as modernism's ambition: a failed agenda, steeped more in suspect ideologies than utopian ideals. Yet, postmodern cynicism and corporate hubris yield to altruism in Peter Fraterdeus's 1996 essay, republished in *Texts on Type*, in which he writes, "There are still some of us who do

Figure 4

believe that the purpose of design is to help make a better world. Perhaps we are those who take seriously the relationship between the culture and the cultural workers whose artifacts help to define the culture. See *www.dol.com/worldstudio*."[25] It's the inclusion of a URL at the end of such a declaration that really caught my eye. Here, again, the network paradigm proves to manifest a venue for alternative viewpoints. The discussion and the networked existence of this designer's response to the discussion are so interrelated that only the Web site can complete his statement.

And so, within networked collaborations, we find our alternative exemplars. Accordingly, one organization refers to itself as nothing less than "Design for the World." Only a network of designers formed by ICOGRADA, the International Council of Societies of Industrial Design (ICSID), and the International Federation of Interior Architects/Interior Designers (IFI) could claim such a monolithic title. Formed in 1998, Design for the World applies its volunteers' expertise in communications, products, and shelter to the needs and emergencies of the developing world: disaster relief, health, education, development, and the widening AIDS crisis.[26] Though nascent, Design for the World is establishing a design purview of tremendous relevance to contemporary global problems.

In contrast to the small army behind Design for the World, a one-person design studio in Richmond, Virginia, is backing the fight against transnational corporate monoculture at home. Inspired by the February 2001 Conference on Technology and Globalization held in New York City, Another Limited Rebellion Design created Designers Against Monoculture (DAM), a "rallying cry, calling designers (as well as art directors, marketers, and copywriters) to take responsibility for the powerful communications skills they wield and to consider carefully their effects." DAM refuses "to create design that furthers the creation of a global corporate monoculture."[27] ALR Design (the studio's abridged moniker) hopes to create an online network of designers who embrace DAM's mission. To augment this effort, ALR Design publishes an e-newsletter and an extensive list of resources.

ALR Design wrestles with the question student readers of this essay are undoubtedly asking: How do I follow my convictions, work as a designer, and, somehow, manage to avoid starvation? Noah Scalin, the studio's founder, posed this question to himself before he founded his business. His answer: list out the methods of doing business that will best support your convictions—i.e., do not work for companies in the midst of labor disputes, and choose clients whose efforts benefit their communities. Impressively, Scalin's rejection of transnational corporations and their fat branding budgets has not sent him to the food bank. In fact, ALR Design takes on precisely the clients he hoped to engage, and generates award-winning design. Scalin will soon bring his philosophy directly to the classroom via a specialized studies course at Virginia Commonwealth University.

Still, in all, corporate design is the bread and butter of our discipline. This truism factors heavily in U.S. design education. Malcolm Grear's tome, *Inside/Outside: From the Basics to the Practice of Design*, and a plethora of textbooks preceding and following it, fully corroborate my assertion.[28] Fortunately, the above examples prove that the same set of skills required for corporate design and branding, so popular with the Diversity School, can also be applied to proactive networks of alternative viewpoints and action within and without the design field. The manner in which those skills are imparted, however, can greatly aid or undermine student awareness of critical issues affecting the field. And it's the students who ultimately must decide, from all the information given and garnered, what to believe and where to place their talents.

Even if a design program stresses nothing but form, skills learned in the classroom are, nonetheless, couched within some sort of verbalized goal, purpose, concept, or discussion. This creates a context for the assignment—determined by the professor—that will either increase or decrease critical thinking and consideration of the foregoing issues.

Designers, educators, and students cannot merely sidestep the forward march of the Diversity School, if for no other reason than typography is now, more than ever, transformed daily into *brand equity*, or the perceived value, minus real assets, of trademarked products and services and the companies that own them. Brand equity is, therefore, the net result of brand- and product-experience design: just the latest means to inculcate and penetrate consumer culture(s).

Type is currency, and this currency runs global trade and affects every nation, business, worker, and consumer it touches. While the exemplars I cite are inspiring, they cannot justify forgetting about the effects of what we know as mainstream design: brand implementation and brand awareness. Instead, the alternative projects I describe respond to dominant forces, whether political, social, economic, or right within the graphic design field itself.

Some educators may regard these examples as too political. Indeed, the papers delivered by educators at the AIGA Chicago's "FutureHistory" conference—a symposium specifically for design educators—were, with just sparse exceptions, devoid of political, ideological, sociological, or cultural concerns. Instead, I sensed an implicit agreement—knowingly or unknowingly—with the philosophy espoused in Marc Tinkler's "Plumb Design Manifesto" (1997):

> . . . there is a distinct groundlessness in the world today, an absence of any visible consensus of authority that might be capable of prescribing the manner in which we should live, communicate, work, and play. In the span of one generation, we have witnessed the death of virtually every external authority that might be described as an "ism" or movement.

He goes on to state:

> In fact, the rapid shifts in the technologies of global communication might allow us to develop an internal individualized authority that helps us navigate the ever-shifting terrain of the information landscape. What is achieved in this glorification of the individual is the possibility of a more direct intuitive relationship between the individual and the media.

And, finally:

> The real challenges that this theory presents are not technical, aesthetic, or even ideological. The challenges we face are to develop new ways of thinking: about culture, technology, and information architecture.[29]

Here, then, in conclusion, are quotes that embody everything I argue against in this essay. "Groundlessness" and the resultant appearance of heterogeneity are a mirage, an implicit part of the surrounding engulfment: the habitat of authority, a housing so large we cannot see it, is shrouded in misleading indices of diversity. The Diversity School praises individuality, and, thus, preys upon the previous postmodern "ism," because networks of dissenting, aware, and educated individuals threaten hegemony. Adherents to Tinkler's theory will sense ideology is dead because they see the mirage instead of the facts.

Ideology is a product of human organization that will play a greater, not lesser, as we come to better understand this period. To wit, the bifurcation of contemporary understandings of Behrens's statement is an echo of larger, specifically ideological, oppositions. Noted political scientist Benjamin Barber goes to great length and depth of detail to portray ideology's role in U.S. conflicts with the Middle East in *Jihad vs. McWorld: How Globalism and Tribalism Are Reshaping the World*. Barber adeptly drives home the relevance of this polemic for designers, educators, and students when he interviews Marim Karmitz, a French film producer.

Of course, the U.S. movie industry is a big business, but behind the industrial aspect, there is also an ideological one. Sound and pictures have always been used for propaganda, and the real battle at the moment is over who is going to be allowed to control the world's images, and, so, sell a certain lifestyle, a certain culture, certain products, and certain ideas.[30]

Well, you didn't expect him to quote a typographer, now, did you? Such anonymity is our cross to bear, and thus, too, our responsibility to make the connections between discourse in other disciplines and questions in our present typographic universe.

This responsibility falls upon educators and students with a heavy set of challenges, the full weight of which can only be estimated. We should not fall prey, however, to dystopian seizures and Blade Runner-*esque scenarios. Today is a very exciting time to be involved with typography—a purposeful moment. Type education and practice are now emboldened with the potential to offer innovative approaches to contemporary problems and crises. Proactive solutions, as opposed to reactive tactics, can form incisive communications while building and/or reinforcing critical networks of access and voice, as the exemplars prove. Yet, there exists a fine line between compromise and coercion when negotiating boundaries.*

Our potential for proactive problem solving can only be realized by investigating the intangible factors constituting the advertised reality of the moment. To do this, educators may have to face the growing complexities of our age without the aid of applicable codified methods, as none exist. And students will have to bring their full intellectual resources to bear in the choices they make—in the classroom and the typographic universe beyond.

Notes
1. Recent country music "jingle" for Ford Motors, 2002.
2. See Corey S. Powell, "The Race to Find Out How the Universe Will End," *Discover* 23, no. 9 (2002): 49–55. See also Brad Lemley, "Guth's Grand Guess," *Discover* 23, no. 4 (2002): 32–39.
3. The titles "typographer" and "graphic designer" have been used interchangeably since the heyday of the International Typographic Style. See Robin Kinross, "Swiss Typography," *Modern Typography: An Essay in Critical History* (New York: Princeton Architectural Press, 1992), p. 123. Additionally, new technologies in

font creation combine the activities of typographers (presently meaning those who arrange type, often in concert with images) and type designers (formerly a separate field of skilled experts) into the present hybridized graphic designer. Erik Spiekermann and E. M. Ginger reflect this change in their choice of the label "graphic design" for the activities covered in their introductory typography text, *Stop Stealing Sheep*, cited below.

4. Philip B. Meggs, *A History of Graphic Design*, 3rd ed. (New York: John Wiley & Sons, Inc., 1998), p. 223.

5. Rick Poynor, "First Things First Revisited," *Emigre*, no. 51 (Summer 1999): 3.

6. Kathy McCoy, "Speaking in Tongues: Audience-Centered Communication and Cultural Sustainability" (paper presented at the AIGA Chicago "FutureHistory" Conference, Chicago, IL, October 2002).

7. Beverly Russell, "A New Summit in Education: How Michael and Katherine McCoy developed a peak experience for learning," ISdesiGNet (2002): *www.isdesignet.com/Magazine/J_A'00/cover.html*.

8. Erik Spiekermann and E. M. Ginger, *Stop Stealing Sheep & Find Out How Type Works* (Berkeley: Adobe Press, 2003), p. 7.

9. Michael Schmidt, "Responsibility Answers Absurdity," in *Citizen Designer*, ed. Steven Heller (New York: Allworth Press, 2003).

10. D'Arcy McNickle, *The Surrounded* (1936; reprint, Albuquerque: University of New Mexico Press, 1992).

11. I'm specifically referring to the international trade agreements NAFTA, FTAA, and AFTA. For instance, McNickle recounts how treaties with the U.S. government, such as the Dawes Land Allotment Act of 1887, promised money, land, and natural resources in return for Euro-American access to reservation lands. The consequences were devastating. The money never came, considerable land was lost, and the wild game died off. As a present corollary, the North American Free Trade Agreement (NAFTA) promised Mexico an improved economy, a looser border with the U.S., and enhanced access to U.S. consumers. As we know, Mexico's economy is still ravaged; numerous immigrants and migrant workers have been murdered, shot, arrested, and sent back to Mexico after attempting to cross their northern border; and sales profits and jobs from the North have yet to be duly realized.

12. Jack H. Williamson, "The Grid: History, Use, and Meaning," in *Design Discourse,* ed. Victor Margolin (Chicago: University of Chicago Press, 1989), pp. 171–186.

13. Williamson, pp. 184–186.

14. Ellen Lupton, "A Post-Mortem on Deconstruction?" in *Texts on Type: Critical Writings on Typography*, eds. Steven Heller and Philip B. Meggs (New York: Allworth Press, 2001), pp. 45–47.

15. Chris Riley, "Sustainable Consumerism," in *Looking Closer 4: Critical Writings on Graphic Design*, eds. Michael Bierut, William Drentell, and Steven Heller (New York: Allworth Press, 2002), p. 69.

16. INTA, *Free Trade of the Americas Draft Agreement: Chapter on Intellectual Property Rights*, prepared by the FTAA Subcommittee (2001): 6–9.

17. See Rudy Vanderlans, "The Trouble with Type," in *Looking Closer 4*, p. 155.

18. Véronique Vienne, "The Spectacle: A Reevaluation of the Situationist Thesis," in *Looking Closer 4*, p. 36.

19. In an e-mail to the author dated November 4, 2002, Victor Margolin pointed out the growing number of design-related papers, publications, and conferences concerned with various aspects of globalization. See *www.drs.org*, and *www.id.iit.edu/phd/Conferences.htm* and *www.id.iit.edu/phd/resources.htm*.

20. Max Bruinsma, "Culture Agents," in *Looking Closer 4*, p. 59.

21. Michael Schmidt, "Word as Image: Traveling Exhibition of Contemporary Graphic Design," *Designer* (Winter 2000/Spring 2001): 28–29. Johnson & Wolverton's work was featured in an exhibition by this same name, cocurated by the author, Sandy Lowrance, and Wendy McDaris.

22. Don DeLillo fans will recognize the implicit reference to "The Airborne Toxic Event" in *White Noise* (New York: Penguin Books, 1985). DeLillo's novel was ahead of its time in its investigation of the "Surround," as opposed to then popular postmodern "Below," e.g., *Jaws I, II,* and *III* (postmodern pop culture examples used in Williamson's essay, cited above).

23. In an e-mail to the author dated November 7, 2002, Scott Stowell described Open's collaboration with Sheila Levrant de Bretteville. See *www.notclosed.com/pages/wemake/work_nion.html.* See also *www.nion.us.*

24. Michael Worthington, "Right On!: Mass-Market Graphic Activism," *Eye* 11, no. 41 (Autumn 2001): 61.

25. Peter Fraterdeus, "Rumors of the Death of Typography Have Been Greatly Exaggerated," in *Texts on Type*, p. 48.

26. Design for the World, *www.designfortheworld.org*.

27. In e-mails to the author dated December 5, 2002, Noah Scalin explained the missions of ALR Design and Designers Against Monoculture (DAM). See *www.alrdesign.com*.

28. See Malcolm Grear, *Inside/Outside: From the Basics to the Practice of Design* (New York: Van Nostrand Reinhold, 1993).

29. Marc Tinkler, "Plumb Design Manifesto," in *American Center for Design Journal: New Media. New Narratives?* (Park City, Utah: American Center for Design's 1998 Living Surfaces Conference Proceedings, 2000), pp. 51–54.

30. Benjamin Barber, *Jihad vs. McWorld: How Globalism and Tribalism Are Reshaping the World* (New York: Ballantine Books, 1996), p. 82.

Traditions and Conventions

What Is a Letter? *Johanna Drucker*

Every technology suggests possibilities for letterform designs: clay and stylus, brush and ink, drawing pens and vellum, metal type, steel engravings, paper and pencil, ballpoint, photography and photomechanical devices, and digital type. But letter design isn't simply determined by technology. Gutenberg's metal characters took their design from preexisting handwritten models, just as surely as photocomposition copied the design of hot metal fonts—in spite of the unsuitability of these models to the new media (Figure 1).

Finding a vocabulary for a new technology takes time. The aesthetics of a medium aren't in any way self-evident—or immediately apparent. How is the metalness of metal to be made use of with respect to the design of letterforms? Can we even speak of an inherent aesthetic of photo-type? And, in the simulacral technologies of digital media, where shape-shifting and morphing are the common currency of image exchange, what defines the technological basis of an aesthetic: the capacity for endless invention and mimicry?

But, more importantly, the question, "What is a letter?" isn't answered just by a history of descriptions of material forms and styles, or production modes. We have to address a second, equally significant question: "What is the concept of a letter at any given moment?"

What does it mean to ask what the "concept" of a letter is? Very simply, it means acknowledging that a letter, like any other cultural artifact, is designed according to the parameters on which it can be conceived. If we imagine, for instance, that a letterform may be shaped to contain an image with a moral tale, or that the letters of the alphabet comprise cosmological elements, designs that

Figure 1: 1880s wood letter series.

realize these principles may be forthcoming no matter what the material. Similarly, a twentieth-century modern sensibility inclined toward seeking forms within the aesthetic potential of materials of production was satisfied by designs that brought forth the qualities of smoothly machined curves, such as those typical of deco forms. Obviously, in any historical moment, competing sensibilities and conceptualizations exist simultaneously. The "modernity" of Paul Rand exists side by side with the pop sensibility of Milton Glaser and the psychedelic baroque style of Victor Moscoso. Can anything be said to unify their sensibilities? At the conceptual level, yes—a conviction that custom design and innovation are affordances is permitted—even encouraged—in an era of explosive consumer culture.

The same two variables are at play, then, no matter what the individual style or cultural trends: the materials of production *and* the conception of a letter. Even at the level of production, where identity seems self-evident, a host of different concepts about what a letter *is* can be identified. A letter may be understood as: 1) a preexisting shape or model; 2) a ductal form created by a sequence of strokes with varying pressures; 3) an arbitrary sign; 4) an image fraught and resonant with history and reference; 5) an arrangement of vectors or pixels on a screen; or 6) a digital file capable of being manipulated as an image or as an algorithm. On the other hand, in conceptual terms, we understand a letter as a function of: 1) its origins (born in flames, traced on wet sand, marked by the hand of god in tablets of stone, reduced from images, invented out of air); 2) its value (numerical, graphical, pictorial); 3) its form (style, history, design); 4) its functionality (phonetic accuracy, legibility); or 5) its authenticity. No doubt other conceptualizations could be added to this list.

The advent of digital modes of production brought many of these issues, long latent in the history of letters and type design, into new, sharp focus. The work of mathematician Donald Knuth provided crucial insight as he explored the computer's design capabilities. In 1982, Knuth introduced the idea of a "metafont." Frustrated by the publication costs involved in the production of his books, Knuth decided to take advantage of the capabilities of digital media to generate the visual letterforms and equations essential to putting his research into print. His programs, TEX and Metafont, evolved directly from these efforts. Knuth proposed that a single set of algorithms could describe the basic alphabetic letterforms. As Douglas Hofstadter later commented, Knuth held out a "tantalizing prospect [. . .]: that with the arrival of computers, we can now approach the vision of a unification of all typefaces" (Figure 2).

Knuth imagined a flexible design capable of creating "a $6\frac{1}{7}$-point font that is one-fourth of the way between Baskerville and Helvetica."[1] Underlying that image were assumptions about the nature of letters as a "set." For an *a* to be described according to its features such that the "Helvetica-ness" of one version could be mixed with "Baskerville-ness" in another required that these characteristics be specifiable (distinct and discrete) and modifiable (available to an algorithmic specification and alteration). Hofstadter argued that letters belong to what are called "productive sets"—sets that cannot ever be "complete," since they are, by definition, comprised of each and every instantiation. Not only do an infinite number of *a*'s exist, but determining precisely what their common features are—or the properties of "consistency" in mathematical terms—is more complicated than it seems.

Their discussion was the expression of a particular optimism about digital media and its capabilities. In 1982, as desktop publishing and design were just coming into view over the horizon, the idea of generating fonts from a set of simple instructions—parameters describing each letter— seemed like just the right fantasy to entertain. The essence of letterforms turned out to be far more elusive than Knuth imagined. But the imagining,

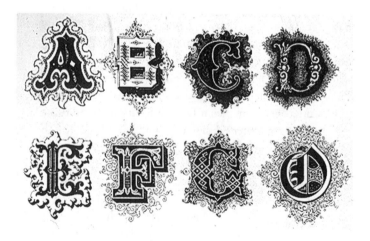

Figure 2: Wood ornamentals.

like so many other moments of intersection between digital technology and traditional practices, illuminated conceptual issues. Conceiving the "essence" of a letter as an algorithm and proposing a "metafont" are ideas with a direct connection to digital media's perceived capabilities.

As it turned out, no single essential *a* exists. A swash letter majuscule *A* in a wildly excessive script face will have elements that could never be predicted from an algorithm responsible for the minimal stroke forms of a three-stroke sans serif *A*.

Why have I spent so long on this example? Because Knuth's concept of letters had everything to do with the technology in which he was imaging their production. The idea of treating letters as "pure" mathematical information suggested that they were reducible to algorithmic conditions. Though this turned out not to be true, the link between the technological possibilities and the framework of imagination was so powerful that the idea of a metafont was brought into being.

What principles can be abstracted from this example? That the technology of production and the frameworks of conception both contribute to our sense of what a letter is. The technology of digital media couldn't produce a genuine metafont, but the context of computational typesetting and design could generate such an idea. The fantasy of digital capabilities pushed font design as programmers sought to accomplish these elusive goals.

This observation is not meant to suggest a techno-determinist view of letter design or conception. Quite the contrary. The limit of what a letter can be is always a product of the exchange between material and ideational possibilities. Sometimes, technology leads. Sometimes, it does not. If we consider the history of letterforms, we can see many moments when one or the other (technological developments or conceptual leaps) gets out of synch with the other. The serifs of Bodoni's seventeenth-century rational modern designs—meant to embody mathematical proportion, reason, and stability in metal type—were prone to break. These forms were better suited to production through photocomposition or digital modes in which their visual fragility could be countered by a technological robustness.

Asking "What is a letter?" is not the same as asking "How is it made?" The answers are never in synch—the questions don't arise from a common ground—but they push against each other in a dynamic dualism. We may imagine a pen, scraping on prepared vellum, held in the competent hand of a scribe whose manual abilities are only partially realized through the graphic vocabulary of his circumstances. Flourishes abound. The hand meanders, weaving fretwork and interlacing in elaborate intricacies. Like some artisanal genius of logic, he imagines the overlaps and underpasses that link conduits of energy in the complex form he brings slowly into being (Figure 3). The well-wrought harmony is articulate, illuminating. But could that same hand produce a row of Hobo? Or snow-capped letters? Technically, of course. Conceptually, probably not.

The conceptual frameworks are missing. The road from illumination to sans serif fonts is a dialogical road, not a material one. And the milestones are not a set of dates with tags: creation of the quill pen, invention of printing, production of the punch-cutting machine. Important as these technological developments are to the transformation of designs in physical, material form, they are modified in relation to the conceptual schema by which the letters may be conjured as forms.

Technological means have their specificity. Skills have a history. The improving capabilities of punch cutters can be dramatically illustrated by the differences between a 1501 sample of Aldine italic and examples by other artists created just a few decades later. What has changed? We'll fall into trouble quickly if we imagine a linear progression with steps toward "improvement." Witness the fantastic ability of Urbanus Wyss, a century earlier than the invention of type, carving samples in wood to demonstrate his virtuosity. Design standards are a function of industrial and engineering capabilities, as well as conceptual and technological ones (Figure 4).

The ways production means limit execution seem apparent, part of the tangible, physical world of things rendered visible. We don't expect to see swash letters carved in stone, or historical initials made of clay. But, where are the limits of conceptual possibilities rendered? How are ways of thinking about what a letter is to be gotten hold of? We have to revisit that second list from above, the table of concepts: myths of origin, of essential value and meaning value, signification of style, functionality, and authenticity—all contribute to the lore about the identity of letters. Separating these from their relation to the history of production is an artificial, but critically useful, exercise.

For instance, when we posit the form of letters in terms of their origin, we are prone to imagine their shapes as an index of those bird tracks, constellations, or arrangements of natural elements from which they

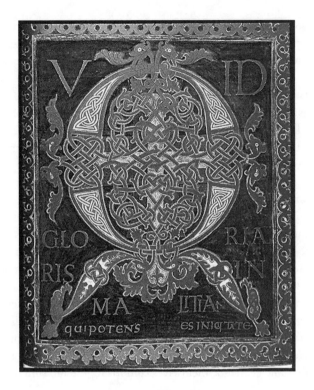

Figure 3: Interlaced initial cap.

Figure 4: Urbanus Wyss, 1459.

were supposed to be derived (Figure 5). Iconographic theories of origin suggest pictorial analogy, so the A, B, and C of our Roman letters are somehow to be reconciled with the elements of Semitic tribal camps from which Hebrew letters took their visual form (Figure 6). Such contorted sets of association and formal comparison include all manner of anachronistic or improbable histories, but the mythic strength of such assertions keeps a tenacious hold on popular imagination. To this day, the notion that the *A* contains vestiges of the ox-head, a horned "aleph," persists. Once fixed in mind, such associations seem so natural that displacing them with mere historical argument and archaeological information is difficult, indeed.

Similarly, the concept of the letters as differentiated tokens of exchange, used in a simple economy of trade in the Mediterranean, has so little allure that its factual basis gains barely a foothold. Who can imagine that seventeen signs, a reduced set of fairly basic marks found almost universally in human mark-making systems, could be established by consensual use among groups trading across linguistic and cultural barriers? The idea of the letter as arbitrary sign, however well it may be reconciled to contemporary semiotics, fares less well as an explanatory mythology.

Sacred origins and occult traditions have long posited the alphabet as a set of cosmic elements, themselves comprising the full sum of compo-

Figure 5: Origins of Chinese characters.

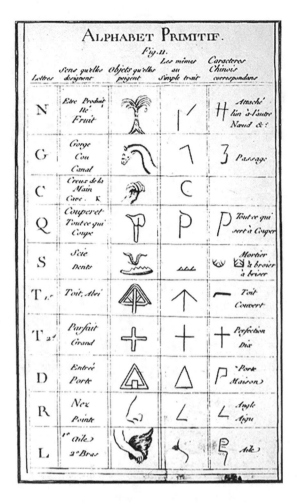

Figure 6: Alphabet history—Gebelin.

nents of the universe (Figure 7). In such a role, the letters are charged to retain their identity for reasons more profound than mere functionality. According to the *Sefer Yetsirah*: "Twenty-two foundation letters: he ordained them, he hewed them, he combined them, he weighed them, he interchanged them. And he created with them the whole creation and everything to be created in the future" (II.2). This *Book of Creation* contains

Figure 7: Kabbala—Kircher.

echoes of the history of Mesopotamian-Persian exile, the Sumerian-Babylonian story of the Flood, the beliefs of the Gnostics, the intellectual life and legacy of Alexandrian Jewry, and the influence of the Pythagoreans. Many cultural legacies consider numbers as qualities, as fundamental elements of creation. How paltry and meager, by contrast, is the notion of tokens and signs. Conceiving of letters as simply functional seems primitive, by contrast, a crude concept, commercial and crass.

Sign, symbol, and metaphor are potent concepts. The legacy of classical antiquity, including misunderstandings about the nature of Egyptian pictorial writing systems, put in the minds of Greek philosophers such as Plato and, much later, Clement of Alexandria the idea of the letters as figures. Hieroglyphics were considered to be occulted signs, capable of revelation and concealment, however little such an idea was grounded in historical reality.

Similarly inspired by recovered remains and ancient texts, the philosophers of the later Renaissance imagined the possibility of letters that might communicate directly to the eye (Figure 8). Visual systems of well-ordered epistemology were to be marked in newly designed universal languages, such as that of Joachim Becker. Far from alphabetic, such

Figure 8: Hypnerotomachia.

written forms have a conceptual base that returns a sense of figurative value to alphabet systems. Geoffrey Tory's letter designs embedded a sense of proportion and balance between the masculine principle of the straight stroke and those of feminine curves. Mystical tales and rational order combine in the well-wrought forms he imagined and engineered.

When the letters became familiar to the nursery and schoolroom, their capacity to carry lessons within their forms was exploited (Figure 9). Pictorial images and small vignettes elaborated the precepts of good behavior. Moral tales and instruments of training, as well as the inculcation into that symbolic order that is language and law—the ideological training of the young—the letters served multiple purposes as they were introduced to the lisping tongues and clumsy fingers of the young.

Even in more restrictively formal conceptions, such ideological notions make their appearance. The notions of a rational order, everywhere in evidence within certain programs of letterform construction, are as much concerned with constraining modes of thought as are the nursery images referred to above. And those diversions and inventions by which constructors of form displayed their virtuoso understanding of perspectival systems? These, too, contain their conceptual lessons, charged as these structured views are with the surveying mastery and scopic control so typical of regimes of optical power. By contrast, the analysis of letterforms, as consonant in shape with the organs of speech by

Figure 9: Nursery rhymes, nineteenth century.

which they are pronounced, suggests a poignant search for organic authenticity (Figure 10). It is as if the body's identity had a natural purity to it that might strip away the ideological layers from the innocent form of letters.

Figure 10: Moussaud.

Perhaps no approach to the conception of letterforms is more telling with respect to modernity and its discontents than that of handwriting analysis. The fetishized systems for analyzing the psycho-expressive form of marks articulates a system of bourgeois individual subjectivity and identity production that grounds identity in an embodied, but class-bound, sense of difference. The self as product and construction, inherent and cultivated, is nowhere more significantly charged than in the economy and legislative attention to forgery. Here, the letterforms enter into a system of currency, and the self as marked in that system is conceived within the act of making those rote forms with enough significant difference to be identifiable as unique, distinct, and individual. So, the letters, those templates of consistent regularity, become the instrumental means for marking uniqueness.

The list of examples of ways letters are conceived could be extended and, at every instance, brought into relation with assumptions about the technology of production.

In contemporary projects involving dimensional modeling, animation, and immersive systems, letters and language become a space to inhabit. The electronic production of Jeffrey Shaw's *Legible City* made a vibrant contribution to the notion of words as objects to encounter in a topographic field. The works of artists and designers frequently leap conceptual boundaries, overstepping perceived technological obstacles. Letter design, at its most expansive, demonstrates that letters are poetical instruments that show the manual imagination in dialogue with a materialized conceptualism.

The concept of a letter, then, turns out to be something other than a form in an idealized sense. No Platonic *a* exists, waiting to be brought into pale reflection through crass embodiment in wood, metal, or digital output that is always inadequate to display its perfection. Rather, the letter is a set of constrained parameters within a defined system of elements, a set of protocols by which a form is called forth. Those protocols are shaped by conceptual and material conditions, and by the imagination, according to which these may be determined to intersect in production.

Notes
1. Douglas Hofstadter, "Metafont, Meta-mathematics, and Metaphysics," *Metamagical Themas* (New York: Viking, 1985), p. 266.

Fine Typography: Is It Relevant? How Can It Be Taught?

Terry Irwin

Is Fine Typography Relevant?

In order to answer that question, let me clarify what I mean by "relevant," and draw distinctions between "good" and "fine" typography.

"Relevance" refers to the value of fine typography. Is it worth learning and practicing, or has it become redundant in this era of fast-changing technology and increasingly ephemeral printing? Is the "printerly care" that was once bestowed upon a page of text a justifiable expenditure of time and effort? It is, in part, that printerly care that distinguishes good typography from fine typography.

"Good" typography refers to the level of quality necessary to reveal and clarify the meaning of the written word. "Bad" typography, on the other hand, can obscure, or even disguise, meaning. "Fine" typography goes beyond these essential requirements and enhances both meaning and legibility, but also imbues the text with a sense of grace and appropriateness that is reminiscent of a finely performed piece of music. It transforms the act of reading into an aesthetic experience, which Beatrice Warde[1] compared to the added appreciation of fine wine provided by a crystal goblet.

Given these distinctions, I believe that as long as clear communication is relevant in our society, "good" typography will remain relevant. The relevance of "fine" typography is a different question, and one I hear debated with increasing frequency both in academia and in practice. Should we continue to teach design students the history and craftsmanship of fine typography? Are classic typographic standards valid, given how linked typography has become to rapidly changing technology? And, finally, how much time can students afford to spend analyzing the space between letterforms, given the larger problems confronting the world? Is it the equivalent of rearranging the deck chairs on the Titanic? As long as a connection to history, pride in craft, appreciation of subtlety, and love of beauty remain relevant, so, too, is "fine" typography.

Fine typography is based upon overarching principles, yet depends upon precision and attention to detail for its success. Fine typography combines art with craft, and is an important link to the history of communication, literature, and book design. It is an essential component of one of our most powerful cultural forces, and the crafting of fine typography requires an ability to focus on large issues and minute details with equal facility. The ability to see the whole and understand the interrelationships of its elemental parts is a universal problem-solving skill that is becoming increasingly important in a world hell-bent on specialization.

There is an element of beauty found in fine typography that is difficult to quantify but is, perhaps, akin to what Vitruvius refers to in architecture as "the element of delight." Frederick Turner, in his book, *Beauty: The Value of Values*, has this to say about beauty:

> Some years ago I bought a set of simple stoneware in a Cretan market, very irregular in form, glazed white with an easy loose pattern of little dark-blue and black arabesques. I bought it from the potters themselves, a dark blond couple, and haggled over the price because the process itself in Greece establishes a human value for a purchase. The stoneware is distinctly odd, but its cups, its jug, its plates look like archetypal cups and jugs and plates, with a generous but simple roundness of bottom made for the comfortable containing of liquid or crumb. It is beautiful in its old strange familiarity, its match with human kinetic expectations and capacities, its friendliness to the leverage of the arm and hand and nervous system. A good typeface has the same beautiful familiarity, even when the language is one unknown to us, say Japanese or Arabic or Sanskrit . . . beauty has about it the quality of inexhaustibility, of depth. It connects to where we are, and indeed evokes our whole past, both of the nursery and of the race. . . .[2]

Turner is writing about beauty, but I think this passage captures the essence and relevance of fine typography. It speaks to subtlety, appropriateness, and ease of use, which are among its key characteristics. A fine typographic solution appears simple, but is the result of mastery of both art and craft.

Who Were Typographers?

I use the past tense intentionally because there are very few true typographers around today. There is an entire generation of practicing designers who have never worked with real typographers and may not know that designers haven't always been responsible for making type look beautiful. Typesetters and printers were the ones who studied fine typography and possessed much of the knowledge found in the books that I now ask my students to read, such as Robert Bringhurst's *The Elements of Typographic*

Style and Rauri McLean's *The Thames and Hudson Typography Manual of Style*. Would-be typographers were required to pass arduous tests before they could join the prestigious typographic union and begin lengthy apprenticeships. My father, who was a metal typesetter, had to apprentice for six years before he was allowed to compose on his own. This meant years of having all of his typesetting proofed by a journeyman typesetter, who, more often than not, would have him reset some part of it. An apprentice entered the trade knowing mastery of craft would take a long time, and they felt a deep sense of pride and accomplishment once it was attained.

Typesetting companies were a wealth of information for designers, and if you developed good relationships with the typesetters, you could learn as much from them as you could in school. Most of the better type-setting houses offered large catalogs of typefaces, with multiple styles for both letter- and word spacing. Typographic subtleties such as these were more widely recognized and addressed. The process of crafting fine typography was complex and took time, by today's standards. It required the collaboration of both the designer and the typographer, and a much higher value was placed upon typographic excellence. This is in stark contrast to the ease with which students and designers alike can distort type with the push of a button or accept whatever random level of quality the combination of software application and digitized font produces. Left to its own devices, the computer usually sets type that is too tightly tracked and too loosely word spaced by classic standards, and that result is anything but fine.

Jack Stauffacher, of *The Greenwood Press*, is a typographer, though he refers to himself with both pride and humility as a printer. Jack has spent his long career in an intimate relationship with typographic form, content, and the craft of assembling letters—one at a time—to create beautiful and meaningful communications that will be relevant five hundred years from now. Jack reads everything more than once before he sets it. He makes sure he has a depth of understanding and an emotional connection to the information he is entrusted to communicate. He approaches his work with a reverence for its power and history, and still delights in the heft of the composing stick in his hand and the heavy clink of the letters as he lines them up. He doesn't work as fast as he can; he knows there is an appropriate pace and rhythm to setting type and making beautiful typography that won't be rushed any more than a fine vintage can be. He is always asking, "Is it beautiful?" and, "Is it appropriate?" Jack cares deeply about civility, and it shows in his manner and in his work. I will never consider myself to be a typographer—I know too much to pretend to possess the depth of knowledge it requires.

How the Computer Has Affected Typesetting and Typography

Our industry is being transformed in both positive and negative ways by technology. If technology has contributed to an overall decline in the quality of typography (and I believe it has), it has also given us greater flexibility and a wider choice of fonts. Many designers have learned their trade on the computer and do not have either the "eye" or the skills to produce fine typography.

The personal computer and software for designing fonts brought typeface design into the mainstream and changed it from a slow, meticulous process, practiced by a small group of specialists, to a fast-paced, style-driven exercise, undertaken by anyone with a computer. Type designers no longer need to carefully consider what kind of font may be useful or take years of meticulous work to bring one to market. Everyone who can afford to purchase software programs such as Fontographer can become a type designer, and scores of distribution companies, such as FontShop, make licensing and distribution easy and lucrative.

An interesting result is that type designers no longer assume their typefaces will outlive them, and distributors and designers alike have begun to view type design as fashion. How many of the digital fonts created in the past decade are likely to endure as long as classic faces, such as Garamond and Bodoni? The traditional view of type and typography as a classic element of communication design, rich in history, with concrete standards for its use, seems to be giving way to a view in which type becomes an ephemeral vehicle of style with no clear guidelines for use or standards for quality. This transition to ephemeral elements is changing both the way in which type is designed and used and our ideas about quality and standards for fine typography.

The number of typefaces that have been designed and distributed in the past ten years poses a significant challenge for design educators as they struggle to establish criteria and standards for good typography. Who is to say what is good or bad, or what works or doesn't work, when practically anything is possible, and experimentation and distortion of letterforms is so easily undertaken? I've never been more challenged as a design educator to redefine the relevance of basic "good" typography, as well as to instruct my students in how to produce it. For the moment, the question of "fine" typography remains even more elusive.

Can Fine Typography Be Taught in Design Programs?
I have been teaching level-two typography for the past fifteen years, and during that time, I have watched my students' attitudes toward it shift significantly. They are less interested in its history and more prone to view it as just one more visual element to be manipulated on the page, rather than as an area of expertise to be mastered. I work harder to instill a love and respect for typography and to discourage thoughtless distortion on the computer with the various options that are available, such as automatic bold and italic commands or tools that allow type to be extended or condensed. Since jettisoning them all into deep space isn't an option, each semester, I must justify why these tools undermine typographic quality, despite the fact that software applications make them available.

I believe one of the most rapidly disappearing aspects of design and typographic education is the mastery of craft. My students often see craft as a set of remedial skills having little to do with concept and design development, and this attitude, naturally, extends to the area of typographic skills. Moreover, many schools no longer teach hand skills, and when students are asked to draw letterforms, they have no confidence that they will be able to do so. As typesetting has migrated to the computer, it has become something we "watch," instead of something that we make with our hands. A host of tools that a typographer once mastered has given way to a keyboard and computer screen. "Craft" has become synonymous with unskilled labor, and the tradition of apprenticeship has all but disappeared from the vocabularies of most professions, and, with it, goes a pride in the making of artifacts that may be woven into the fabric of fine typography.

Craft seems to represent the antithesis of technology, which is changing so rapidly that it can't help but impose its speed of change upon our design programs. The computer compels us to reexamine how and what we teach each time a new software version is released. More than once, I've had a student ask me why quotation marks should "hang" outside the left text margin if Quark doesn't make it easy to do so—a logical question for someone who grew up with computers. Each time significant changes in the software occur, the pressure increases to eliminate classes in drawing or color theory, or even a third semester of typography, in order to replace them with classes in computer skills. It is particularly challenging to introduce students to the subtleties, rich history, and meditative quality of making fine typography within the context of a chaotic, ill-lit, and understaffed computer lab. My lectures on the accomplishments of Robert Granjon or the beauty of a page of type set by Claude Garamond just don't seem as relevant when they are directed to a room of shadowy figures, whose faces are lit with the blue glow of computer screens.

The quality of typography that Jack Stauffacher creates, or that some of us were able to order up like steak from typesetting companies, is a thing of the past, and the task of preserving that knowledge (or redefining more relevant standards) may fall to design instructors who, themselves, were never trained as typographers.

So, what can we do? I don't have answers, as evidenced by the sub-heads in this essay—I'm sharing my questions. Here are some of the things I do in my own search:

Try to Get Very Good at Teaching One Thing

I have taught level-two typography for fifteen years because it is often the point at which students develop a deep and abiding love of type that will last their entire careers. If they can master the subtlety of typography, they usually can elevate all of their abilities as a designer.

Remain in an Inquiry

I'm always honest with my students, and discuss my own confusion and search for relevance. I discuss the changes that have occurred in my career and the dilemma that rapidly changing technology imposes upon areas of specialty. I encourage them to discuss the issues in their theory and critical-thinking classes. I find students are very willing to engage in a process of inquiry and join me in a search for new criteria and standards.

Keep Your Own Passion Alive

Students smell it if you're not passionate about what you teach. I love letterforms and typography, and I try to communicate that love and respect for the printed word to them. The history, craft, and power of words on paper: I bring in diverse examples of typography I love, talk to them about my own criteria for quality, and encourage them to develop their own.

Create the Right Atmosphere in Which to Teach Typography

I try to create a quiet atmosphere in which we can work, for typography cannot be learned within a noisy, chaotic, and overly technical environment. For three hours, we all agree to leave our other deadlines and concerns at the door, and we enter a quieter space that moves slowly and requires us to listen more closely. There is a quality of grace that surrounds fine typography. Andre Guertler, who taught me letterform design at the Basel School of Design in Switzerland, used to make us light a candle while we were doing calligraphy. At first, I thought he was a few letters shy of a full font, but eventually, came to understand that it was all in the service of attaining the mood or mind-set essential for creating sensitive and beautiful forms.

Keep an Open Mind

Embracing the technology is essential; however, keeping it in its proper place is difficult. Having an open mind means remaining students ourselves and being open to the innovation and change that is affecting typography. Staying abreast of technical innovations, as well as what new, young designers are doing, is essential if we are to develop relevant standards for fine typography, and I resist the temptation to dismiss some of the more experimental, computer-based work. Sometimes, this is difficult.

When I feel the urge to pine for "better days," I remember a story Josef Müeller-Brockmann once shared with a small group of designers who had gathered to hear him speak in Los Angeles in the late 1980s. He said he believed that, as we get older, our scope of acceptability narrows—it is simply human nature. But, he maintained, as designers, we must resist this at all costs, lest it handicap us as professional communicators. He described how each day, he would take some time to put on his Walkman and listen to rap music because he absolutely hated it. He wanted to keep looking at what was new and fresh out in the world and remain willing to step out of his comfort zone. I always picture that elegant, elderly Swiss gentleman sitting in his studio, rocking to a new and strange beat to keep his mind open. Redefining the relevance and quality standards for fine typography may challenge us in similar ways.

Notes
1. Frederick Turner, *Beauty: The Value of Values* (Charlottesville: The University of Virginia Press, 1992), pp. 1–2.
2. Beatrice Warde, *The Crystal Goblet: Sixteen Essays on Typography* (Cleveland: World Publishing Company, 1956).

The "Crystal Goblet" as a Teaching Tool *Shelley Gruendler*

Beatrice Warde's essay, "The Crystal Goblet or Printing Should Be Invisible," argued for clarity in typographic book design. She utilized a metaphor that communicated to her audience, and provided a goal to work toward: the message should be prioritized over the typographic structure that imparts it. The strength of the essay lies in its accessibility, not its theoretical foundation, and although the concept was not entirely original, it can still be used as a catalyst for discussion with typography and graphic design students.

The "Crystal Goblet" text first appeared as a lecture on October 7, 1930, when Warde gave a speech titled, "Printing Should Be Invisible," to the recently formed British Typographers' Guild at the St. Bride Institute in London.[1] Six days later, the lecture was published in *The British & Colonial Printer & Stationer*, a weekly printing trade journal. In 1932 and 1937, the Marchbanks Press, a small private press in New York City, published the lecture as a booklet that doubled as a Press publicity piece. From then on, Warde's essay was published as "The Crystal Goblet *or* Printing Should Be Invisible." In 1955, the essay gained an even wider audience when it appeared as the first essay in her book, *The Crystal Goblet: Sixteen Essays on Typography*, published in England by the Sylvan Press. (The first United States edition was released in 1956.) The popularity of the "Crystal Goblet" continues even today, for it is still mentioned in literature, on Web logs, and at conferences.

The "Crystal Goblet" essay is centered around a metaphor of wine in a crystal goblet, and the symbol proved to be so effective and convincing that the concept itself became known as "the Crystal Goblet." Warde reasons that "almost all the virtues of the perfect wineglass have a parallel in [book] typography." She uses wine to symbolize the author's words and intentions, and the goblet represents typography and the book itself.[2] Warde presents the choice of drinking wine from a transparent crystal goblet or an exquisite solid gold one, and contends that she would know if the wine drinker was an amateur or connoisseur simply by their preference. According to Warde, a wine expert would never opt for the solid gold chalice because it would impair the drinker's visual experience, which contributes to the enjoyment of the wine. Similarly, a typographer or practiced reader would not allow for an overdesigned book that inhibits the reader's grasp of the author's thoughts.

In the essay, Warde further expanded this idea to relate it to an additional, yet similar, metaphor of a transparent window.[3] She viewed the window as a vessel for transporting the reader into the arena of the author's meaning, and described different styles of windows, with their particular characteristics and how they coincided with book typography. She first describes a window made of stained glass, symbolizing overly expressive book typography, and promptly labels it "a failure as a window," since the colored window evolves into a thing to be "looked at, not through." Her next example is of a window that is so completely transparent that it allows for no remembrance of the window whatsoever—only of the view, which symbolizes her definition of truly functional printing. She continues describing a third window comprising of small panes of glass, signifying "fine printing." While viewing this variety, one is aware of the window's high quality, but the awareness never completely overtakes the view that is its intended function.

The beginning student often has difficulties with theoretical concepts, and the "Crystal Goblet" is usually the first serious reading on the subject to which the students are exposed. The tone is accessible— although noticeably *bourgeois*—and it is likely that this is the reason why it is as easily understood now as it was in 1930. The language used throughout echoes the original lecture format, and perhaps this is what the students identify with so quickly.[4] When compared to other essays of the period, its mood is almost casual, and the metaphors of both the wine and the windows are well defined and self-explanatory.

The "Crystal Goblet" can be a successful point of discussion, but one must acknowledge what the essay lacks. It is neither profoundly philosophical nor accurately academic, and cannot withstand intense scrutiny, especially among higher-level students; however, the essay could be revisited at varying levels of the education process to measure the students' new design experience and skills.

Warde revelled in sparking controversy, and often instigated discussions knowing that they would lead to heated debates. She wanted people to deliberate ideas, whether historical or contemporary, and believed debate to be a characteristic lacking in both the professional and the educational printing and typographic environments. Beatrice Warde viewed her role in the field as the "instigator," even more so than the "communicator," as she publicly referred to herself. By utilizing a metaphor that communicated a theoretical typographic concept in an easily understood format, as well as providing a goal to work toward, Beatrice Warde's essay is an excellent starting point for the beginner in typography and graphic design.[5] What the "Crystal Goblet" does is inspire dialogue and provoke reactions—which is surely one of our primary goals in studios and classrooms.

Notes

1. In its 1955 publication, this was dated 1932, but the *British & Colonial Printer & Stationer* appearance clearly indicates that 1930 is correct.

2. "Bear with me this long-winded and fragrant metaphor; for you will find that almost all the virtues of the perfect wineglass have a parallel in typography. There is the long, thin stem that obviates fingerprints on the bowl. Why? Because no cloud must come between your eyes and the fiery heart of the liquid. Are not the margins on book pages similarly meant to obviate the necessity of fingering the type-page? Again: the glass is colourless or at the most only faintly tinged in the bowl, because the connoisseur judges wine partly by its colour and is impatient of anything that alters it. There are a thousand mannerisms in typography that are as impudent and arbitrary as putting port in tumblers of red or green glass! When a goblet has a base that looks too small for security, it does not matter how cleverly it is weighted; you feel nervous lest it should tip over. There are ways of setting lines of type which may work well enough, and yet keep the reader subconsciously worried by the fear of 'doubling' lines, reading three words as one, and so forth." ("The Crystal Goblet," paragraph 2.)

3. "The book typographer has the job of erecting a window between the reader inside the room and that landscape which is the author's words. He may put up a stained-glass window of marvellous beauty, but a failure as a window; that is, he may use some rich superb type like text gothic that is something to be looked at, not *through*. Or he may work in what I call transparent or invisible typography. I have a book at home, of which I have no visual recollection whatever as far as its typography goes; when I think of it, all I see is the Three Musketeers and their comrades swaggering up and down the streets of Paris. The third type of window is one in which the glass is broken into relatively small leaded window panes; and this corresponds to what is called 'fine printing' today, in that you are at least conscious that there is a window there, and that someone has enjoyed building it. That is not objectionable, because of a very important fact which has to do with the psychology of the subconscious mind. This is that the mental eye focuses through type and not *upon* it. The type which, through any arbitrary warping of design or excess of 'colour,' gets in the way of the mental picture to be conveyed, is a bad type. Our subconsciousness is always afraid of blunders (which illogical setting, tight spacing and too-wide unleaded lines can trick us into), of boredom, and of officiousness. The running headline that keeps shouting at us, the line that looks like one long word, the capitals jammed together without hair-spaces—these mean subconscious squinting and loss of mental focus." ("The Crystal Goblet," paragraph 12.)

4. "There is no end to the maze of practices in typography, and this idea of printing as a conveyor is, at least in the minds of all the great typographers with whom I have had the privilege of talking, the one clue that can guide you through the maze. . . . And with this clue, this purposiveness in the back of your mind, it is possible to do the most unheard-of-things, and find that they justify you triumphantly. It is not a waste of time to go to the simple fundamentals and reason from them. In the flurry of your individual problems, I think you will not mind spending half an hour on one broad and simple set of ideas involving abstract principles." ("The Crystal Goblet," paragraph 8.)

5. "Printing demands a humility of mind, for the lack of which many of the fine arts are even now floundering in self-conscious and maudlin experiments. There is nothing simple or dull in achieving the transparent page. Vulgar ostentation is twice as easy as discipline. When you realize that ugly typography never effaces itself, you will be able to capture beauty as the wise men capture happiness by aiming at something else. The 'stunt typographer' learns the fickleness of rich men who hate to read. Not for them are long breaths held over serif and kern, they will not appreciate your splitting of hair spaces. Nobody (save the other craftsmen) will appreciate half your skill. But you may spend endless years of happy experiment in devising that crystalline goblet which is worthy to hold the vintage of the human mind." ("The Crystal Goblet," paragraph 14.)

Convention and Creativity in Typography *David Jury*

Preamble

This (heavily reworked) article[1] was originally published in response to the design proposal by The Designers Republic (TDR) that was adopted for issue 58 of *TypoGraphic*, the journal of the International Society of Typographic Designers (of which I am editor). Each issue is designed by an invited designer who is given a free hand in return for free design. The designers are chosen for their attitude and/or working methodology, in sympathy or empathy with the theme of the issue, which, in this case, was "Too much noise." TDR was invited to design this issue because if noise is whatever comes between author and reader—"interference," in the classic Shannon and Weaver model of communication[2]—TDR are long-term, expert exponents.[3] Their solution was to wipe the journal clean of type and transfer it all to the journals' wrapper. This irreverent (but also appropriate) treatment of the text created the biggest response of any issue of *TypoGraphic*.

Convention

The necessity of formality (or rules) in many of the circumstances where typographic communication is required has, at best, been downgraded in the teaching of typography. With all printed information, the predictability offered by conventions (rules) is essential for accurate and speedy comprehension. Because the conventional is predictable, and, therefore, easy to comprehend, it follows that an author, editor, or typographer who deviates from convention—who breaks the rules—knows that, in so doing, the information to be communicated will require additional effort by the recipient if it is to be understood.[4]

Rules are generally associated with the formal experience of learning, regardless of the subject, except for the visual arts. Here, rules (conventions) are too often looked upon with disdain, mistakenly considered to be the antithesis of creativity. Besides architecture, music, and dance, there is no other branch of the creative arts where the elementary rules are considered anything other than an essential part of creative endeavor. Every problem requires its own very specific solution, so, if a "conventional" appearance is required, this will rarely be achieved by using existing conventional idioms.

The role of convention is to diminish the influence of noise. "Noise" might be defined as anything that comes between author and reader: poor light, uncomfortable chair, bad printing, errors of fact, unconventional (and therefore, unpredictable) layout, etc. If, despite an unconventional presentation, clarity of content is a prerequisite, to compensate, the information itself must be written in as simple and conventional a manner as possible. For example, if a telephone line is distorting sound, we repeat words, and, if asked to spell something, we will say, "A for apple. . . ." Any information that has to function in a stressful, busy environment must be simple, repetitious, and highly predictable.

Similarly, formal, familiar design helps to overcome the problems of transmitting unfamiliar, and, therefore, less predictable, information. If the intended audience is more heterogeneous, the importance of formality in the presentation tends to increase. Alternatively, information we expect to receive plenty of uninterrupted attention, such as that in a highly specialized journal, can be written and designed in a less predictable, more challenging way, in the belief that the reader will enjoy investing the extra intellectual (and, perhaps, physical) effort necessary for its comprehension. Such a reader might be expecting, and, indeed, seeking the challenge of the unpredictable. But, of course, this additional effort will only be rewarded—deemed worthwhile—if it leads to an enhanced understanding of the text. The element of surprise, even initial confusion, will only be acceptable if, finally, it is deemed a legitimate and intrinsic enrichment of the information. (The role of the author is, rather pointedly, ignored here.[5] While I sympathize with those who find this regrettable, my only excuse for the time being is that personal experience suggests that this accurately reflects the current low status of the author, and the correspondingly high status of marketing departments within the publishing industry.)

Structuring information according to an established pattern or convention is a standard method of decreasing the possibility of confusion by increasing predictability. Such "patterns" can also offer an aesthetic aspect to the information. In writing, for instance, the repetitious and, therefore, predictable patterns of rhythm and rhyme can increase both pleasure and comprehension. In fact, with poetry and song, much of the pleasure comes directly from the anticipation of a repeated note or phrase. In typography, the grid achieves many of the same qualities, encompassing and holding together all the disparate parts of, for instance, a book, in a prearranged, formal, and easily comprehendible manner. For the reader, understanding the structure and the hierarchy of the information provides the pleasure that comes from ownership, access, and control. The comfort of unbroken rhythm, of knowing that everything is in the right (predictable) place, should not be underestimated.

The means of delivery is also influential. "Difficult" information presented in a book can be reread as many times as is necessary, and at the reader's convenience. The same information delivered through speech would need to be slow and precise, because there is clearly a socially defined (if vague) limit as to how many times you can ask someone to repeat himself!

For a "mass audience," information is generally designed to be highly predictable in both form and content. Mainstream pop music and television soap operas offer few surprises. More demanding information, which, by definition, is less predictable, might be presented in a less formal way, especially when the audience is a more specialized group. However, the context and orientation of "demanding information" is always evolving, even for mass audiences. Any audience will learn, over time, to understand and enjoy what was initially considered to be a "difficult" subject. New conventions can, and are, learned and accepted all the time. Challenging "norms" is essential for social and cultural development. But where a challenge has been successfully achieved, inevitably, "redundancy" follows. Initial reactions to the Surrealists were, understandably, hostile, because they went out of their way to ensure that their working methods and public events would stimulate an adverse reaction. Today, many of their "affronts to public decency" appear childish—at best, amusing in their rather obvious attempts to shock. Similarly, people who grew up in the punk era find it demeaning to hear "their" music played on mainstream radio and even in supermarkets.

The conventions of typography become tradition, and tradition, by definition, is predictability. In the recent (essentially, pre-digital) past, predictability also had two practical functions. It enabled compositors, proofreaders, and printers to know, without needing to ask, what everyone else was doing. It streamlined training and production, made errors easier to recognize, and, in so doing, guaranteed a level of quality at a predictable cost that, in turn, guaranteed a profit—"well-tried, well-reasoned principles of text construction whose survival would depend on their effectiveness in practical situations."[6]

Convention also has certain important benefits for the reader. When the text looks familiar, there is nothing about the text itself to divert the reader's focus of attention. Eliminating typographic uncertainty allows the receiver to read "automatically." This does not, of course, mean mindless reading—quite the opposite. It means the reader can concentrate on what the author is "saying" without distraction. Convention reduces interference (noise) to a minimum.

Convention, or tradition, requires time spent with a stable working methodology to become established. To the layman, there has probably been very little discernible change in the design and arrangement of type in the five hundred years between the quasi-calligraphic use of black letter and the invention of digital technology. And yet, for a brief period after the invention of moveable type, printers such as Gutenberg, Plantin, and Manutius must have been aware that they were among the most progressive communicators of their day. In a largely preliterate world, they swiftly embedded the written word into a universal structure and gave it a state of permanence. The types and the arrangements they developed continue to be models for most typographic endeavors today.

By the late fifteenth century, the conventions had been set. It is easy to imagine that, because there was so little discernible change over such a long period of time, *design*, as we use the term today, played little or no part in the process of making and printing books. Certainly, a major part of typographic craft is making text easy to read—normal, conventional, and traditional—which means keeping both the effort afforded to its design, and the design itself, hidden. This is incomprehensible to a typographer who has been educated to believe that the function of the designer is to be an innovator, an arbiter of change.

Creativity

What students have in mind when they (inevitably) describe themselves as "creative" is someone who challenges the status quo. This has, at least in part, to do with the perceived value of "status." To set out to design "change" is also to crave attention. The concerns that initially lead many students into design—humane, political, social, and practical—are, too often, later replaced by design at its most intrusive, short-lived, and disposable form. The very idea of design being a public service could not be further from most students' minds. The celebrity status that too many consider a representation success does not easily equate with the concept of service.

Challenging the status quo is, undoubtedly, part of the service provided by graphic design. But here, we need to distinguish between creativity and originality. It is possible for originality to be no more than the rearrangement or a recombination of existing elements into a different pattern. Originality alone is vacuous, since a "solution" need only be unconventional or different to be original. A creative solution will have varying degrees of originality, but it will always have purpose and be useful. With creativity, I see no reason to differentiate between fine art and applied art. In fine art, just as in typography, surely, originality alone is banal, no more than novelty. To be creative, originality must serve an intellectual and/or practical purpose.

To be applied effectively, it is generally accepted that creativity needs to be incorporated into a range of expertise. Design companies are fully aware of the necessity of acquiring the "right mix" of abilities and attitudes, and, yet, attempts to establish what creativity *is* exactly can prove elusive. In studies of the working patterns of leading artists and scientists, it has been found that the only common characteristic is a willingness to work hard for long hours. Such a characteristic is, of course, likely to contribute to success in any area of activity, but, at least, it refutes the oft-repeated cliché that "creativity" offers an alternative to hard work.

As well as being hard work, creative endeavor in a commercial context can also be expensive. To be creative, the designer must be allowed to think, but, too often, "time to think" is considered a luxury. And yet, without time to think and reflect, mere novelty—often disguised as creativity—tends to be the result. When pressure is caused by volume of work and lack of time, there is a tendency for the typographer to switch to "automatic." This is unfortunate, but also inevitable. In education, typographic students are encouraged (I hope) to think creatively and unconventionally, and, of course, are given the time and the appropriate circumstances to do so. But when the commercial world cannot allow this, switching to "automatic" is the only alternative. It is then that typographers may have to rely on the essential conventions—rules—(I hope) they were also taught as students; the tradition, the essential orthodoxy, of how type works. Substantial anecdotal evidence describes how, in the recent past, the compositor achieved the "traditional" appearance of type, honed to varying degrees of finish depending on how much time could be allowed—all of which, of course, was dictated by how much the customer was willing to pay. Doing repetitious work, but with varying deadlines, quickly establishes what is absolutely necessary and what is "extra."

The unconventional is risky. But a few design companies (usually smaller ones) are able to work in this way. This is not easy and requires a rare, intellectual rigor if such an approach is to be maintained. Generally, as habits are formed, there is less likelihood of attaining a creative solution. It is not surprising, therefore, that it is often the newcomer who displays the greatest creativity, suggesting that, for typographers to produce successful work, they must be knowledgeable about their subject, capable of seeing the familiar afresh and able to recognize merit in the work of others, particularly when such work challenges personal orthodoxy. Not surprisingly, an alternative methodology will be a major reason for employing newly graduated students. The ability and confidence to apply a personal "voice," even when working within rigorous conventions, is seen by many in the design profession as a valuable aspect of typographic education.

Conclusions

Reading and readability are not, by any means, the only function or criteria of typography. Elements that attract also have a role to play in communication. In historical terms, this requirement is most clearly identified in the use of display type, designed to attract and divert the viewer from whatever else he or she might be doing. But also, on a more subtle level, there is little doubt that visual attraction, created by the use of prearranged signals, a germane arrangement of text, or simply good-quality printing on appropriate stock, can divert and persuade a reader to invest time (and, perhaps, money) in order to read more. Every piece of printed matter must clearly convey the reason for its existence: why it is appearing now, and why it looks the way it does. The conventional requirement—that there should be a connection or coherence between purpose, content, and form—remains an essential criterion. But, at the same time, there is so much more that is possible; print is cheaper and more versatile, and digital technology offers endless options. However, this technology also requires the same high standards of skill and knowledge as all previous methods of setting and arranging type stretching back over 550 years. It certainly offers no excuses for the acceptance of lower standards!

The function of the typographer is often described as being a "form-giver."[7] At the early stages of any project, there are many options. The process of elimination, achieved by the relentless adherence to the needs of the message and of the reader, will continue until only the essential ingredients remain. If the form loses contact with the message, that form will degenerate into novelty. It must be remembered that looking at a page of text is very different from reading a page of text. A critical appraisal cannot, finally, be made only by looking. Composition, proportion, balance, rhythm, tone, and texture—all of these are important. But the intimate level of intellectual engagement—reading—is where the most important appraisal is made, and, importantly, that judgment is not made by the designer.

While textual typography requires anonymity, the purpose of generating printed text is never to remain anonymous. If printed matter is to exist, it must be made into something, an object that can attract the attention of those whose attention is sought. In short, it must solicit. But the means of attraction must not sacrifice the message. Irrelevance will inevitably be betrayed by superfluous design. For the typographer, the functions of convention and creativity are often almost indistinguishable.

Notes

1. David Jury, "Predictability," *TypoGraphic* 58 (2002). The Designers Republic's design proposal for *TypoGraphic* 58 meant that no illustrative material could be included, and, as a result, two of the planned articles had to be pulled (a third contributor "withdrew" his article on seeing the design proposal). So, I wrote "Predictability" to fill the space.

2. C.E. Shannon and W. Weaver, *The Mathematical Theory of Communication* (University of Illinois Press, 1949).

3. The Designers Republic is based in Sheffield, U.K. In *Emigre* 29, which they designed in 1994, Ian Anderson, TDR founder, described their work thus: "There is no conscious effort to create a new movement or style, just a continuing desire to work further into what we do . . . to constantly reinvent and reinterpret . . . and to take ideas beyond logical extremes" (page 3).

4. David Jury, *About Face: Reviving the Rules of Typography*, chapters 12 and 13 (Rotovison Books, 2002).

5. In the meantime, here is an excellent description of the relationship between author and typographer, offered by Stanley Morison: ". . . a 'fine' book is more than 'something to read.' The amateur of printing looks for character in the product. The book, therefore, which essays to rank above the commonplace must, while not failing in its essential purpose, transport the personality of its maker no less surely, though certainly less assertively, than that of its author and its subject. The problem of the typographer, therefore, is to achieve an individual book without doing violence to the essential purpose of the author. . . . Thus the whole mystery of fine typography lies in the perfect reconciliation of these several interests. There is no master formula: every book is a challenge to the artist-typographer." Stanley Morison, *Four Centuries of Fine Printing*, student edition (London: Ernest Benn Limited, 1960), p. 12.

6. Paul Stiff, quoting Robert Waller in "Instructing the Printer," *Typography Papers*, no. 1 (Department of Typography and Graphic Communication, University of Reading, 1996), 35. On the same page, Stiff offers another quote, this time from Brooke Crutchley, who was university printer at Cambridge during the 1950s, describing the practical function of tradition, "because everyone working at the press knew how to deal with typographic detail and elaborate instructions were unnecessary, it was possible for one full-time designer and five or six copy-editors . . . to deal with two hundred books and as many journal issues in a year." Taken from Brooke Crutchley, "Design and Production: A Cambridge Experience," *Scholarly Publishing* (July 1973): 303–7.

7. Karel Martens, *Printed Matter/Drukwerk* (London: Hyphen Press, 1996), p. 129.

Back to Basics: Stopping Sloppy Typography *John D. Berry*

There's a billboard along the freeway in San Francisco that's entirely typo-graphic, and very simple. Against a bright blue background, white letters spell out a single short line, set in quotation marks: "Are you lookin' at me?" The style of the letters is traditional, with serifs; it looks like a line of dialogue, which is exactly what it's supposed to look like. Since this is a billboard, and the text is the entire message of the billboard, it's a witty comment on the fact that you *are* looking at "me"—that is, the message on the billboard—as you drive past.

But, as my partner and I drove past and spotted this billboard for the first time, we both simultaneously voiced the same response: "No, I'm looking at your apostrophe!"

The quotation marks around the sentence are real quotation marks, which blend in with the style of the lettering—"typographers' quotes," as they're sometimes called—but the apostrophe at the end of "lookin'" is, disconcertingly, a single "typewriter quote," a straight up-and-down line with a rounded top and a teardrop tail at the bottom.

To anyone with any sensitivity to the shapes of letters, whether they know the terms of typesetting or not, this straight apostrophe is like a fart in a symphony—boorish, crude, out of place, and distracting. The normal quotation marks at the beginning and end of the sentence just serve to make the loud "blat!" of the apostrophe stand out. If that had been the purpose of the billboard, it would have been very effective. But unless the billboards along Highway 101 have become the scene of an exercise in typographic irony, it's just a big ol' mistake. Really big, and right out there in plain sight.

The Devil Is in the Details

This may be a particularly large-scale example, but it's not unusual. Too much of the signage and printed matter that we read—and that we, if we're designers or typographers, create—is riddled with mistakes like this. It seems that an amazing number of people responsible for creating graphic matter are incapable of noticing when they get the type wrong.

This should not be so. These fine points ought to be covered in every basic class in typography, and basic typography ought to be part of the education of every graphic designer. But clearly, this isn't the case—or else a lot of designers skipped that part of the class, or have simply forgotten what they once learned about type. Or, they naively believe the software they use will do the job for them.

Maybe it's time for a nationwide—no, worldwide—program of remedial courses in using type.

Automated Errors

As my own small gesture toward improvement, I'll point out a couple of the more obvious problems—in the hope that maybe, *maybe*, they'll become slightly less commonplace, at least for awhile.

Typewriter quotes and straight apostrophes are actually on the wane, thanks to word-processing programs and page-layout programs that offer the option of automatically changing them to typographers' quotes on the fly. (I'm not sure what has made the phenomenon I spotted on that billboard so common, but I've noticed a lot of examples recently of text where the double quotation marks are correct but the apostrophes are straight.) But those same automatic typesetting routines have created another almost universal mistake: where an apostrophe at the *beginning* of a word appears backwards, as a single open quotation mark. You see this in abbreviated dates ('99, '01) and in colloquial spellings, like 'em for *them*. The program can turn straight quotes into typographers' quotes automatically, making any quotation mark at the start of a word into an open quote, and any quotation mark at the end of a word into a closed quote, but it has no way of telling that the apostrophe at the beginning of 'em isn't supposed to be a single open quote, so it changes it into one.

The only way to catch this is to make the correction by hand—every time.

Anemic Type

The other rude noise that has become common in the symphony hall is fake small caps. Small caps are a wonderful thing, very useful and sometimes elegant; fake small caps are a distraction and an abomination.

Fake caps are what you get when you use a program's "small caps" command. The software just shrinks the full-size capital letters down by a predetermined percentage—which gives you a bunch of small, spindly-looking caps all huddled together in the middle of the text. If the design calls for caps and small caps—that is, small caps for the word but a full cap for the first letter—it's even worse, since the full-size caps draw attention to themselves because they look so much heavier than the smaller caps next to them. (If you're using caps and small caps to spell out an acronym, this might make sense; in that case, you might want the initial caps to stand out. Otherwise, it's silly. (And—here comes that word again—distracting.)

If it weren't for a single exception, I'd advise everyone to just forget about the "small caps" command—forget it ever existed, and never, ever, touch it again. (The exception is Adobe InDesign, which is smart enough to find the real small caps in an OpenType font that includes them, and use them when the "small caps" command is invoked. Unfortunately, InDesign isn't smart enough, or independent enough, to say, "No, thanks," when you invoke "small caps" in a font that doesn't actually have any. It just goes ahead and makes those familiar old fake small caps.) You don't really need small caps at all, in most typesetting situations; small caps are a typographic refinement, not a crutch. If you're going to use them, use real small caps: properly designed letters with the form of caps, but usually a little wider, only as tall as the x-height or a little taller, and with stroke weights that match the weight of the lowercase and the full caps of the same typeface. Make sure you're using a typeface that *has* true small caps, if you want small caps. Letterspace them a little, and set them slightly loose, the same way you would (or at least should) with a word in all caps; it makes the word much more readable.

Pay Attention, Now

There are plenty of other bits of remedial typesetting that we ought to study, but those will do for now. The obvious corollary to all this is, to produce well-typeset words, whether in a single phrase on a billboard or several pages of text, you have to pay attention. Proofread. Proofread again. Don't trust the defaults of any program you use. Look at good typesetting and figure out how it was done, then do it yourself. Don't be sloppy. Aim for the best.

Words to live by, I suppose. And, certainly, words to set type by.

The Language of Letters *Max Kisman*

Letters of Identity

When I was a teenager I loved to draw letters. In my school diaries and notebooks, and on my schoolbags. It was one of my favorite activities. Basically, I copied the lettering of the record sleeve designs of *Rubber Soul* and *Revolver* by the Beatles, *White Room* by Cream, the Who, and albums by the Dutch group, Cuby and the Blizzards. Lots of drippy-drop, psychedelic lettering. It made it to the cover of the school paper and, later, a few posters.

Unconsciously, and by trial and error, I discovered the essence and power of "custom" lettering: the expression of identity.

It became obvious to me that, by drawing my own letters, I became part of them. Or, they became part of me. It was my drawing, and I made it. It was me. This awareness made me become more interested in lettering and letters. I hadn't yet heard the word *typography* whispering in the distant future.

At art school, graphic design became my main focus. During my education, I had four professors who taught me various aspects of lettering and typography. In 1970, at the Academy for Art and Industry in Enschede, Abe Kuipers, a well-known Dutch typographer and graphic artist, was the first to stimulate working and designing with lead type for the book press. But first, he made us draw the letterforms and layouts by hand.

As an artist, his paintings, silk-screen prints, and sculptures were an important example of mixing fine art and applied art. Book designer Sien ten Holt, my second teacher, forced me to break with my "psychedelic" approach in the core year at the Gerrit Rietveld Academy in 1971, by teaching the basic letterform construction of the Roman capitals and the essence of letterspacing. The next couple of years, Charles Jongejans, my third teacher and mentor, placed typography in a broader cultural and social context.

His involvement in the earlier developments of the profession of the typographer and graphic designer showed a strong affection and cultural integration of typography in society.

Finally, Gerard Unger introduced me to the more detailed aspects of letterforms and type design (1975–76). He was young and entertaining.

He designed brand names and logos with classical type. I thought that wasn't modern enough. I wasn't sure if I liked his typography class that much, but because I liked him, I did my best. Unger taught me the very basics of typeface design: when and where to pay attention, what to look out for, and where to be modest. His specialty, the curves, had my interest, too, especially the female curves. What other reason can one have to design letters? The hallway of his house had the curves of his wife's calf. Most importantly, I learned to change the look, appearance, and meaning of a message with typography, the manipulation of the good, bad, pretty, ugly, legible, illegible, provocative, and conservative.

After my formal education, when I was art director for *Vinyl* magazine (Amsterdam, 1981–1986), we deliberately changed the headline typeface every month as a matter of style. It was quite experimental and appealing to my generation: a hardcore group of fans of the post-punk and new-wave movements. You could say it was the *Raygun* of the eighties. We would draw our letters, or write them in script, use photocopy machines, very early Linotype digital typesetting, optical modification techniques, and early dot matrix printouts, all as manual artwork and a lot of darkroom repro stuff. *Vinyl*'s design expressed the shifting conventions of typography and graphic design that illustrated the individualization of the lifestyle of the youth in the eighties. While the seventies were very much about collective idealism, the eighties—the precursor to the computer era—were known as the "Me" generation.

With *Language Technology*, the first magazine completely produced with computers (Amsterdam, 1986), I started to digitize typefaces with the earliest versions of font software. Soon, I started to apply the technology to all my work for posters, books, and other graphic designs. No more darkroom days, ever again! A new era was born. *Language Technology*, with its desktop publishing production, shook a rusted graphic industry to its foundation.

The field was cracked wide open, and so was the source code. New freedoms, new forms. By gluing parts of two existing typefaces together, I created the "Fudoni" in 1990. It was the first reassembled, remixed typeface of its genre, instantly devaluating established conventions of the industrially produced letterform.

The secrets of producing type production were gone. The technology was accessible to anyone. For the graphic designer, type design had become another aspect of the broad field of the profession. Type became an illustrative element in graphic design. With custom-created alphabets, the graphic designer could give a strong and recognizable identity to the graphic product. Typography had become lettering again.

Hindsight

To become a professional typographer, you will need to develop an eye and feel for every aspect of typography and applied lettering. You need a basic appreciation in the matter that can originate from various fields of interest, like writing, painting, or drawing: the content and/or the form of communicating messages.

Then, you'll need to get focused on more specific aspects and details. Good teachers will inspire you to explore your own talents and will help direct you in an appropriate direction.

Also, you'll need to locate yourself in the professional landscape. Who is doing what, and where? Who are your friends and allies? Who are your competitors? What do you want to achieve with all the energy you will put into your work?

Then, you will have to look for the opportunity to jump on an assignment and use it to accommodate your client's goals, as well as your own. Try to be at the right place at the right time. You might get lucky.

So, don't sit and wait. Start and do. Know that not everything you touch will become a work of art. You will fail, sometimes, but all failures will lead to more successes. The more you produce, the closer you'll get.

Edit Your Design Decisions

One of my philosophies (which is rather concise) is: "The quality of talent is within its limitations, not with its possibilities." It means that in dealing with the physical limitations of reality, the professional designer often has to be inventive and improvise to solve a problem within a limited time frame. He needs to be practical and efficient. He needs to know what to look for, but, more importantly, when to stop.

The design process is one of decisions. Every decision has its own direct consequence, and, ultimately, its long-term consequences and outcomes. Once you know where you want to be in a certain time frame, it is easier to make your decisions. When you visualize the design process in a schedule, scheme, rough setup, or outline, you will be able to take your steps with a strong sense of direction.

Outlining is essential in the design process. And, it literally can be anything. To me, it is drawing or sketching. For somebody else, it might be writing, or a list, or charts. What is important is that these are all manual reflections of thoughts. Mind maps, brainstorms, and doodles. They are, at best, physical interactions with the spirit. The spirit of each individual is influenced by the spirit of mankind. Your own hand, as limited as it is in its skills, interprets your individual style. You become the visual translator of your thoughts, which nobody else will ever be able to replicate. Experience will build up confidence. What once seemed to be awkward and strange becomes special. That's where originality originates.

Language Is Reference

Communication is language, whether it consists of words or visuals. When we communicate, we understand the use and meaning of the words or visuals. Why? Because, we learned them at a certain stage in our lives. If we do not communicate, we don't know anything about the use and meaning of the words or visuals. Why? We do not have any reference material to fall back on.

Meaning is a value given to something previously meaningless and abstract. Meaning is subjective, because it could have been something else, too. Subjectivity is culturally dependent; thus, meaning is culturally dependent. Communication uses cultural references. When references aren't shared completely, they'll create misunderstanding and opposition. Most problems we encounter individually, locally, or globally are based on not sharing cultural, religious, or economical references, unintentionally or deliberately.

The easiest way to communicate is using values that everybody recognizes. These overused values are the clichés of communication. A lot of our language is cliché, whether we like it or not. But, there is nothing wrong with clichés. They are very digestible.

Is the easiest way to communicate also the best way? Is there a hard way to communicate? If you know whom you are talking to (what reference group your audience belongs to, culturally, politically, mentally, spiritually, and economically), you will use a language of reference to communicate. The wider your audience is, the more your reference groups will build up, and the reference material you use will be less specific. You will compromise more to general references, and, probably, clichés.

By using clichés in your own personal style vocabulary, you will be able to translate them according to your own interpretation skills. By appropriating them, you make them your own.

Our book of reference is very much time dependent. Insights, knowledge, experience, and understanding are constantly changing. These changes are the living organisms of our way of thinking about and looking at the world around us. That will never stop. Our references will change and extend. And, so, our language will change and extend. As long as we develop our personalities, and our individual characters, we will see different and new interpretations of the references we live by. This applies to images, drawings, and paintings, lettering and letterforms, typeface design, typography, music, dance, writing, photography, literature, science, business, economics, politics, religion, industry, trade, travel, and everything else that is humanly created.

The Voice of Type

A letter speaks to us, because we know it is a letter. It was given a label, which merged into the letter. Certain letters are created in certain times. They are historical, they are "old"; sometimes, they are "classic" because of how they were produced. Sometimes they are modern because of the way production has changed. Sometimes they are crap because everybody and anybody can make them. But still, they all are letters. The styles of letter reproduction tell us they want to look different than the others. They say whether they are sophisticated, angry, obnoxious, or gracious. They say: "Use me for your specific purpose."

And you have a purpose! You have a poem, so you'll choose a poem typeface. You're writing for a grocery store, so you'll choose a grocery typeface. You are part of a revolution, so you choose a shouting typeface. If you have something to sell, choose the typeface that sells it the best.

Does the style choice matter? No, as long as it sells your thought, idea, or message within the context that used and shaped it. Communication is selling. And a listening consumer is your reward.

Type Casting *Steven Brower*

My first job in book design was at New American Library, a publisher of mass-market books. I was thrilled to be hired. It was exactly where I wanted to be. I love the written word, and viewed this as my entrance into a world I wanted to participate in. Little did I suspect at the time that mass-market books, also known as "pocket" books (they measure approximately 4" × 7", although I have yet to wear a pocket they fit comfortably into), were viewed in the design world as the tawdry stepchild of true literature and design, gaudy and unsophisticated. I came to understand that this was due to the fact that mass-market books, sold extensively in supermarkets and convenience stores, had more in common with soap detergent and cereal boxes than with their much more dignified older brother, the hardcover first edition book. Indeed, the level of design of paperbacks was as slow to evolve as a box of Cheerios.

On the other hand, hardcover books, as if dressed in evening attire, wore elegant and sophisticated jackets. Next in line in terms of standing, in both the literary and design worlds, was the trade paper edition, a misnomer that does not refer to a specific audience within an area of work, but, rather, to the second edition of the hardcover, or first edition, that sports a paperbound cover. Trade paperbacks usually utilize the same interior printing as the hardcover, and are roughly the same size (generally, 6" × 9").

Mass-market books were not so lucky. The interior pages of the original edition were shrunk down, with no regard for the final type size or the eyes of the viewer. The interiors tended to be printed on cheap paper stock, prone to yellowing over time. The edges were often dyed to mask the different grades of paper used. The covers were usually quite loud, treated with a myriad of special effects (i.e., gold or silver foil, embossing and de-bossing, spot lamination, die cuts, metallic and Day-Glo pantone colors, thermography, and even holography), all designed to jump out at you and into your shopping cart as you walk down the aisle. The tradition of mass-market covers had more in common with, and, perhaps, for the most part is the descendant of, pulp magazine covers of earlier decades, with their colorful titles and over-the-top illustrations, than that of its more stylish, larger, and more expensive cousins.

What I Learned

So, when I made my entry into the elite world of literature, I began in the "bullpen" of a mass-market house. I believed I would be afforded a good opportunity to learn something about type and image. Indeed, in my short tenure there, I employed more display typefaces in a year and a half than I will in the rest of my lifetime. And, I abused type more than I ever dreamed possible.

There, type was always condensed or stretched so the height would be greater in a small format. The problem was that the face itself became distorted, as if it was put on the inquisitionist rack, with the horizontals remaining "thick" and the verticals thinning out. Back then, when type was "spec'd" and sent out to a typesetter, there was a standing order at the type house to condense all type for our company 20 percent. Sometimes, we would cut the type and extend it by hand, which created less distortion but still odd-looking faces. Once, I was instructed by the art director to cut the serifs off a face, to suit his whim. It's a good thing there is no criminal prosecution for type abuse.

The art director usually commissioned the art for these titles. Therefore, the job of the designers was to find the "appropriate" type solution that worked with these illustrations to create the package. It was here that I learned my earliest lessons in the clichés of typography. Mass-market paperbacks are divided into different genres, distinct categories that define their audience and subject matter. Though they were unspoken rules, handed down from generation to generation, here is what I learned about type during my employ:

Typefaces	Genre
Square serif	Western
Script and cursive	Romance
LED faces	Science Fiction
Nueland	African (in spite of the fact that the typeface is of German origin)
Latin	Mystery
Fat, round serif faces	Children's
Sans serif	Nonfiction
Hand scrawl	Horror
1950s bouncy type	Humor/Teen titles

And so it went. Every month, we were given five to six titles we were responsible for, and every month, new variations on old themes hung up on the wall. For a brief period I was assigned all the romance titles, which, themselves, were divided into subgenres (historical, regency, contemporary, etc). I made the conscious decision to create the very best romance covers around. Sure, I would use script and cursive type, but I would use *better* script and cursive type, so distinctive, elegant, and beautiful that I, or anyone else, would recognize the difference immediately. (When, six months after I left the job, I went to view my achievements at the local K-Mart, I could not pick out any of my designs from all the rest on the bookracks.)

Soon after, I graduated to art director of a small publishing house. The problem was, I still knew little of and had little confidence in, typography. However, by this time, I *knew* I knew little about typography. My solution, therefore, was to create images that contained the type as an integral part of the image, in a play on vernacular design, thereby avoiding the issue entirely. Thus began a series of collaborations with talented illustrators and photographers, in which the typography of the jacket was incorporated as part of the illustration. Mystery books especially lent themselves well to this endeavor. A nice thing about this approach is that it has a certain informality and familiarity with the audience. It also made my job easier, because I did not have to paste up much type for the cover (as one had to do back in the days of t-squares and wax), since it was, for the most part, self-contained within the illustration. This may seem like laziness on my part, but hey, I was busy.

Eventually, my eye began to develop, and my awareness and appreciation of good typography increased. I soon learned the pitfalls that most novice designers fall into, like utilizing a quirky novelty face does not equal creativity and usually calls attention to the wrong aspects of the solution. The importance of good letterspacing became paramount. Finding the right combination of a serif and sans serif face to evoke the mood of the material within was now my primary concern. The beauty of a classically rendered letterform now moved me, to quote Eric Gill, as much "as any sculpture or painted picture." I developed an appreciation for the rules of typography.

The Rules

As I've said, it is a common mistake among young designers to think a quirky novelty face equals creativity. Of course, this couldn't be farther from the truth. If anything, for the viewer, it has the opposite of the intended effect. Rather than being the total sum of individual expression, it simply calls attention to itself, detracting from, rather than adding to, the content of the piece. It is no substitute for a well-reasoned conceptual solution to the design problem at hand.

As a general rule, *no more than two faces* should be utilized in any given design, usually the combination of a serif face and a sans serif face. There are thousands to choose from, but I find I have reduced the list to five or six in each category that I have used as body text throughout my career:

Serif
Bodoni
Caslon
Cheltenham
Garamond

Sans Serif
Franklin Gothic
Futura
Gill Sans
News Gothic
Trade Gothic

You should *never condense or extend type*. As I stated, this leads to unwanted distortions. Much care and consideration went into the design of these faces, and they should be treated with respect. There are thousands of condensed faces to choose from without resorting to the horizontal and vertical scale functions.

Do not use text type as display. Even though the computer will enlarge the top beyond the type designer's intention, this may result in distortions. *Do not use display type as text*. Often, display type that looks great large can be difficult to read when small.

Do not stack type. The result is odd-looking spacing that looks as if it is about to tumble on top of itself. The thinness of the letter *I* is no match for the heft of an *O* sitting on top of it. As always, there are ways to achieve stacking successfully, but this requires care. Also, as I noted, much care should be given to letterspacing the characters of each word. This is not as simple as it seems. The computer settings for type are rife with inconsistencies that need to be corrected optically. Certain combinations of letterforms are more difficult to adjust than others. It is paramount that even optical (as opposed to actual) spacing is achieved, regardless of the openness or closeness of the kerning. It helps if you view the setting upside down, or backwards on a light box or sun-filled window, or squint at the copy to achieve satisfactory spacing.

I would caution you in the judicious use of *drop shadows.* Shadows these days can be rendered easily in programs such as Adobe's Photoshop and Illustrator, and convincingly, too. The problem is, it is so easily done that it is overdone. Thus, the wholesale usage of soft drop shadows has become the typographic equivalent of clip art. Viewers know they have seen it before. Rather than being evocative, it mainly evokes the program it was created in.

Hard drop shadows, ones that are 100 percent of a color, are easily achieved in Quark and placed behind the main text. This method is generally employed when the main text is not reading against the background, because of a neutral tone or an image that varies in tone from dark to light. The handed-down wisdom is: *If you need a drop shadow to make it read, the piece isn't working.* These solid drop shadows always look artificial, since, in reality, there is no such thing as a solid drop shadow. There should be a better solution to readability. Perhaps the background or the color of the type can be adjusted. Perhaps the type should be paneled or outlined. There are an infinite number of possible variations.

If you must use a solid drop shadow, it should never be a color. Have you ever seen a shadow in life that is blue, yellow, or green? It should certainly never be white. Why would a shadow be 100 percent lighter than what is, in theory, casting the shadow? White shadows create a hole in the background, and draw the eye to the shadow, and not where you want it to go: the text.

Justified text looks more formal than flush left, rag right. Most books are set justified, while magazines are often flush left, rag right. Centered copy will appear more relaxed than asymmetrical copy. *Large blocks of centered type can create odd-looking shapes that detract from the copy contained within.*

Another thing to consider is the point size and width of body copy. The tendency in recent times is to make type smaller and smaller, regardless of the intended audience. However, the whole purpose of text is that it be read. A magazine covering contemporary music is different from the magazine for The American Association of Retired Persons.

It is also common today to see very wide columns of text, with the copy set at a small point size. The problem is that a very wide column is hard to read because it forces the eye to move back and forth, tiring the reader. On the other hand, a very narrow measure also is objectionable, because the phrases and words are too cut up, with the eye jumping from line to line. We, as readers, do not read letter by letter, or even word by word, but, rather, phrase by phrase. A consensus favors an average of ten to twelve words per line.[1]

Lastly, too much leading between lines also makes the reader work too hard jumping from line to line, while too little leading makes it hard for the reader to discern where one line ends and another begins. The audience should always be paramount in the designer's approach, and it is the audience—not the whim of the designer, or even the client—that defines the level of difficulty and ease with which a piece is read. As Eric Gill said in 1931, "A book is primarily a thing to be read."[2]

A final consideration is the size of the type. As a rule of thumb, mass-market books tend to be 8 point for reasons of space. A clothbound book, magazine, or newspaper usually falls into the 9.5 point to 12 point range. Oversized art books employ larger sizes—generally, 14 point to 18 point or more.

Choosing the right typeface for your design can be time-consuming. There are thousands to choose from. Questions abound. Is the face legible at the setting I want? Does it evoke what I want it to evoke? Is it appropriate to the subject matter? There are no easy answers. When a student of mine used Clarendon in a self-promotion piece, I questioned why he chose a face that has 1950s connotations, mainly in connection with Reid Miles' Blue Note album covers. He answered, "Because I thought it was cool." I lectured him profusely on selecting type simply based on its "coolness." Later, I relayed the incident to Seymour Chwast, of the legendary Pushpin Group (formerly Pushpin Studios). He observed that Clarendon is actually a Victorian face, which he and his peers revived as young designers in the 1950s. When I asked him why they chose to bring this arcane face back to life, he replied, "Because we thought it was cool."

Breaking the Rules

Of course, there are always exceptions to the rules. An infinite number of faces can be used within one design, particularly when you employ a broadside-style type solution, a style that developed with the woodtype settings of the nineteenth century. Another style, utilizing a myriad of faces, is that influenced by the Futurist and Dada movements of the early twentieth century. As Robert N. Jones stated in an article in the May 1960 issue of *Print* magazine: "It is my belief that there has never been a typeface that is so badly designed that it could not be handsomely and effectively used in the hands of the right . . . designer."[3] Of course, this was before the novelty type explosion that took place later that decade, and, again, after the advent of the Macintosh computer. Still, Jeffery Keedy, a contemporary type designer whose work appears regularly in *Emigre*, concurs: "Good designers can make use of almost anything. The typeface is the point of departure, not the destination." Note the caveat "almost." Still, bad use of good type is much less desirable than good use of bad type.

When I first began in publishing, a coworker decided to let me in on the "secrets" of picking the appropriate face. "If you get a book on Lincoln to design," he advised, "look up an appropriate typeface in the index of the type specimen book." He proceeded to do so. "Ah, here we go—'Log Cabin!'" While, on the extremely rare occasion, I have found this to be a useful method, it's a good general rule of what *not* to do.

Notes
1. Eric Gill, "An Essay on Typography" (Sheed and Ward, 1931), p. 136; (Godine, 1988).
2 and 3. Richard Hendel, *On Book Design* (New Haven: Yale University Press, 1998).

Adapted from Publication Design *(Delmar Learning, 2004).*

My Backward Step to Lettering *Art Chantry*

When I began pursuing graphic design as an interest, I was unaware of typography as a field of art and craft. I just looked at words as lettering. They were just elements to work with—like photos, illustration, color, etc. Of course, as I dug deeper, I discovered that typography was a whole new world to explore. It was a world containing its own science and language and art, and it was a world critical to the development of graphic design. In fact, I can easily argue that the entire basis for what we've considered "good graphic design" for the last century is based in the founding principles of typographic artistry.

So, during the second "phase" of my development as a designer, I studied the wonders of typography. My mentors switched from comic book artists like Steve Ditko and psychedelic poster artists like Victor Moscoso to advertising typographers like Herb Lubalin and Lou Dorfsman. As my studies expanded to include the thinking behind the art of the likes of Marcel Duchamp and Andy Warhol, I soon discovered the areas where art and typography met in the work of Lester Beall and Robert Massin.

Typography was a field unto itself. It had dictums and heroes and adventurers and a legion of high craftsmen. I began to use typographers to help create my work (like I used photographers and printers) because I had realized how badly I needed them to execute my ideas. I also had discovered my limitations as a typographer (I couldn't run a Compugraphic Editwriter 750, for instance, but I could tell the operator what I wanted him to do), and needed the high skill levels of my typesetters to achieve my aesthetic goals.

One of my great professional sorrows is the loss of the typographer/typesetter in contemporary graphic design. With the advent of the computer and the death of the type shop, all graphic designers had to be their own typographers. I learned that graphic designers are not typographers. The mere fact that all graphic designers now have to act as their own typographers has, in effect, tossed out five hundred years of expertise and replaced it with a level of amateurism and experimentation that is going to take decades to absorb. I've noted that every time new technology enters the field of design, there is a huge learning curve that has to be overcome. It took well over a decade for cold type to be absorbed into design circles, and graphic design went through a seriously bad period of low typographic quality as a result (in the late sixties and early seventies; think "souvenir"). Computers are such powerful design tools that it may take many decades to get past the "bad type/bad design" learning phase.

For example, the tidal wave of terrible typeface designs (please don't call them "fonts." That word has a different meaning) is on par with, or is worse than, the deluge of awful designs we experienced when cold type first allowed amateur typeface designers to cannonball into the waters. Typeface design has almost nothing to do with design or function at this early stage, but it has everything to do with decoration and fad. Because typography is such a powerful tool of designers, the hubris bred by these "design decisions" has resulted in an enormous dumbing down of the standards of good and bad design and typography. Just look at design in the 1990s (at the influence of David Carson, for instance).

Enter my current phase. I have quit doing typography. It no longer interests me as a province of graphic design—any more than, say, photography. I've stepped backwards into what is best referred to as "lettering." As a designer, I no longer attempt to practice typography; I do lettering now. If you examine my work—particularly over the last three years, it becomes apparent to me that I have become a letterer. I no longer even attempt to create what I used to consider "quality designed typography"; I just make the words fit my ideas—however that is achieved. I carve it out of whatever seems appropriate to the idea I'm trying to get across. Sure, at times, classic "typography" is the desired goal, but it's just another thing—like another piece of clip art—needed to express the idea with accuracy.

I think this philosophical shift has become increasingly obvious to me as I've worked alongside my partner, Jamie Sheehan (who is one of the best classic typographers I've known personally). I can see how differently she thinks about and approaches graphic design. We collaborate steadily, but my work has become free from the rules that act as her mantra, and my work has taken off in directions that I'm not quite able to describe. It seems my vocabulary has to be somewhat rewritten to describe what I'm doing now with my design. Give me another year, and I can talk about it intelligently. In short, "typography" no longer describes what I'm doing, but "lettering" does.

Typographic Narratives

The Value of the Narrative in the Education of a Typographer

Chris Myers

Old libraries smell of dust, a particular sort of decay that is subtly moist but feels dry, and of aged wood. The chairs scrape when they move, from the friction of wood against wood. It is a pleasant friction that may, by accident, set off a high-pitched squeak and a dozen raised eyebrows—a rondo in the key of quiet. The checkout desk is as high as a pulpit, where you offer up your books to the circulation librarian. "Please, madam, may I have more?"

It is fitting that our libraries look like churches and temples. The smallest of the Carnegie libraries[1] in small towns across America refer, in some small way, to the public buildings of Athens and Rome. This is where the community keeps what it knows is important today, and hopes will be important to someone tomorrow, or forever. Sometimes, I recognize the name of someone I know on the borrower's slip of an old library. I feel I know something secret about them. Sometimes, I see no one has borrowed the book that I have selected for over fifty years. I feel a strange ownership over this neglected work. Everything I read, I consume. It becomes the biggest part or the smallest part of who I am.

How could there be a greater wonder of the world, ancient or not so ancient, than the Library of Alexandria?[2] It carries the mystery of those who die young. What if . . . what if? Oh, what if? I have dreamed of it as the very center of the marvelous. There are rumors of cures, mathematic systems, languages, and histories that had been placed there for safekeeping. What did we learn later that had already been there for the asking? What answers disappeared? Are we asking the right questions to find out what someone already knew and left for us there? In that torchlight, we are like children waiting for the presents that will never arrive. So many needles. So many haystacks.

I am under the illusion that all libraries and their contents belong to me.

In older, nomadic society, the shaman held the wisdom and the balance of power. Less exalted, but essential, was the keeper of the fire, who was responsible for carrying the live coals from camp to camp when the people moved, or for keeping the sacred flame lit in sacred places in settled, agrarian society. The keeper is the one upon whom the community's survival might have been staked. The success of the keeper was the hinge on which the shaman's power turned.

Today, we are nomads again, members of unsettled society. We roam in constant communication with others across fractured time spans. We seem to be looking for acknowledgment of ourselves: announcing our arrivals, departures, potential arrivals, potential departures, and our smallest thoughts, most of which fall through the archives of conversation. The great man of psychology, Shakespeare, speaks of "Necessity's sharp pinch,"[3] and here is where it comes into play. We have an insatiable need to explain ourselves. We are rigorously self-referential. The highest standard we hold for truth is that which is derived by comparison to what we already know. It is the test of fire between merely accepting something as truth and knowing it is so.

Writers—of our books, of our grand electronic array, of our ballads, of our screenplays, of our music—are our shamans. They provide us with knowledge. If there is magic today, surely, they are the ones who keep it. They are among the chosen who have the power to cast ideas across time beyond themselves. The typographer is a guide between this knowledge and that memory. He is a keeper of the fire. Without one who can mark a record of our thoughts, surely, they will dim and become lost. He has worked consistently and quietly throughout time. We have also called him scribe, calligrapher, brother, abbé, and stonecutter. His lineage is long. The earliest of this tribe might be the Nameless Ones, whose work is found in blood, carbon, stone, and clay on rock walls and deep in dark caves, and whose ambiguous marks may be pictures and more.

Our ongoing collective task has been to try to understand ourselves. We Americans are a manifestly religious people. Whoever picks up coins only if they have fallen "heads up," or avoids passing under a ladder, has unconsciously acknowledged belief in a power greater than himself. Who imagined the order of the colors of the rainbow? Does the wild rabbit have a soul? Can the dead see the living? Is the love of my family written into my hands?

In a continuous century-spanning search, we have celebrated religion and invented science to explain our mysteries. It is a testimony to our persistence, endurance, and instinct. Chronicles, myths, theorems, and fables have been the currency in trade to accomplish this. Whoever has learned at the foot of their parents or grandparents learned through stories.

Whoever believes or believed in a god or gods found their way to their deities through stories. Simply put, we have an inherent understanding of the complex and the abstract when it lies within the architecture of a story. All of these narratives are either parables or testimonies. A parable shapes imagined circumstance in order to tell truths. Testimony asserts that it is the truth embodied. I do not know if we dwell in a world circumscribed by storytelling through dint of instinct or comfortable tradition.

A narrative witnesses real or imagined change. What is felt along the heart of a good story is the knowledge that it has no meaning unless it is shared, and that its life expectancy is measured by its worthiness to be shared. It is the typographer who archives our attempts to concretely document these obsessions. Through him, the thoughts belonging to others might become part of how we think and understand our world. The typographer and his art glide us back to the past and beckon us to fall into the future. Typography becomes a sixth physical sense, whether it is floating on the surface of the printed page or radiant on a computer screen.

The democratic access to the digital manufacture of typography has expanded the potential and range of typographic authority for the typographer, but, at the same time, it has shifted a once-shared editorial responsibility to him alone. The respected expertise once delivered by the now-lost professions of the proofreader and the typesetter has vanished. Everyman has been empowered with the vocabulary of the typographer. And Everyman has pressed his advantage and embraced his possibilities with hurricane force. Personal Web sites and tribute sites (a form of religious expression) blow like so much dust across cyberspace. Everyman attaches a site counter to his biography to see how many folks are knocking at the front door of his posted life. Self-published novels and treatises fly out of ink-jets. The proliferation of electronic correspondence compounds response upon response upon response through software that recapitulates every previous thought. It offers the casualness of telephone conversation voiced in a typographic key—communication without the rigor of correspondence set on stationery. It is the confusing flotsam and jetsam of what is important and unimportant. Absolutely nothing can be lost or forgotten. Here is the detritus of communication without the meaning.

The education of the typographer without a greater appreciation of the written word is incomplete. The classic narrative structure is shot through our lives. It is a three-part structure: the setup, the difficulty or conflict, and the resolution. The cinematic story celebrates it, as does the popular ballad and the Beethoven symphony. In this atmosphere of increasing digital democracy, where information is often delivered in story form, the typographer's lack of understanding of narrative structures verges on incompetence. Three years ago, I was invited to direct a course at the University of the Arts that attempted to address these issues. The following thoughts were founded in that experience.[4]

Typographers must be aware of the strategies and genres of the narrative: the dramatic narrative, the how-to, the instructional narrative, the comic narrative (the most difficult and, therefore, perhaps most appreciated), the coming-of-age story, and that particularly American favorite, the on-the-road saga that traces itself back to the mythic quest. Typography must extend beyond the craftsmanship of typography and aesthetic invention. A typographer's education should include writing as a developmental process. This is central to the education of a typographer: there is a need to investigate the situational aspect of text, to move from form and content to form and context.[5]

To this end, typography students should attempt to write text that they will design. The autobiographical sketch will serve this purpose well. The subject matter is familiar to the author, and it offers a window into the shadow line that lies between fiction and nonfiction. There is also a higher stake when the subject offered to the world is oneself. There is a respect for words when they are your own that a student will not often confer upon the work of strangers.

There may be a strong, initial resistance to writing among students. A common belief among design students is that they are incapable, biologically, to confront the difficult task of writing and setting down critical arguments. The theory of left- and right-brain development, and its relationship to visual acuity and intellectual ability, has been applied to the detriment of the art and design student. It is a modern conceit to disconnect intellect from artistic vision. If we accept that interpretation of science, we have backslid to the notion of the designer as a visual sycophant. If the past two centuries of art history have told us anything, it is that the independence of the visual artist, artistically and financially, has come from the interwoven forces of intellect and visual perception. This is the wall over which today's typography teacher must drag himself and his students—sometimes, kicking and screaming. In these matters, one needs to engender a faith in the process of writing. In a sense, "the affirmation comes before the knowing."[6]

A studio course can be developed as an experimental laboratory. This way, the responsibilities are revealed clearly, while the results can be unpredictable. By holding several initial parameters stable, light can be shined on the effect of isolated variables on the presentation of the text.

The course should be progressive and move from an initial casting of the text in typography through a typographic grammar of increasing visual complexity. All experiments should be played along a matrix that attempts to separate the conceptual dichotomy of informational emphasis and editorial emphasis. Informational emphasis attempts to highlight the objective aspects of the narrative: the title, the author, and the consecutive progression of the story line. Editorial emphasis selects aspects or sections of the text and signals that selection for special notice. Editorial emphasis can override the original intent of the author. It may exist as repetition within the text, as scale change within the text, or as a pull-quote (a selected quotation separated from the text in the tradition of tabloid and magazine journalism). Editorial emphasis reframes the context for the reader to a specific viewpoint based on the visual cues designed by the typographer.

The course might progress to the addition of imagery, which can also be approached within controlled experiments. The syntax of imagery can be investigated: scale, vignette, color, cropping, and bleeds. Image research should be linked to visual strategies such as iconology, the metaphor/analogy, the historical parallel, and the visual pun. The student of typography should experience the confusion, the clarity, the misdirection, the expansion, the unexpected subversion, the shifting emphasis, and the damage he might bring to text as he shapes its visual form. While these lessons reside in virtually any typographic problem, they are especially critical in the design of narratives because narratives are most often sequential and progressive in nature. The notion of linear time in classic narrative structures adds complexity and greater potential for mishap. There is no better lesson than when the assailant and the victim are one and the same.

Since this course was conceived as a laboratory, its primary objective is to design experiments, execute them, and evaluate the consequences of the elements brought together. The value of the course lies in the ability to create the broadest landscape of valid interpretations of the text at hand and to attempt to learn how the visual choices redirect, subvert, or amplify the text. Sooner or later, each student will come across the limits of the English language. (The difficulties of the English language for both the writer and the designer are well chronicled.) By taking the broadest approach toward narrative—a story with a beginning, middle, and end—the implications for these studies rapidly unfold. Diagrams, family trees, and timelines tell stories. The architecture of a Web site can follow narrative structure. An image can supply the implication of an occurrence off-stage, a back story behind the curtain.

In an open investigation, what, then, is held sacred? The answer is a pathway through the words in consecutive order, without ambiguity, and the responsibility to the reader. Without the reader, the text has no purpose. The physical legibility of the consecutive text and informational retrieval from line to line should be inviolate. How will the interpretations be evaluated? The touchstone is the text. "All permissions spring from the text."[7] If the conventions of reading are to be questioned, and the editorial choice of the designer is to be validated, the source of justice is the text. To this end, it is wise to invite a professional writer into the studio process, and give that writer authority equal to that of the visual arts instructor. The writer can serve as an antidote to the natural proclivities of designers to become visually enchanted, to the detriment of textual comprehension. We are ultimately chasing that elusive prize: bringing the savage engagement of today's distracted reader to the text.

It is the middle of the night. I am flying more than six miles above America. That is almost the distance from my childhood house to my grandmother's house. I am traveling at 550 miles per hour. I realize I do not know what this means. When I drove my high school car at 115 miles per hour on country roads, I had an exhilarating sense of speed. It appears now as if I am suspended, motionless above the earth. It is so very dark. I trust I am crossing a continent, but I cannot feel I am. This cabin has lost its fuller context. Speed that heats the blood requires a sense of time and distance. Here, there is nothing to provide those coursing rhythms. All time references are manmade and unnatural, and tied to distractions: the length of a cycling sound tape, clock-time, or the length of a video. I am shipped in a container traveling to somewhere better. The best gauge of time is what I remember—how I order my experiences. That is what sets this time in place and gives it context. In this isolation, I am aware that I am the keeper of my own history.

Over thirty years ago, a young Native American woman recast the keeper of the fire as a contemporary, cultural custodian, carrying the important memories and rituals of the community from camp to camp, or keeping sacred things alive in sacred places. She redefined the sacred fire as memory. She presciently forecast the analogy to the typographer's tasks and his history, borne in the heat of hot metal and shot into the digital fire careening across wires and no wires.

He's as heavy as a lead weight, baby.
He's as skinny as a wire.
He's a prophet of a new day, baby.
He's a keeper of the fire.[8]

There is no evidence of anything below us. My small son sits next to me. We are going to visit his grandmother. We are together and alone. He is watching an in-flight movie with headphones; I am listening to the country-western channel on my headset:

Hey, Jesus, it must have been some Sunday morning.
In a blaze of glory:
We're still tellin' your story.
I might not go down in history,
I just want someone to remember me.[9]

We know we remember. We just are not clear exactly how we do it. How much of us is in the present, and how much of us is constructed out of memories? Our gift among the creatures of this earth is that we can remember things we think are special, and combine them with other cached thoughts to create new arguments and possibilities. We relentlessly recombine our memories to rival and challenge our contemporary experiences. We also desire to be appreciated, to be noticed, to be remembered. The typographer, perhaps unwittingly, ends up at this crossroads of desire, knowledge, and memory. How he might spin these stories is both his lure and his lore.

Up here, in dark suspension, I comb through these thoughts. I keep returning to the mission of typography, sometimes battered and broken, but still good.[10] Still powerful, even in partially deciphered runes or ruins:

Stop. I want to tell you something I know.
It might be something I remember.
And as soon as you look at this, and read this—
now it is also about you.

Notes:

1. Joseph Frazier Wall, *Andrew Carnegie*, 2nd ed. (Pittsburgh: University of Pittsburgh Press, 1989). In the nineteenth century, industrialist Andrew Carnegie offered to build a free library in interested communities throughout the United States. The fund to establish the library was usually estimated to be about two dollars per resident. The agreement between the community and Carnegie required that the community raise approximately 10 percent of the original grant yearly to be set aside for maintenance, operation, and improvement of the library's collection. It is thought that Carnegie built 1,946 free libraries in the United States and 2,811 libraries worldwide.

2. It is thought that the Alexandrine Library, certainly the largest documented repository of knowledge in the ancient world, was founded in the third century B.C. by Ptolemy II Soter, a Greek. Although its existence is well documented, as is its destruction, the circumstances surrounding its demise are less certain. It is thought that it was ravaged as many as three times between A.D. 47 and A.D. 640 by, consecutively, Julius Caesar, Patriarch Theophilus, a Christian religious fanatic, and Caliph Omar of Damascus, a Muslim conqueror. The last known entry in the chronicles has Caliph Omar ordering the remaining library scrolls to be used to heat the public baths, declaring, "they will either contradict the Koran, in which case they are heresy, or they will agree with it, so they are superfluous."

3. William Shakespeare, *Hamlet*, act V, scene 4, ln. 214.

4. These thoughts are based upon my participation in a section of a fourth-year course in graphic design at the University of the Arts in Philadelphia. This course sprang from an initial capstone project devised by Kenneth Hiebert, and was modulated by Inge Druckrey and Hans Allemann into a course exploring the design of narratives. I am particularly indebted to Sherry Lefevre, a professor of writing at the University of the Arts and a documentary filmmaker, for her tenacious defense of text and narrative architecture within our laboratory course, and also to Joseph Mitchell, writer.

5. I am crediting this expression to Meredith Davis, professor of design at North Carolina State University. If she is not the original source, she is my first contact. Whereas Meredith sees the conceptual shift as driven by sociocultural trends, I believe it was the more recent, technological revolution and democratic access to higher technology that forced the cultural shift.

6. I attribute this statement to Denise Levertov, poet and educator. The open, organic form of her poetry and her open way of teaching clearly embraced this necessary moment of acceptance without validation as a window to new knowledge or experiences.

7. I first came across this expression about ten years ago in a conversation with Ken Hiebert, author, educator, and designer. Ever since, I have been attracted to the simple eloquence of the dictum.

8. Buffy Sainte-Marie, "He's a Keeper of the Fire," *Gypsy Boy Music* (BMI, 1969). Dr. Sainte-Marie, adjunct faculty member in fine arts at Evergreen State College and York University, is a social activist specializing in experiential learning in elementary and intermediate education. She has developed a nationally recognized, cyber-assisted, educational project, the Cradleboard Teaching Project, which addresses the cultural history and contemporary issues of aboriginal peoples. She has also collaborated with the Children's Television Workshop to produce educational broadcasts.

9. Brett Beavers and Tom Douglas, "Something Worth Leaving Behind" (Nashville: Tree Publishing Company, 2002).

10. Dean DuBlois, Chris Sanders, and Alan Silvestri, *Lilo and Stitch*, screenplay (Burbank, Calif.: Walt Disney Pictures, 2002). The paraphrase is close enough to merit documentation. The tone of this film narrative and its purposefully flawed characters sharply veer from the contemporary formula of past Disney successes.

The Letter as Such: Aleksei Kruchenykh as Closet Typographer

Jared Ash

*It has always been my dream that someone would study the graphic life of letters,
this "voice from the depths of the grave" that resounds with a passion for metaphysics. So many signs—musical, mathematical, cartographic, etc.—languish in
the dust of libraries. I understand the cubists when they incorporate numbers in
their paintings, but I don't understand poets' estrangement from the aesthetic life
of all these*

$$\int \quad \sim \quad + \quad \S \quad X \quad ♂ \quad ♀ \quad \sqrt{} \quad = \quad > \quad \Delta$$

and so forth and so on.

—Nikolai and David Burliuk, "Poetic Principles," 1914[1]

It may seem odd, at first, to suggest that serious typophiles should direct
their attention to Aleksei Kruchenykh, a Russian futurist. Why
Kruchenykh, rather than those more commonly recognized in typographic
surveys and sourcebooks as pioneers of typographic innovation in 1910–20
Russia (namely, Vladimir and David Burliuk, Vasilii Kamenskii, Igor
Terent'ev, and *le maitre*, Il'ia Zdanevich)?[2] Didn't Kruchenykh denounce
mechanical type as incapable of capturing the vitality of a written work,
and urge "wordwrights" (poets and writers) to entrust their works to
"artists, rather than typesetters,"[3] to be copied in longhand and printed
lithographically?

 With no disrespect to (and complete disclosure of my own adulation
for) the Burliuks, Kamenskii, Terent'ev, and Zdanevich, I am suggesting
Kruchenykh as a figure worthy of attention, for the very fact that, as an
artist whose most acclaimed works were created as deliberate alternatives
to typography and mechanical reproduction, he has languished in obscurity
and remained overlooked in studies of avant-garde typography; however, as
this essay affirms, Kruchenykh is a figure in whom even the most ardent,
hard-hearted typographer and typophile will recognize a kindred spirit,
fellow traveler, and true lover of letterforms.

 In explaining the initial motivation behind the turn to book production by Russian futurist painters and poets in 1910, Vasilii Kamenskii

recalls in his autobiography: "The success of art exhibitions was far from enough for us; and now, having pooled our strength and organized ourselves into a strong, focused and intimate group, our literary faction decided to throw a bomb into the sleepy, cheerless streets of everyday."[4] The bomb took the form of *A Trap for Judges (Sadok sudei)* (St. Petersburg: Zhurval', 1910), a literary anthology financed by artist and composer Mikhail Matiushin and his wife, Elena Guro, a poet and painter. Printed by a German newspaper in St. Petersburg, *Petersburger Zeitung*—the only newspaper that would do it[5]—*Trap for Judges* featured poems and/or prose by Kamenskii, Guro, David and Nikolai Burliuk, Velimir Khlebnikov, Sergei Miasoedov, and Ekaterina Nizen (Guro's sister), and illustrations by Vladimir Burliuk.

Generally recognized by contemporary scholars and the creators themselves as the first literary publication of the Russian futurists, *Trap for Judges* was intended to lay a "granite" foundation for the "new epoch" of literature. Among the resolutions that Kamenskii and the group set forth for the collection were:

> *To destroy the old orthography—to throw out the tiresome letters* yat *and the hard sign [Ъ]; To print a book on the reverse undecorated side of cheap wallpaper—as a symbol of protest against sumptuous bourgeois publications; [...] To select a wallpaper pattern that one would find in the average, squalid apartment, and to leave the design untouched on the left side of the pages as ornamentation; [...] To try to avoid probable persecution, censorship and confiscation of the book by including only lyrical material; [...] [and] upon its publication, to show it to as many people as possible [...] and propagandize the advent of the futurian [*budetlian].[6]

Despite being printed on wallpaper, bound in wallpaper covers, and bearing a letterpress title piece glued by hand to the front cover, *Trap for Judges* failed to elicit the outrage for which its producers had hoped: "The Symbolists hardly noticed, taking a bomb for an ordinary little children's firecracker."[7] Nevertheless, the collection remains significant for having brought together poets and painters of the emerging avant-garde, and launching a strong tradition of collaboration and camaraderie. Most importantly, it created an outlet for poets like Velimir Khlebnikov—whose neologistic, innovative poems strayed far beyond the bounds of symbolism—to publish their works.

The drive to criticize and challenge accepted conventions and common trends in art persisted: two years later, a second volume of *Trap for Judges* appeared (which was also bound within wallpaper covers), in addition to *A Slap in the Face of Public Taste: In Defense of Free Art (Poshchechina obshchestvennomu vkusu: v zashchitu svobodnogo iskusstva)* (Moscow: G. L. Kuz'min, 1912), a collection of poems, verse, and critical essays, that was bound in a coarse, sackcloth cover. While the materials on which these publications were printed were certainly unconventional, the typography itself remained rather unexceptional.

When Kruchenykh embraced the practice of using lithographically reproduced manuscript text for his self-published books, *Old-Time Love (Starinnaia liubov)* (Moscow, 1912) and *A Game in Hell (Igra v adu)* (co-authored with Khlebnikov; Moscow, 1912), he was motivated by more than merely the desire to perpetuate the assault on traditional book design aesthetics. Recognizing the extraordinarily expressive character of words and letterforms in ancient texts, ideographic writing, and hieroglyphics, Kruchenykh and others devoted themselves to achieving the same degree of expression through the graphic form of their own texts.

In a manifesto, "The Letter as Such," Kruchenykh and Khlebnikov argue that typography lacks the ability to fully realize the dignity and dynamism of words and letterforms. They write:

> *The word is still not treasured, only tolerated!*
> *Would it still be wearing a convict's gray garb, otherwise?*
> *You have seen the letters in their [the Symbolists'] words—stretched out in a row, sullen, with heads shorn, and all equally colorless and glum— they are not letters, but stains! [...] I suppose you would enshroud all your beautiful women in identical government-issue caftans?*
> *No way! They would spit in your eyes; but the word—it keeps quiet. For it is dead (like Boris and Gleb), around you the word is stillborn.*[8]

As examples of works in which the energy and vitality of letters are depicted effectively, artists and poets pointed to traditional Russian art forms, such as painted shop signs, popular woodcuts, and Old Russian illuminated manuscripts—works in which they recognized "the life of letters" to be particularly well understood, noting that letters and text were "embellished and fortified" with the same "great love" as the illuminations.[9]

The aesthetic value of handwritten text was well established among Russian artists by 1910, and authors' manuscripts were even included in modern art exhibitions. Kruchenykh and Khlebnikov further affirmed the advantages of text written in longhand over typography in another manifesto, "The Word as Such." They cited the capacity of handwritten script to convey the emotion and mood of its scribe, and argued that, in reproducing the text and illustrations in a manual, rather than mechanical, process, the work remained closer to the hand of the author, and that a more direct connection to the reader could be achieved without the depersonalization of typography.

A wealth of innovative achievements and applications of avantgarde aesthetics to the book medium proceeded from these principles. Many of the best-known artists of the early Russian avant-garde (including Kazimir Malevich, Natal'ia Goncharova, Mikhail Larionov, and Olga Rozanova, among others) were drawn to the book by Kruchenykh's invitation and initiative. Each artist responded to the project in his or her own unique manner, and found a different solution for combining text and imagery and imparting the entire work with energy and dynamism.

One of the best demonstrations of the theory that different hands convey different moods is *Worldbackwards (Mirskontsa)* (Moscow, 1912), a collection of poems and prose by Kruchenykh and Khlebnikov, transcribed and illustrated by four artists (Larionov, Goncharova, Vladimir Tatlin, and Nikolai Rogovin). Not all of the text in *Worldbackwards* is manuscript; in fact, in producing this book, Kruchenykh happened upon a type process that, at last, seemed as novel, innovative, and playful as the poems themselves. Interspersed amongst the lithograph pages are text pages, printed by Kruchenykh using a handheld, children's typesetting kit and different color inks.[10]

Kruchenykh defies the dominant designation of typography as a means for utilitarian efficiency and expedience, and explores the expressive potential of letterforms and the process itself. While the text of the stamped pages is identical in each copy of *Worldbackwards*, the layout varies from one copy to the next. As Gerald Janecek illustrates in his essay, "Kruchenykh contra Gutenberg," a comparison of the "same" page in three different copies of the book, reveals variations in the spacing between characters and lines of text, and an arbitrary and inconsistent capitalization system (i.e., a word rendered in one copy with one scheme of uppercase and lowercase letters, and use of spacers and ornamental asterisks, may appear in an entirely different configuration in the corresponding location in another copy), thereby suggesting that during the process of printing the edition's worth of a particular page (220 copies), Kruchenykh rearranged and reset the type periodically, switching uppercase and lowercase letters (seemingly) arbitrarily.[11] By frequently recomposing the type, Kruchenykh identifies and activates the latent aesthetic potential of the materials, and demonstrates a more creative and artistic approach to typography. Each page of stamped text is as unique as the collage on the book's cover.

An even greater range of variation can be seen in copies in which a certain poem is rendered entirely in type in one copy, and in a combination of type and hand-drawn, potato-cut letters, in sizes and colors that dominate and contrast sharply with the stamped type.[12] As the reader adjusts to the unconventional stamped and manuscript texts, a turn of the page throws him or her off balance again: an oversize *O* calls out from the middle of a word, its form sharply distinguished from its co-letters by its darker color, crude appearance, and diminishing size. Kruchenykh's techniques elevate the letter to an unprecedented place of prominence, and force the reader to give it more consideration than he or she would otherwise give it. He asserts the letter's duality: it is a component of a larger organism (the word), as well as an individual, self-sufficient entity with the ability to capture a reader's attention on its own.

One of the monuments of Russian avant-garde book design is Kruchenykh's *Universal War: Ъ (Vselenskaia voina. Ъ)* (Petrograd: Andrei Shemshurin, 1916).[13] Printed in an edition of one hundred copies, the album is comprised of letterpress covers, two pages of text, and twelve primarily abstract collages by Kruchenykh. Despite the album's (relatively) wide renown, mention is rarely made of its subtitle: the Russian letter Ъ (*tverdyi znak*—hard sign), a silent letter, used only after a consonant to indicate the consonant's hardness. The hard sign figured significantly in the heated campaign for Russian orthographic reform; it was a letter whose obsolescence or preservation held significant economic, educational, and societal implications.[14]

Even without delving into the possible political or social connotations of the subtitle, the typographic dynamics of the cover are profound. The hard sign's position on the cover of *Universal War* is prominent: it stands alone, centered starkly in the middle of the cover, black against white, in a size three times larger than the main title above it. Kruchenykh presents the sign on its own, even though it has no practical purpose unless preceded by a consonant. Stripped of its utilitarian function, and with no sound of its own to be spoken or pronounced, the hard sign Kruchenykh presents is a purely visual letter; precisely, a "letter as such."

Kruchenykh's appreciation and reverence for the physical form of the written word is further apparent in the editions he created between 1917 and 1921. He continues to explore letters as visual materials, creating graphic compositions, rather than phonic or literary ones, especially in a series of hectographic booklets of hand-drawn poems.[15] The primary aesthetic principles of these editions are the same that served as the foundation for avant-garde painting and poetry—an economy of means and primacy of materials: in books such as *Kachildaz* (Tiflis, 1918), Kruchenykh presents minimalist page compositions consisting of two single lines on different angles, set above two roughly drawn letters; in *F/nagt* (Tiflis, 1918), one poem consists entirely of five diagonal lines arranged at different angles.

Even though the text is hand-drawn, Kruchenykh seems to have designed the layout of these books with a typesetter-like approach, limiting himself to primary type elements—letters, ornaments, spacers, and bars, as well as mathematical signs, like those mentioned in the epigraph of this essay. A number of pages practically call out to be transferred to a printer's line or grid; whether the results would have retained the warmth, charm, and dynamism of the longhand originals is debatable.

Kruchenykh did attempt to realize in type a composition similar to those of his hectographic books in *To Sofiia Georgievna Melnikova: The Fantastic Tavern* (Tiflis, 1919), a thick collection of poetry, prose, and graphics by a large number of contributors.[16] A true landmark of futurist typography, the collection features an incredible array of Russian and Georgian type designs by Kruchenykh, Igor Terent'ev, and Il'ia Zdanevich, set by Adrian Ternov. By exploiting outline type, Kruchenykh achieves expressiveness not possible with manuscript text. In a composition similar to those of his hectographic publications, Kruchenykh presents a poem comprised of five letters (*m, u, z, k, a*), set in various sizes and styles, in a circle-like arrangement. Whether the magic is Kruchenykh's alone, or Kruchenykh and Ternov's, the effect achieved reveals a true sensitivity and understanding of the unique aesthetic properties and potential of type.

When one reads or rereads El Lissitzky's writings on typography, or looks at *Of Two Squares (Pro dva kvadrata)* (Berlin: Skify, 1922), certain principles or practices addressed by Kruchenykh from 1910–1920 are bound to seem reflected: concerns about the limitations of type in its existing state; the importance of economy, purity, and simplicity; the striving for an optical, rather than phonic, transmission of ideas. Kruchenykh's use of letters of contrasting colors, his unconventional use of capitalization and varying type sizes, and other techniques by which he successfully drew the reader to consider the letter as a self-sufficient entity are precisely those for which *Of Two Squares* and *For the Voice (Dlia golosa)* (Berlin: Gosizdat, 1923) are most often praised.

Kruchenykh is an example of someone who, while rarely thought of as a typographer, played an essential role in providing precedents and creating an environment that encouraged innovation and experimentation with letterforms. Including Kruchenykh in studies of typographic history illustrates the importance of expanding the field of focus to include artists who may have worked primarily outside the margins of typography, yet whose aesthetic theories and creative explorations resonated within the discipline.

Kruchenykh is the first of a number of artist-designer-typographers whose significant contributions to typographic innovation and advancement in Russia between 1910s and the 1930s are not yet entirely recognized or even known. Kruchenykh is a teaser—a taste of what is to come; for example: introductions to lesser-known artist-designers of the 1920s and 1930s, such as Nikolai Il'in and Mikhail Tarkhanov, who were considerably more involved in typographic artistry than their more widely recognized colleagues; more information and examples of works by Aleksei Gan, Solomon Telingater, and others, whose recognition by the field has been impeded by the limited availability of their works and lack of reference material; and better insight into the major issues, trends, practices, and principles involved in typography at the time, which are coming to light thanks to the diligence and dedication of Russian scholars such as Selim Khan-Magomedov, Vladimir Krichevskii, and Alexander Lavrentiev.[17] Those with the foresight to foster and encourage the research of these scholars and others, and the willingness to accept and incorporate new findings, corrections, and clarifications, will be rewarded handsomely.

Notes

1. Nikolai and David Burliuk, "Poeticheskie nachala," *Futuristy: pervyi zhurnal russkikh futuristov 1-2* (Moscow: D. D. Burliuk, 1914), p. 82. An English translation may be found in *Russian Futurism through Its Manifestoes, 1912–1928*, ed. and trans. Anna Lawton and Herbert Eagle (Ithaca: Cornell University Press, 1988), pp. 82–84.

2. Illustrations of all works mentioned in this essay may be found in Margit Rowell and Deborah Wye, eds., *The Russian Avant-Garde Book 1910–1934* (New York: The Museum of Modern Art, 2002). For more

detailed discussion about the typographic work of these artists, see: Gerald Janecek, *The Look of Russian Literature: Avant-Garde Visual Experiments, 1900–1930* (Princeton: Princeton University Press, 1984); Alexander Lavrentiev, *Laboratoriia konstruktivizma. Opyty graficheskogo modelirovaniia* [The Constructivist Laboratory: Experiments in Graphic Design] (Moscow: Grant, 2000); Tatiana Nikol'skaia, *"Fantasticheskii gorod": Russkaia kul'turnaia zhizn' v Tbilisi (1917–1921)* ["'Fantastic City'": Russian Cultural Life in Tbilisi"] (Moscow: Piataia strana, 2000); Vladimir Poliakov, *Knigi russkikh kubofuturizma* ["Russian Cubo-futurist Books"] (Moscow: Gileia, 1998); and Patricia Railing, *From Science to Systems of Art: On Russian Abstract Art and Language, 1910–1920* (Sussex: Artists Bookworks, 1989).

3. Aleksei Kruchenykh and Velimir Khlebnikov, "Bukva kak takovaia" [1913], *Neizdannyi Khlebnikov*, ed. by Kruchenykh (Moscow: Gruppa druzei Khlebnikova, 1930), vol. 18: 7. An English translation may be found in Lawton and Eagle, pp. 63–64.

4. Vasilii Kamenskii, *Put entusiazta* (Moscow: Federatsiia, 1931), p. 113.

5. Mikhail Matiushin, "Russkie kubofuturisty. Vospominaniia Mikhaila Matiushina," in N. I. Khardzhiev, *Stati ob avangarde v dvukh tomakh*, V. Rakitin and A. Sarabianov, eds. (Moscow: Arkhiv russkogo avan-garda, 1997), vol. 1: 158.

6. Kamenskii, p. 113.

7. Matiushin, p. 158.

8. Kruchenykh and Khlebnikov, "Bukva kak takovaia," p. 7.

9. N. Burliuk and D. Burliuk, "Poeticheskie nachala," 82. For more on the links between the Russian avant-garde and Old Russian manuscripts and art forms, see Jared Ash, "Primitivism in Russian Futurist Book Design 1910–14," Rowell and Wye, pp. 33–40.

10. The conclusion that a child's typesetter was used for the stamping was made by Vladimir Poliakov, based on the asterisk employed (see *Knigi russkikh kubofuturizma*, p. 243). Other books by Kruchenykh in which he used stamped text in a similar manner include: *Explodity (Vzorval)* (St. Petersburg, 1913); *Transrational Boog (Zaumnaia gniga)* (Moscow, 1915); and *F/nagt* (Tiflis, 1918).

11. Janecek, "Kruchenykh contra Gutenberg," Rowell and Wye, p. 44.

12. Compare the example reproduced in Rowell and Wye, p. 69, upper-right corner, which is composed by stamped text of two colors, with the variant of the same page illustrated in Janecek, *The Look of Russian Literature*, p. 78, in which four single letters executed by potato-cut are interspersed throughout the stamped text.

13. Illustrated in Rowell and Wye, pp. 103–106.

14. Among those who supported striking the hard sign from the alphabet are the collaborators on *Trap for Judges* (as mentioned above), and Vladimir Mayakovsky, whose attempt to publish a book of his own poems without using the letter was considered tantamount to treason (Kornei Chukovskii, *Sovremenniki* [Moscow: Molodaia gvardiia, 1967], p. 337, quoted in Janecek, *The Look of Russian Literature*, p. 16). For more on the issues surrounding orthographic reform and the hard sign, see Janecek, *The Look of Russian Literature*, pp. 12–18.

15. The specific hectographic compositions discussed in this essay are illustrated in Rowell and Wye, pp. 112–115. The most extensive collection of Kruchenykh's editions from this period is held by the Mayakovsky State Museum, Moscow; see *Knigi A. E. Kruchenykh kavkazskogo perioda iz kollektsii Gosudarstvennogo muzeia V.V. Maiakovskogo: Katalog (A. E. Kruchenykh's Caucasian Period Books from the Collection of the V.V. Mayakovsky State Museum: Catalogue)*, ed. A. P. Zimenkov (Moscow: The V. V. Mayakovsky State Museum, 2002).

16. Illustrated in Rowell and Wye, p. 123.

17. Among the most significant recent contributions to the field are: Selim Omarovich Khan-Magomedov, *Pionery sovetskogo dizaina (Pioneers of Soviet Design)* (Moscow: Galart, 1995); *Iugo-lef i konstruktivizm: po materialam arkhiva N. Sokolova (Southern-LEF and Constructivism: Materials from the Archives of N. Sokolov)* (Moscow: Lad'ia, 2000); Vladimir Krichevskii, *Oblozhka: graficheskoe litso epokhi revoliutsionnogo natiska 1917–1937 (The Book Cover: The Graphic Face of the Revolutionary Onslaught Epoch 1917–1937)* (Moscow: Samolet, 2002) and Nikolai Il'in: *"U menia est' koe-kakie mysli otnositel'no nabornoi oblozhki" (Nikolai Il'in: "I Have a Few Ideas Concerning the Printed Cover")* (Moscow: Samolet, 2000); and Lavrentiev, *Laboratoriia konstruktivizma* (see note 2). Although the texts of these books are in Russian, some have captions or summaries in English. Those that lack English entirely will still be useful as visual references.

Alef-Beit: A Typographic Journey *Martin Mendelsberg*

The letters are to the Torah as the foundation is to the building.
(R' Bechaye, IV, 25)

As a young child, I remember watching and listening to the *minyan* (ten Jewish men) follow weekly prayer services in my parents' home. Synagogue politics moved my father and his friends to start their own traveling *Shabbat* morning services. Instead of wandering in the desert seeking the Promised Land, we moved from house to house with books, head coverings, prayer shawls, arc, and scrolls. It was in these prayer books and *Torah* scrolls that I became fascinated with the abstract forms and counterforms of the *Alef-Beit*.

As a first-year student at Minneapolis College of Art and Design, I studied letterform construction with master calligrapher Ruth Justice. My left hand was tested in every way as I struggled to reproduce the classical proportions of Arrighi's *La Operina*. Little did I know that years later, as a Hebrew calligrapher, I would be producing letters by moving my hand from right to left, as the language is read.

Years later, I was reading and examining the origins of the Hebrew letters in a study group, where I met Dr. David Sanders, a brilliant student of Talmudic and Chassidic thought. We discovered that the Hebrew letters are not merely a convenience of language, but are considered in Jewish tradition to be essences that sustain the structure of the world. The shape, name, and numeric value of each letter have lessons to teach us about our spiritual and religious lives. These studies moved me to develop a digital Hebrew font based on the best scribal models.

A thorough search of digital Hebrew fonts in Israel and America revealed the absence of high-quality traditional typefaces. I realized none of the existing digital fonts exhibited the grace and beauty of the letterforms found in the Torah. My process began with the quill guided by earlier studies with Rabbi Menachem Goldberger, a *sofer* (scribe) trained in Israel. I was also very fortunate to find a Hebrew/English edition of the *Mishnas Sofrim* (now published by Feldheim in Jerusalem), which is a teaching manual for the scribes who write Torahs in Israel. This document contains a detailed examination of the creation of each letter, beginning with a set of detailed instructions on how to prepare the writing quill.

As I completed the hand-lettered alphabet, I examined original Torah scrolls, as well as published exemplars. I found a limited edition *Tekun* (printed Torah) by the noted sofer, Menachem Davidovich. Here were some of the best models I had ever seen. Once my "left-handed" work was complete, the original drawings were scanned and transformed into digital files. I worked with paths in Adobe Illustrator, then imported the documents into Fontographer to produce the first postscript samples.

The ancient Hebrew alphabet is essentially twenty-two letters, with five final versions. The tenth letter of the alphabet, *Yud*, is the smallest, and looks like a floating comma. *Yud* is the nucleus of every letter. Its form gives birth, metaphorically, and, in the hands of the scribe, it is the first mark drawn when building any letter. In Kabalistic terms, it is the Soul. Most of the letters fit inside a perfect square divided into nine grid fields. One ascending letter, called *Lamed*, rises above all others like a majestic king. There are five descending letters, final *Kaf*, final *Nun*, *Ayin*, final *Pei*,

Figure 1: Alef. (© *1993 Martin Mendelsberg*)

Figure 2: תורה Torah. *(© 1993 Martin Mendelsberg)*

and final *Tzadik*. Crowns (called "tags") can be seen in nine of the letters. It is impossible to give a true picture of the conceptual layers and formal elements in this brief writing.

In 1994, I met Rabbi Yitzchak Ginsburgh, author of *The Alef-Beit, Jewish Thought Revealed through the Hebrew Letters*. Rabbi Ginsburgh examined my first digital files very carefully. He encouraged me to complete work on the project, even though he had reservations about the translation of "sacred letters" into a computer font. Ironically, hand-produced Torah scrolls, new and old, are currently checked for accuracy via digital technology. Since the meeting with Rabbi Ginsburgh, I continued to work and rework the letters until I felt the look and feel of the alphabet reflected the nuances found in these "sacred letters." I had to deal with the problem of transforming a biblical script into a digital typeface without contrivances (remember Zapf Chancery?) Since 1995, I have used the completed Macintosh Postscript font for limited-edition books, fine-art prints, logotypes, and environmental signage.

After more than ten years of sustained work, Torah font will be marketed and distributed worldwide, via Masterfont Ltd. Studio Rosenberg. Established in 1986, in Tel Aviv, this typeface distributor produces some of the best Hebrew fonts available. Zvika Rosenberg, lead designer, and his team are now converting my files to work seamlessly with Israeli keyboards, word processors, and output devices. The fonts will soon be available in TrueType, and in Postscript versions for Macintosh and PC workstations.

References

R. Yitzchak Ginsburgh, *The Alef-Beit: Jewish Thought Revealed through the Hebrew Letters* (New Jersey: Jason Aronson, Inc., 1992).

R. Aryeh Kaplan, trans., *Sefer Yetzirah* (Maine: Samuel Weiser, 1991).

Michael Munck, *The Wisdom in the Hebrew Alphabet* (New York: Artscroll, Mesorah, 1988).

David Sanders and Martin Mendelsberg, *Neshama: The Journey of the Soul*, (Denver: Black Fire/WhiteFire, 1996).

Mishnas Sofrim (Jerusalem: Feldheim, 1997).

Charting a Course for Arabic Typography *Tarek Atrissi*

The education of an Arabic designer/typographer is no different than the education of a Western one. It includes a basic introduction to Latin typography, as well as major historical styles and movements presented in theory and in practice. Arabic typography is, in fact, something of an afterthought that follows a more Western tradition, making the learning process more complicated and more demanding. There are no programs or schools solely dedicated to Arabic type or type design, but just like many Western schools, most of the existing Arabic graphic design schools take typography as their primary focus.

Yet, the reason both Arabic and Latin typography are equally important is that many Arabic countries are bilingual. It is also because many of the instructors who formed the first generation of modern Arab graphic designers studied design in American and European schools.

Given this cross-pollination, a viable course must include the following: separate introductory typography classes in Arabic typography and Latin typography, and courses that cover the historical development of two different writing systems. At an advanced stage, Arabic and Latin typography need to come together when the focus shifts toward adapting the two scripts together, which is often the case. Logos, for example, especially typographical ones, are often adapted in two languages; corporate identities often work in two scripts, yet look cohesive and consistent. And, perhaps, this is one of the most important factors in studying Arabic typography: the integration of Arabic and Latin alphabets for different communication needs.

It is also important to learn the difference between calligraphy and typography—knowing the characteristics of each discipline and how to use them separately. Arabic lettering is built on the calligraphic rendering of form. Calligraphy is handwritten, and more of an artistic practice, with a rich history for Arabs, that has always been closely related to religion. Typography, on the other hand, is machine-made and an offspring of calligraphy, as a result of the evolution of printing.

Young designers do not have to learn calligraphy, because it is a practice that needs specialization and long years of practice, and a skill not directly useful to the contemporary field. Designers should, however, have an acute understanding of calligraphy in order to know how to use it for their specific needs. They must be able to communicate to the (craftsman) calligrapher what they need, or push his skills into challenging results. Indeed, it is similar to hiring an illustrator or a photographer, but in that context, the use of calligraphy is very related to the typographical aspect of design.

Even when a designer is involved in the design of a magazine or newspaper masthead in Arabic, he might need to initially work with a calligrapher and, later, abstract this calligraphy to create the typographical letter.

But beyond understanding calligraphy, the major focus of the designer should be on typography itself. To be able to work successfully with Arabic type is necessary to understand all the problems, in order to bypass them and eventually solve them. Unlike Latin fonts, Arabic fonts have many problems, which makes the task of creating good design and typography a hard one.

The main problem of Arabic fonts is availability. Compared to the uncountable number of Latin fonts available in the market and emerging every day, Arabic fonts are pretty insignificant. The "less is more" theory does not apply here, because out of the relatively small existing palette, only ten fonts are up to a high typographic standard,[1] and, therefore, difficult to have enough faces to be expressive or novel. Typography can be defined either as type design or as design with type. In the West there is a wide selection of available typefaces, and designers can be satisfied using these "ready-made" fonts.[2] In the Arab world, however, there are so few fonts that the designer's involvement with both "type design" and "designing with type" is more likely to happen. Yet, availability is not the only problem; many of the existing fonts merely, and poorly, attempt to imitate the traditional calligraphic style. The result is a failure to preserve the beauty and fluidity of calligraphy. Moreover, typefaces that are stuck in the past and fail to respond to the contemporary needs of our modern times, like legibility in small sizes or efficiency in New Media application,[3] are inefficient, at best. It is hard to use typefaces successfully as graphic elements, which makes it very difficult to find good Arabic design composed solely of type. I have never seen an Arabic typographical poster that could be compared to those by Paula Scher, who uses letters as a major source of graphic elements.

Learning type in Arab countries is even more challenging because the graphic and typographic design profession is still young enough not to have a rich heritage of masters to emulate. A very effective way to create innovative graphic and typographical language is to make use of the cultural, social, historical, and geographical factors—to make the visual expression a true reflection of its context. There is a thin line between being inspired by the West and trying to randomly apply a foreign approach in an inappropriate context. That is why the critical mission in teaching Arabic typography is not only to educate how to juggle between two alphabets, but is also to create a delicate mix of Western and Eastern charm, making the best out of the two sides while keeping the local flavor. When such an approach is taken in design and typography education, a more inspiring quality of work will be the result.

Like anywhere else, culture, religion, and politics exert a major effect on lettering and typography. The conservative attitude that governs these three sectors in the Arab world is reflected in type, which remains a very traditional field, not open for innovative contributions.[4] The shift toward globalization—particularly through the Web—should have a positive impact, bringing in foreign cultural trends[5] that will bring about positive progress—if incorporated well with every country's own cultural heritage and the visual form of its written and spoken language. Academic institutions should stress, however, that in the world of Arabic typography and design, renewing should not be just for the sake of renewing, but, rather, for solving current problems—to take Arabic typography a step further.

Perhaps when academic institutions can afford a bigger focus on Arabic type design, a new generation of Arabic fonts will arrive and make things much easier. This could happen with the introduction of graduate school programs in Arabic type design, to prepare the students to fully explore all aspects of Arabic type design, particularly the neglected technical aspects that are complicated by a script like Arabic. It is only then that radical progress will happen: when specific software and technical solutions are created in the Arab world, instead of the West, taking into consideration the real problems facing Arabic type designers, and breaking the technical limits that are imposed nowadays by big Western software companies.[6] Designers then will know how to make their creations fully operational on computers.

Undergraduate studies in design will never have enough time to fully focus on type design, but they can prepare designers to do so in the future, if that is their interest.[7] A clear description of the responsibilities of making type design, as well as a better overview of the technical and production side of it, will be a useful addition to the smaller attempts and exercises in designing letters, words, or titles. However, in order to have more people interested in further focus on type design—thereby creating educational systems especially dedicated to respond to this need—copyright issues and intellectual property laws should witness a major reform. Piracy of fonts is too damaging for the industry in the Arab world, and it seems that the efforts and responsibilities are not only in the hands of the designers, but, equally, in the hands of the consumers.[8]

The constant struggle to try to make effective modern Arabic graphic design was the springboard for a project I developed over the last two years. It is a Web site about Arabic typography (*www.arabictypography.com*), aimed to create a modern user interface to prove that existing problems with Arabic fonts should not limit the creation of fresh typographically designed pieces. The main function of the site is to play the role of communication platform for Arabic type and, hence, to exchange ideas between various people interested in the field—designers, calligraphers, typographers, technical people, and more—to create discussion and awareness of what it will take to solve the problems in the absence of major Arabic type or graphic design associations.

With the emergence of a fast-growing community of Arabic designers, interest and individual efforts in the field of Arabic typography are highly needed. When these various individual efforts are brought together, higher standards will be generated and teamwork will eventually produce a stronger educational system for the Arabic designer/typographer, who will then be more ready to break all the current limitations and carry the industry to the next step.

Notes

1. Interview with Samir Sayegh.
2. Interview with Habib Khoury.
3. *Arabic Typography*, a comprehensive sourcebook by Huda Smitshuijzen Abifares (Saqi Books, 2001).
4. Interview with Huda Smitshuijzen Abifares.
5. Interview with Habib Khoury, AvanType.
6. Interview with Thomas Milo, Deco Type.
7. Interview with Mamoun Sakkal, Sakkal Design.
8. Interview with Habib Khoury, AvanType.

Digital Literacy

Digital Type Decade *Emily King*

For a short period between the buoyancy of the late 1980s and the economic downturn of the early 1990s, there existed an unprecedented typographic euphoria. Suddenly, for a relatively small investment in hardware and software, designers were able to marshal the industry's standard type technology from their desktops (thanks in part to the de-encryption of Adobe's PostScript Type 1 software). For a few years, this capability was exploited to the full, and the result was an exhilarating rush of intensive typographic invention.

A 1992 article by Robin Kinross (*Eye*, vol. 2, no. 7) described the heady early years of device-independent digital type and a newly reordered typographic landscape, in which traditional firms (such as Monotype, Berthold, and Linotype-Hell) had been forced to slim down, merge, or seek out niches in a market they had formerly dominated. In their place had emerged software firms (Adobe, largely, and Apple and Microsoft, to a lesser extent) who had arrived at type almost inadvertently through the development of desktop publishing technology and now were required to take up the slack. Most revolutionary of all was the rise of the independent type designer: individuals, such as Zuzana Licko, who had seized the design initiative. Kinross called the then-current changes "as profound as any in the course of [typography's] 550-year history."

The digital technologies introduced in the late 1980s did not just change the conditions in which type was being designed and distributed, they also changed dramatically the circumstances in which type was being used. Although it had seemed, in the early years, as if the software giants were going to occupy the typographic high ground left vacant by the demise of the old guard, it soon became apparent that this was not going to be the case. Since 1992, many of the traditional type firms have been reduced to venerable labels attached to static libraries, and, although Monotype continues to thrive in the guise of Agfa Monotype Corporation[1] (a wholly owned subsidiary of the Agfa Corporation, which has been picking up other firms along the way, including ITC), it does so in a form that bears little resemblance to its former self. Where Monotype once targeted marketing at a community of type professionals, it now works with operating systems manufacturers to supply core fonts: this is the means to desktop publish and assemble workable Web sites.

Over the past decade, it has become evident that software companies will never become the white knights of typography. In the example of Adobe, it seemed the software created by the type team was at odds with the software products made by the rest of the firm; the former targeted the specialist, while the latter aimed to open up the activities of design and print to as broad an audience as possible. Given commercial imperatives, these companies have the resources to create fantastic products; remove the profit motive, and their attention strays elsewhere. Interviewed in 1995, Adobe's Bur Davies recalled a period between 1989 and 1991 (when the sale of Adobe's PostScript types went "through the roof") that was followed by a sharp downturn in 1992, when economic recession and competition combined to slash revenues. The consequences were immediate; the type team was cut to twelve people, and their design program was considerably reduced. By the mid-1990s, the beautiful type booklets that Adobe had once produced to promote their Originals range had been replaced by glossy leaflets selling Fun Types.

The current emphasis of type design at Adobe, where a few key members of the original heavyweight type team continue to work, is to showcase developments in type technology, in particular, those technologies that are unwieldy and forbidding to independent type designers. The most important of these is OpenType. Announced in 1997, this font format was developed jointly with Microsoft to address the problem of cross-platform incompatibilities of the existing PostScript and TrueType formats. Its goal was later extended to work with the larger international standard character set of Unicode, which is designed to support the interchange, processing, and display of written texts of all languages. Unicode v.3.1 accommodates 94,140 characters—enough for all the languages in the world.

Major recent additions to the Adobe type library include: Robert Slimbach's "full-featured, state of the art OpenType family" Warnock—a typeface that brings together classic proportion and contemporary detail—named after the cofounder of Adobe Systems, John Warnock; and Carol Twombly's Chaparral, an OpenType face that combines sturdy slab serifs with varying letter proportions. Both are accessible faces imbued with all the features that the OpenType format allows.[2]

As well as creating designs in new font formats, an area in which the big software companies continue to make the running is the design of type for the screen. Among the most widely used and widely admired of contemporary screen fonts are Matthew Carter's designs for Microsoft:

Verdana (sans serif) and Georgia (serif). The manner in which these fonts are distributed has echoes of the proprietary models that were the norm in the pre-PostScript era: just as fonts were once sold in conjunction with typesetting equipment, Carter's fonts are distributed by Microsoft alongside their browser. The dominance of the software companies in the field of screen fonts seems likely to continue, as only these companies have access to the extremely wide channels of distribution that are required if such fonts are to be successful.

The underlying method behind all of Carter's Microsoft fonts was the same. Starting out by making basic bitmap fonts at the three sizes that Microsoft considered to be the most important for text on the screen, Carter embellished these fonts with bitmapped italic, bold, and bold italic versions. It was only after these bitmap fonts had been approved that Carter wrapped a vector outline around them and passed them on to Tom Rickner, an expert in hinting type for the screen, who created the scalable versions. Carter has argued that the chief virtue of working this way is not so much evident in the forms of the letters, but in their spacing, which remains regular in accordance with their underlying bitmap.

The information design consultant Andrew Boag, of Boag Associates, describes Carter's method as "bottom-up" design. Although he acknowledges the need for Carter's fonts and the considerable merit of the designer's work, Boag argues that the bottom-up approach has its limits: there is a ceiling on the number of different letterforms you can make from a restricted grid. As an alternative, Boag recommends the "top-down" approach, which involves hinting traditional typefaces for screen use.

One of the core techniques of the top-down approach is "grayscaling"—rendering letterforms in pixels of varying levels of intensity. This is a technique that comes into its own on low-resolution, color screens of the kind that are the norm on desks around the world, particularly when appearance is more important than absolute legibility. Boag's writing about this is included in his Web site.[3]

Other developments in screen type include the typefaces designed for handheld screens, such as those on mobile phones and Palm Pilots. As these devices are used as a means of access to ever-wider sources of information, their typographical qualities become more and more important. Because they are used at preset sizes and need not be scalable, the fonts that appear on these screens are relatively easy to design. Nevertheless, when looked at en masse, they demonstrate commendable ingenuity in the face of low resolution. Peering at jaggy type on tiny black-and-white screens may have become an increasingly common activity, but this doesn't mean the long-term goal of making the screen as comfortable to read as the printed page has been abandoned.

The most significant development in this area is ClearType, a technology that is being developed by Microsoft. Combining insights into the nature of screen display with an understanding of visual perception, the technologists and designers behind ClearType hope to exploit the properties of commonplace screen technology to create a more fluent reading experience.[4]

At present, ClearType is available exclusively as part of Microsoft Reader, and only a small selection of existing typefaces have been adapted to the technology (including Berling and Frutiger), but many, including the technological commentator Nico Macdonald,[5] believe that this type technology is set to become the on-screen standard.

Far away from the major software companies and the large-scale type distributors, the independent digital foundries (the new kids on the block in the early 1990s) continue to proliferate. The typography section of the Microsoft Web site carries a list of more than six hundred small-scale type foundries.[6] To a large extent, this section of the type industry has flourished against the odds. After the initial joy of gaining access to the tools to make and distribute type, the mood of many designers took a nosedive when they realized how difficult it would be to earn sufficient revenue from their type-design labors. The primary threats to the independents were (and still are) software pirates and competition from larger companies, who sell type in cheap packages, or even bundle it free with other software. Small type foundries have adopted a range of different strategies in their efforts to overcome these circumstances. Some, such as the Dutch foundry Enschedé,[7] have chosen to aim for the top end of the market by charging high prices for their fonts and offering quality and "exclusivity" (their inverted commas) in return. Others, such as Rian Hughes's Device,[8] thrive on the quantity and immediacy of their output.

Another route taken by a number of independent foundries has been that of custom type. Making faces for publications or corporations has become the staple for companies such as Dalton Maag[9] in London (whose clients include BT, Hewlett-Packard, and Lego), and the Hoefler Type Foundry[10] in New York (clients include *Harper's Bazaar*, *Martha Stewart Living*, Tiffany & Co., and the Guggenheim Museum). A unique typeface has become a must-have accessory among contemporary brands. It is partly due to the expansion of client-initiated design that the flow of new typefaces prompted by the technological changes of the late 1980s has continued unabated into the new century. "What's a brand without a type-face?" cries the cover of Dalton Maag's brochure.

Yet, the frenzy around type that was so much a part of the early-1990s graphic design scene is now somewhat dulled. Explanations for the dampening down of typographic excitement might include the threats of software piracy and cut-rate competition mentioned above, market saturation, or even economic cycles, but more likely than any of these factors is the reassertion of a couple of basic truths: type is complex and time-consuming to make, and requires an adherence to principles that put a damper on revolutionary ambition. What we are experiencing right now could be described as a second digital wave.

To a great extent, many of the directions being explored in type design now appear to be edited down, hemmed-in versions of design initiatives that arose in the early years of PostScript. For example, the digital type magazine *Fuse*, launched in 1991, has just released its eighteenth issue, the first in several years. Taking the theme "Secrets," *Fuse* 18's editorial describes a world in which information has obscured meaning, and its typefaces reflect that theme to a greater or lesser extent. The strongest fits between theme and font are Matthew Carter's contribution, DeFace, which explores the communicative and destructive properties of graffiti, and Jake Tilson's httpwc MEN ONLY, which turns the keyboard into a means of revealing codes. Fuse produces typefaces that only qualify for that description in the loosest possible sense and continues along an already established path, marshalling those designs in the service of its apocalyptic message.

At the other end of the type-design spectrum, the exploration of various chapters in typographic history continues apace. In particular, the merging of two quite disparate typographic styles into a single traditional-looking, yet distinctive, face—a significant theme in type design since the introduction of PostScript—remains a popular tack. This approach informed both of Adobe's major new OpenType typefaces, Twombly's Chaparral and Slimbach's Warnock. Also dealing in typographic history is Jeremy Tankard, who has delved into medieval manuscripts (Alchemy), the Grotesque and Egyptian lettering styles associated with the industrial revolution (The Shire Types), and is currently looking at the typography of the 1901 Doves Bible with the aim of creating a new typeface for publishing use. Tankard's most visible face is the sans serif Bliss (used by British Midland Airways, Foxton's estate agent). The Bliss typeface is the outcome of the assessment of five sans serif faces: Gill Sans; Syntax; Frutiger; Edward Johnston's Underground typeface, and Kinneir and Calvert's Transport typeface (see *Eye*, vol. 9, no. 34). The result is a design that answered the current quest for "a new simplicity." It is a face that seems straightforward because it is imbued with so much we already know.

Parallel to official typographic history, another area that seems to be proving endlessly fruitful to contemporary type designers is typographic popular culture. This is a broad field that ranges from the comic book to the commonplace and functional—the car number plate, source of Conor Mangat's Platelet[11]—and into the fantastic and the camp, a route comprehensively explored by the U.S. outfit House Industries.[12] The mood in the popular culture camp is upbeat. House Industries employ an indeterminate 1960s and 1970s nostalgia, a longing for a time of burbling TVs, snack foods, and reclining leather chairs—an era when commercial culture was titillating and innocent, rather than manipulative and scary. All this frothiness is a bit foolish, but it does make a change from the decayed, abject thing that characterized many of the forays into pop-culture typography of the early 1990s. While typefaces such as Barry Deck's Template Gothic (1990) or Smoke Bomb's Backspacer (1993) had us all teetering on the brink of unstoppable cultural decline, House Industries' Latin types speak of nothing more disquieting than "bongo madness."

The split between typographic history and popular culture is far from unimpeachable: there's an apparent distaste on the part of many typographic commentators for all of postwar consumer culture. As the recent past becomes more historicized, the popular/historical gap may gradually erode. Lucas De Groot's Pistol fonts are examples of designs that might qualify for inclusion in the typographic history section. Drawn from Jamie Reid's ransom-note lettering for the Sex Pistols, and referring strongly to the design language of the punk fanzine, they seem sufficiently allied with grassroots, political radicalism to be allowed some kind of worthwhile typographic meaning.[13]

The idea that letterforms could communicate independently to the texts they spell out—though it dates from the earliest manuscripts—is heavily associated with the early years of PostScript. It is the outcome of the coincidence between the emergence of the software and the adoption of postmodern theory in U.S. art schools. And, while this is no longer big typographic news, it has become a broadly accepted truth. House Industries exploited this fact as part of the promotion of their recent sans serif face Chalet by inventing a designer, René Albert Chalet, and a story that touched some of type history's favorite bases: modernism, Switzerland, and venerated French type foundries.

In a related, but more earnest vein, in March 2001, the Bilbao cultural organization Consonni, in collaboration with artist Hinrich Sachs, offered for sale at auction the international copyright and software versions of fourteen traditional Basque typefaces known as the Euskara types. As an element of Basque folk culture, these letterforms carry a political charge, particularly in the light of their censorship during the Franco period. The Consonni auction traced questions about meaning and ownership that might be relevant to the typographic community on a broader political map.[14]

If there is a style of letterform that is particularly associated with the end of the twentieth century and the beginning of the twenty-first, it is the gauche, techie look that has become visible in contemporary display type. The awkward, geometric faces that are part of this look are often the outcome of a systems approach, a method whereby the designer establishes the rules at the outset, and allows form to be determined by those rules. For example, many of the typefaces distributed by Christian Küsters's Acme foundry are designed according to a set of principles that all but eliminate formal choice.[15]

According to Küsters, the point is not how these typefaces look, but the "idea" that lies behind them. Other designers working in this way include Julian Morey of Club Twenty-One, who takes inspiration from the crudest of vernacular types—in one instance, the lettering on stationery delivery notes, and works these ideas up into full alphabets. The systems approach to type design implies scant attention to how letterforms might perform in a typographic context, and, as such, has little to do with traditional typographic value, but they have created a current typographic mood. Perhaps it is a perverse response to the seemingly endless formal choice that was offered by PostScript technology.

Another approach is to take the technology apart and craft new software that will make things interesting once again. This is the long-term strategy of the Dutch designer duo Erik van Blokland and Just van Rossum, and their invention appears unstoppable. The most recent recipients of the Charles Nypels Prize for typography (see *Eye*, vol. 10, no. 39),

Van Blokland and Van Rossum, were the originals in this field (see *Eye*, vol. 2, no. 7), and with recent projects such as Federal, a font that takes on more detail at larger sizes, they remain at its forefront.[16] The most significant development in contemporary type may be the emergence of the aforementioned Unicode,[17] a system of encoding that will encompass a large part of the world's written languages and promote the cause of global typography.

But, to return to the more local view, for many of the type designers who create the faces that we see around us, these developments are of limited relevance. Jeremy Tankard has written a short paper for new type users on the trials and tribulations of the technology, in which he describes the incompatibilities and glitches that are the constant hazards of contemporary type designers and typographers. As far as Tankard is concerned, OpenType simply is not happening yet; he doesn't have the time, and his customers don't have the applications. Maybe, once this gap closes, we will witness a surge of innovation comparable to that of a decade ago.

(Thanks to Phil Baines and Nico Macdonald.)

Notes

1. *www.agfamonotype.com.*
2. *www.adobe.com.*
3. OpenType: *www.microsoft.com/typography/otspec.*
4. *www.boag.co.uk.*
5. *www.research.microsoft.com/~jplatt/cleartype.*
6. *www.spy.co.uk.*
7. *www.microsoft.com/typography.*
8. *www.teff.nl* (or, via their U.K. agents, *www.boag.co.uk*).
9. *www.devicefonts.co.uk.*
10. *www.daltonmaag.com.*
11. *www.typography.com.*
12. *www.emigre.com.*
13. *www.houseindustries.com.*
14. *www.thetypes.com/www.fontfabrik.com.*
15. *www.consonni.org.*
16. *www.acmefonts.net.*
17. *www.letterror.com.*
18. *www.unicode.org.*
19. The concept of a world character set had already been recognized by the ISO: ". . . develop the ISO standard for graphic character repertoire and coding for an international two byte graphic character set . . . Consider the needs of programming languages to have the same amount of storage for each character. . . ." [iso/tc97/sc2 n1436, 1984]. Groundwork for the Unicode project began in late 1987 with initial discussions between three software engineers: Joe Becker of Xerox Corporation, Lee Collins, who was then with Xerox, and Mark Davis, then of Apple Corporation. The Unicode Standard began with the publication of a paper written in February 1988 by Joe Becker, Unicode 88. (Contributed by Phil Baines)

Originally published in Eye, *vol. 10, no. 40 (Summer 2001).*

Learning Curves: Teaching Typography with the Computer

Katherine McCoy

Today, typography can be taught almost without pencil, ruling pen, brush, or X-acto knife. We just might be able to throw away our gouache and plaka, tracing paper, and art board. Traditional materials, tools, and hand skills are largely irrelevant for today's typographic education and practice. The computer is a far more powerful learning environment for students and teaching tool for educators.

This contention will set off many alarms among the best of our educators. Disturbing as this sounds, there must also have been consternation when moveable type began to displace the calligraphic pen. Technology has always been intrinsically related to the forms, processes, and output of communication design.

The past ten years of digital technology have given designers good screen resolution, WYSIWYG display, responsive software, and excellent desktop output, enabling the precise manipulation and visualization of typographic forms. For students, these tools are not only useful, but also accessible and relatively affordable.

Yet, few educators have truly harnessed this power. It is time to recognize that the computer provides design education with an excellent tool that supports deeper and quicker progress for the student. The computer is now the tool, and the required hand skill is mousing. In fact, mousing *is* a hand-eye skill and can be an essential part of the development of the visual sensibility so essential for fine typography.

These contentions come from a relatively traditionalist designer. I cherish the noble history of typography rooted in the Renaissance, and revere the classic fonts that took lifetimes to perfect. When the Mac burst on the scene, I had been immersed in typographic practice and education for twenty years, using all the traditional hand skills. Yet, from the first, I found that the computer's typography, drawing, and page design tools are rewardingly accurate mirrors of my precomputer design processes, fluidly supporting concept sketching and the immediate visualization of emerging ideas and forms. Clearly, the profession has adopted this, too, since it is nearly impossible to practice communication design today off-computer.

Yet, we continue to teach typography using traditional techniques. Many of the most rigorous programs do not allow students to touch a computer for one or two years, as if hand skills were a sort of "learn to walk before you can run" issue. Is the computer just too much too soon?

This seems like blaming the pencil for being erasable—too convenient or too responsive. Certainly, we see serious problems associated with students' use of computers, including badly distorted type forms and clichéd effects. But aren't these more the result of permissive teaching and lack of a rigorous methodology for using computer software, rather than the computer itself?

Can we teach typography without resistant and labor-intensive hand processes, while retaining the essential goals for typography? If one analyzes any rigorous typography curriculum, I think that every goal can be supported far more effectively using the computer as the main tool. All our best projects can be taught better by using the computer.

For instance, I have long admired the highly refined sensibility and visual discipline of the rigorous Basle-based graphic training. Those goals of a deep understanding of letterform structure and nuance, the subtleties and accelerations of curves, and two-dimensional composition, including proportion, rhythm, progression, and contrast, can be taught extremely well on the computer.

Letterform design and structure are well supported by computer drawing tools, including the bezier curve system, which reveals the wonderfully elastic nature of lines. Learning to manipulate bezier curves simultaneously imparts key visual sensitivity to the character of curves. In fact, I cannot imagine a better method—this is where I find I am finally reaching my personal goals for understanding curves, after years of experience with brushes, pens, and French curves. The ability to immediately examine one's drawing at all scales, from extreme magnification to tiny text, is also a great asset.

Typographic structure and text organization in two-dimensional space are far better taught using the page-design software and laser printer output. Using the computer, I find that project exercises that previously required weeks to produce a refined solution, using the old tools of type indication, transfer lettering, photo typesetting, and photostats, now take a fraction of the time to achieve the same educational goals.

The computer and laser printer output enable students to explore many iterations. Educators understand how important the feedback loop is for the learning process. Running through the project cycle from concept to visualization to revision is essential. Nothing provides this more effectively than the computer, since this process greatly increases the number of iteration cycles.

Students benefit immensely from immediate visual feedback about their choices, with the "what you see is what you get" nature of the electronic display of typography. Noncomputer methods for designing textual typography involve massive guesswork. Only the actual typesetting of running text in a lead or photo type shop can provide the same WYSIWYG information about the actual appearance of one's type choices. Laborious character counting and highly abstracted type indication provide only the roughest approximation of reality. Without a computer, students rarely actually know the results of their typographic choices and what they might actually look like if their project was real. Is 10- on 12-point a better choice than 10-point solid? Or, maybe, 9- on 13-point is actually more legible? The computer provides the opportunity for rapid and accurate exploration of all typographic variables, including font, size, weight, slant, case, letterspacing, and line spacing.

These same tools support abstract composition and graphic translation exercises. Studies of rhythm, progression, and contrast can be drawn and visualized in rapid iterations, enabling the student to concretely see the results of their choices, evaluate them, and choose the best for further development. The result is a rapid improvement of their skills and a deeper grasp of these visual concepts.

Perhaps we are thinking that time and labor, rather than iteration and feedback, are the essential ingredients of learning. Is typography a "no pain, no gain" sort of thing? I don't think so.

In fact, the computer enables a far fuller understanding of typography and two-dimensional composition far more quickly, and without the frustrations of manipulating resistant and messy materials. What it loses is the time-consuming waste of blood, sweat, and tears. It also eliminates the ruined piece just before completion, and the jeopardy of a failed experiment. And, we all know how students can become married to weak concepts when they have invested huge amounts of time in them.

Noncomputer projects delay feedback while the student labors with hand processes. The opportunity to iterate an extensive sketch progression with immediate feedback yields far more educational growth and a much better understanding of the criteria of fine typography.

Another great benefit is that digital design files are always editable. A project can be continually refined and improved, incorporating feedback from faculty and critiques even after the final class presentation.

This editability of files also allows the teacher to demonstrate the possibilities of alternate approaches in real time. Sitting with the student at the computer to review an emerging project solution is a powerful teaching situation. The teacher can quickly demonstrate the visual possibilities of variations with immediate WYSIWYG feedback. And the student can also make changes in real time and receive faculty feedback. After this sort of exploration, one can instantly return the student's original solution with a keystroke.

The real-time demonstration of alternative possibilities in digital files can also be projected for the entire class via an LCD projector. As educators know, one student's project critique frequently demonstrates concepts that can be generalized to apply to the entire class. Digital files projected in a classroom overcome the legibility limitations of graphic design's inherently small scale in a group situation, and allow the entire class to see dynamic real-time WYSIWYG visualization of changes that result in refinements of the project solution.

But, we should not throw the baby out with the bathwater. What is the actual value of those hand skills we have traditionally emphasized? Thumbnail conceptual sketching for ideation capitalizes on important hand-eye-brain connections. However, mousing and tablet input using drawing software can achieve much the same benefit as hand sketching, while also immediately describing accurate type forms. In fact, we educators need to develop new methods for digital conceptual sketching to harness this potential.

This is not to say that drawing and other hand gestures no longer have a place in communication design. Life drawing, especially quick "gesture drawing," continues to be great training for designers, helping us understand the body's connection to visual form.

Many educators complain that student work executed on the computer is just too "computery," with too many canned software tricks and a thin glossiness. However, this problem is easily countered by carefully conceived projects and clear faculty input. Some of the most interesting work moves fluidly in and out of the computer. A very interesting example of "in and out" is Jeff Keedy's course, at the California Institute of the Arts, that incorporates traditional calligraphy into his computer-supported type-font design curriculum. This close blending of computer processes with selected traditional techniques can be applied to all typographic courses, and might be the key to a more effective typographic curriculum.

It is time to effectively embrace the impact of digital technology on our discipline and its potential for education. A great deal of typography will never leave the screen, since increasing amounts of output are screen display. Yet, even for print, the computer is the best tool I have encountered to date for teaching typography.

Using the computer as a teaching tool is not a cause for guilt. This is not about speed, ease, and sleaze. Although I have mentioned speed many times in this essay, speed is just part of the means, not the end. This is about progress and learning. When typographic fundamentals take less time to master, students will achieve greater expertise and will move on to more advanced conceptual levels of communication design, emerging from their education far better prepared for significant professional practice. So, I urge design educators to retool their project sequences to harness the assets of computer-supported typographic design, starting from day one. The computer is not just a professional's design tool, but, also, a powerful educational process.

Originally published in PRINT *(Jan/Feb 2003).*

The Newness in the New Typography *Teal Triggs*

Earlier this week, I cut out of London underground's daily *Metro* news-paper a little story about the new phenomenon of "slebbing"—that is, taking pictures of celebrities and sending them as images on your mobile phone. The article started off observing that, "In a style of communication where text is abbreviated to 'txt' to save time, it was perhaps inevitable that words would eventually disappear altogether."[1] Based upon Cockney rhyming slang—London's East End coded language—you can send an image of Britney Spears to a friend, for example, and mean, "Fancy a beer?" If an image of the sitcom *Friends'* star Jennifer Aniston is received from your potential date, it might take on a negative connotation, and could be understood as, "Let's just be friends." On the other hand, an image of Leslie Ash, who just had plastic surgery on her lips, and stars in the U.K.'s prime-time soap drama, *The Bill*, might translate as, "You look like a trout." The trouble with this practice is that the images of celebrity are not fixed, and their meanings change with both time and how many column inches they have had in the tabloid press. It's a humorous device, but is certain to be a short-lived one.

However, in this media-driven world, the image is undoubtedly taking precedent in some sectors over the typographic word. We are con-stantly bombarded with images from television, LED signage, the Internet, and, as the theorist and critic Jon Thompson has written, "images and technologies of image-making and image-dissemination play an increasing role" in our social world.[2] If, indeed, our understanding of the typographic form is returning to its most basic roots of symbolic image—reminiscent of glyphs and pictograms—consideration must be given to how we might understand "representational meaning"—that is, the way in which forms gain meaning. The "linguistic paradigm" is, by now, omnipresent, with design practitioners and theorists alike attempting to decipher the relation-ship between words and images, and, indeed, "pictorial meaning," itself.

On the other hand, employing semiotic analysis has become increas-ingly significant, particularly as the debate surrounding "type as image" rapidly unfolds. Yet, in the field of fine art, Thompson observes that many artists still question the relationship between the signification of words and images "mainly on the grounds that the address that we make to the image is of an entirely different character to the address that we make to a text; that similarly, the address the image makes to us—the way in which it inhabits the eye—is entirely different to the way a text sits before the reader's eye."[3]

In the move from pictorial art to language, and, in the case of "slebbing," the process of the image moving into language, "reading" occurs in two stages. In the first instance, the viewer establishes the form, which is instantly recognizable as representing an object or idea. The second stage occurs when meaning is ascribed to that form. The typographic mark is a visual code, and is matched within this process, to a specific meaning. In the same way that the philosopher Richard Wollheim suggests that "a painting represents what it does in part because of how it looks,"[4] typographic materiality is highlighted through type size, weight, spacing, and shape, etc., and must also be taken into account.

At the same time, consideration must also be given to the way in which "representational meaning" is culturally mediated and produced, as well as the context in which it is presented. How many TV soap addicts outside of the U.K. would know the story behind the image of Leslie Ash, for example? It may also be argued that a relationship exists between theory, practice, and the way in which we not only "read" meaning but the processes through which we understand the production of meaning within the new typography. Communication is an "ongoing, fluid process of exchange taking place in a communicative field in which such things as beliefs are continuously renegotiated."[5]

German Bold Italic

In 1998, the pop superstar Kylie Minogue, in collaboration with the experimental musician Towa Tei, released "GBI (German Bold Italic)". The lyrics went something like this:

My name is German Bold Italic
I am a typeface
Which you have never heard before
Which you have never seen before.

I can complement you well
Especially in red
Extremely in green

Maybe in blue, blue, blue.

You will like my sense of style.[6]

"German Bold Italic" is an interesting song for two reasons: first, that such a song even exists; and, second, that typography could be so "hip" that Kylie would consider writing a song about the subject at all. On one level, "German Bold Italic" suggests the way that typography has become "visual fashion"—a sort of *typotainment*—notable by its style of delivery and focus on "display." Equally, Kylie's "German Bold Italic" is interesting in the way the lyrics imply that the typeface is a complement to something else—that is, a complement to meaning. The referents are clear. Kylie is a complement to her male counterpart—an accessory of adornment, which even appears in complementary colors. The typeface would be selected for its stylish attributes and is a complement to the word. The lyrics exemplify the way in which typography has been embedded with cultural authority, and there are "ways of reading" that help us interpret meaning.

I am reminded here of Roland Barthes' analysis of the "decorative complexity" represented in the image-based letterforms drawn by the artist Erté. Erté was a fashion illustrator for *Harper's Bazaar*, who provided the magazine with its quintessential Art Deco woman—elegantly drawn and draped in a whimsical neoclassical garment. For the alphabet, Barthes notes that each letterform was created as a "mixture of a woman's body and adornment," where "the body and garment *supplement* each other. . . ."[7] For example, the letter *Z* is formed by the posture of the female figure, whose pleated garment accentuates a position of submissiveness as she kneels with her arms outstretched, leaning back in order to replicate the letterform's shape. Barthes observes that,

> *In Erté's generalized alphabet there is a dialectic exchange: Woman seems to lend her figure to the Letter; but in return, and more certainly, the Letter gives Woman its abstraction. . . ."*[8]

Such an analysis is useful in highlighting the relationship between what might be considered typographic style and its interpretation, and that meaning that is generated by the word itself. In other words, "typefaces and their configurations contain meaning that is distinct from the words they create. Certainly, calligraphy, decorative type, and italic or bold letterforms have long served to express tone or heighten the impact of words."[9] However, we might ask, can a typeface be something more than a "complement," in Kylie's words?

The New Typography Then

The new typography is a simultaneous experience of vision and communication.
—Laszlo Moholy-Nagy, 1923.

Parallels may be found between the new typography of the 1920s and what we might consider the newness in the new typography of recent years. The new typography of the 1920s was a movement sought to "express the spirit, life, and visual sensibility of the day." It was fuelled by the transformation of the social, cultural, and political climate sparked by an emerging set of technologies fostering notions of standardization and functionalism. In Europe, artists and designers, including El Lissitzky, Jan Tschichold, and Moholy-Nagy, rejected ornamentation in favor of rational design. Whereas the old typography had been about "beauty," the form of the new typography emerged as a result of its function. The new machine age needed to be expressed in the dynamics of the page using an asymmetrical design of contrasting elements. It was on the page, where typography had to be economical, both visually and financially. And, with a reductiveness of form, it avoided reference to any previous historical style or fine art calligraphy. Such formal properties of the new typography would facilitate communication democratically and more universally.

In 1923, Moholy-Nagy wrote in his essay, "The New Typography":

> *Typography is a tool of communication. It must be communication in its most intense form. The emphasis must be on absolute clarity since this distinguishes the character of our own writing from that of ancient pictographic forms.*[10]

The typographical image should achieve for the reader what is conveyed by voice and gesture for the listener. But, for many of the designers during this period, typography also included the use of photography, which was seen as a precise and objective form. In this way, the photograph was preferred over the use of illustration, much in the same way that the expressive letterform had been rejected in favor of the sans serif.

However, in terms of layout, the inclusion of the photograph, situated in close proximity to the appropriate textual passage, was frequently under scrutiny. It was argued by some proponents of a pure modernism that any such typographical layout would be visually confusing and would create a "psychological tension between text and illustration."[11] But, what happens when the conventional boundaries between image and text are blurred?

The New Typography Now

My starting point for a definition of *new* for typography today is that which is about to begin or has just begun. For example, this could be a new year; a new town; a new style; or, in this particular case, a new typography. Typography, for our purposes here, is concerned not only with the designing of type, but also with designing *with* type. My definition of a new typography also embodies aspects of what Theo van Leeuwen has described in the rise of a new semiotics—a form and method which combines not only theory and practice, the intellectual and aesthetic, but moves across the confines of conventional boundaries.[12] Designers and typographers have become more aware of the link between craftsmanship and historical understanding, between cultural and technological issues, the aesthetics and function of type, and the importance of language and meaning.

At the same time, the broader audience has become more sophisticated in its ways of reading, and more accepting in the way alternative models of visual communication may be presented. The experience of the dialectic is no longer confined to the flat two-dimensional page, but, instead, has increasingly become much more about considering the totality of a spatial environment. The educator and designer Katherine McCoy has acknowledged that, with interactive electronic communication design, a "shift from the verbal to the sensory" had led us "to the experiential."[13] It may also be suggested that the new typography moves beyond just image or just type and embraces color, texture, lighting, three-dimensionality, and motion. It blurs the boundaries between language and image, creating new visual identities and a new visual syntax for words and phrases expressing ideas and feelings—on pages, screens, and all around us in the everyday environment.

Designers now require a better understanding of the way in which language works. That is how we notate, interpret, and communicate through written and spoken codes and the ways in which meaning is produced. Meaning is produced from the visual arrangement of the text, and through the hand of the designer or typographer acting as a mediator of the client's message. As Gunther Kress and Theo van Leeuwen have suggested, "The grammar of visual design plays an equally vital role in the production of meaning," in that it "points to different interpretations of experience and different forms of social interaction."[14] Communication is the result of meaning understood through the conventional use of words and where meaning attains form through letters.

In the move from print- to screen-based mediums, viewers are no longer passive receivers of information; instead, they have become interactive participants in the communication process. The publisher and historian Robin Kinross has written, "The designer acts as an interpreter of the meanings of images; and it is in such moments that theoretical understanding comes to play its part in practical design work."[15] He continues with the example of the way in which designers make decisions about how to deploy images through cropping and framing, which may be informed by their theoretical understanding.

Theorists, such as Gui Bonsiepe, have long argued for research into a semantic typography, suggesting that typography is a "constituent element in the reception and production of texts." The use of the type form as a passive receptacle is no longer applicable. As Bonsiepe suggests, "The wave of 'new typography' is making use of the new possibilities of digital technology,"[16] but, also, is a fresh look at how conventional technology may be used in a new way, offering the designer new possibilities for the development of "new" visual language systems.[17] It is here that theory and practice converge, and the theories and methods for analyzing language, as well as the visual elements of spoken, written, and audiovisual communication come into play. And, based upon the notion that all communication is multimodal, there is potential to be found in exploring the areas where different disciplines cross over.

The New Typography and Education

But how might we begin to teach this new typography? Increasingly, we have already seen a gradual division between what might constitute a suitable curriculum for interactive design, and that of traditional print-based design. As technology has continued to develop, so, too, has students' need for specialist knowledge and skills in order to enter successfully into the current job market. However, as the nature of communication problems becomes more complex, the formation of multidisciplinary teams, or designers undertaking postgraduate education to supplement their first degrees in related disciplines, may be potential solutions.

In addition, developments in the new typography offer educators an opportunity to review traditional pedagogical approaches. The greatest effect will be upon the idea of time, visual images, narrative structures, and the organization of given information. Consideration may be given to developing programs that may choose to focus on the research and developmental process in realizing a "solution," rather than on the final product itself. As such, curricula will need to place greater emphasis on the expansion of appropriate research methods training. While the basic theoretical tenets of post-structuralism and deconstruction have found a place in typographic education, Katherine McCoy, for example, has also argued that, in the new area of interactive electronic communication design, additional methodologies are required that could be drawn from the disciplines of social science, anthropology, cognitive and perceptual psychology, and ethnography, as well as information design.[19]

Equally, programs may have an opportunity to develop cross discipline matrices, which offer students from across different disciplines the scope to work in team situations. For example, the faculty of art, design and music at Kingston University is running a year-long postgraduate interdisciplinary research methods course, which provides a forum for M.A. and Ph.D. students in architecture, art and design Theory and History, Fashion and Graphic Design, Illustration, animation, and curating contemporary design, as well as production and screen design, to come together to discuss relevant and mutual research methods that, hopefully, feed back into how they work in their specialist disciplines.

Sven Birkerts, writing in *The Gutenberg Elegies* states, "The context cannot but condition the process." As the culture of print is supplemented by the culture of digital screens, and the visual supplemented by the aural, reading and writing will, necessarily, be redefined. Equally, the transformation from local to global highlights the need for further understanding of the context in which language and cultural identity operate. Although many of the basic communication models will remain the same for the typographer and graphic designer—sender, mediator, and receiver—the underlying assumptions of communication will take on new significance.

Notes

1. "Slebbing: Do You Get the Picture?" *Metro*, March 10, 2003, p. 3.

2. Jon Thompson, ed., *Towards a Theory of the Image* (Maastricht: Jan van Eyck Akademie Editions, 1996), p. 8.

3. Ibid., p. 9.

4. Richard Wollheim, "On the Assimilation of Pictorial Art to Language," in Jon Thompson, ed., *Towards a Theory of the Image* (Maastricht: Jan van Eyck Akademie Editions, 1996), p. 29.

5. Jon Thompson, p. 10.

6. "GBI (German Bold Italic)", lyrics by Towa Tei and Kylie Minogue, music by Towa Tei (*Sound Museum*, East West Japan, Inc. and A Warner Music Group Company, 1998).

7. Roland Barthes, *The Responsibility of Forms: Critical Essays on Music, Art, and Representation* (Berkeley and Los Angeles: University of California Press, reprint 1991), p. 120.

8. Ibid., p. 113.

9. Stephanie Zelman, "Looking Into Space," in Gunnar Swanson, ed., *Graphic Design and Reading: Explorations of an Uneasy Relationship* (New York: Allworth Press, 2000), p. 51.

10. Michael Bierut, Jessica Helfand, Steven Heller, and Rick Poynor, eds., *Looking Closer 3: Classic Writings on Graphic Design* (New York: Allworth Press, 1999), p. 21.

11. Steven A. Mansbach, *Visions of Totality: Laszlo Moholy-Nagy, Theo van Doesburg, and El Lissitzky* (Ann Arbor: UMI Research Press, 1980), p. 102.

12. Theo van Leeuwen, unpublished notes to author, 2003.

13. Katherine McCoy, "Recent Directions in Graphic Design Education," in Steven Heller, ed., *The Education of an E-Designer* (New York: Allworth Press, 2001), p. 4.

14. Gunther Kress and Theo van Leeuwen, *Reading Images: The Grammar of Visual Design* (London: Routledge, 1996), p. 1.

15. Robin Kinross, *Unjustified Texts: Perspectives on Typography* (London: Hyphen Press, 2002), p. 314.

16. Gui Bonsiepe, *Interface: An Approach to Design* (Maastricht: Jan van Eyck Akademie Editions, 1999), p. 67.

17. Ellen Lupton and J. Abbott Miller have proposed that we have moved toward a model of typography that now merges biology and technology, citing the typographic examples of *Beowulf* (LettError), *Narly* (Zuzana Licko), and *Template Gothic* (Barry Deck). Ellen Lupton and J. Abbott Miller, "Laws of the Letter" in *Design Writing Research: Writing on Graphic Design* (New York: Princeton Architectural Press, 1996), p. 61. More recently, Diane Gromala has introduced *Biomorphic Typography*, where she uses biofeedback responses from the user's continuously changing physiological state, which "morph" in real time. She writes, "I am concerned with reconsidering legality in our technologically mediated context—legibility of the typeface and text, physiological and sensory legibility, and the cultural legibilities of our bodies" (e-mail to author, 2002). For typography, an understanding of technology no longer means the development of a skill base, but, rather, a theoretical positioning.

18. Sven Birkerts, *The Gutenberg Elegies: The Fate of Reading in an Electronic Age* (London: Faber & Faber, 1994), p. 128.

19. Katherine McCoy, "Recent Directions in Graphic Design Education," in Steven Heller, ed., *The Education of an E-Designer* (New York: Allworth Press, 2001), p. 5.

This is an expanded version of a paper given at "The New Typography: An Interdisciplinary Symposium," held on March 12 and 13, 2002, in London, sponsored by the faculty of art, design and music at Kingston University.

Hearing Type *Frank Armstrong*

Her head is bobbing rhythmically between earphones, her fingers unconsciously tapping her desktop; her knee and heel are furiously bouncing, like
the needle of a sewing machine. At the same time, her eyes and mind race
to capture, process, and understand fleeting patterns of light displayed on a
video screen. Like the form of the media itself, the ways we read and
experience information are changing. Complementing our newly acquired
multitasking abilities, we've become adept at multisensory perception—
hearing and seeing digital media as a single unified experience.

Since the invention of movable type, typography has been a relatively static visual language of letterforms embedded in passive, two-
dimensional surfaces. However, digital technologies have recently enabled
designers to create kinetic typography, letterforms moving fluidly within
four dimensions: a virtual three-dimensional space and time.
Unfortunately, traditional methodologies for understanding typographic
design, based on principles of two-dimensional visual composition,
are not adequate for students learning to create dynamic time-based
visual communications.

Film, a medium that integrates audio and visual components, provides a model for the macro-aesthetics of kinetic typography: structure and
narrative. Music seems to be an excellent paradigm for the micro-
aesthetics: visual and temporal properties, syntactic relationships, and
interaction between visual elements moving through both space and time.
Could analogies between music and typography provide the foundation of
a new methodology for perceiving and understanding both kinetic and
static typography?

Sound is produced by a vibrating object that transmits waves (alter-
nating high and low pressure areas of molecules) through an elastic
medium, such as air.[1] Our ears detect fluctuations in air pressure, and
translate them into electrical signals our brain understands.[2] A chaotic
group of random sounds, lacking organization, is perceived as noise.
Conversely, music could be described as sounds that have been structured
by their wavelength (frequency or pitch) and time (duration) in a two-
dimensional acoustic field.

173

One description of typography could be visualizing language through the hierarchical organization of glyphs in a spatial field. Our perception of shapes, such as glyphs or letterforms, is based on the contrast between form and counterform colors, produced by different wavelengths of light. Similar patterns of light waves influence our ability to recognize the glyphs within a typeface.

Music and typography are temporal experiences and forms of communication, expressing ideas through different languages. Although they occur in different dimensions, aspects of structure, motion, and time are common to both languages. Music and typography have a common ancestry: spoken language. Originally based on the rhythms of speech, music is a form of storytelling that is structured by phrasing acoustic information. Since typography is the visualization of a spoken language, a notion of time and grammatical syntax are inherent to the process of reading a composition of typographic elements.

Music notation is more directly comparable to typography—both are visual notational systems of symbols that represent elements of their respective acoustic languages. Phil Baines and Andrew Haslam have recently defined typography as the "mechanical notation and arrangement of language,"[3] a concept that could also describe music notation.

According to Robert Bringhurst, "Typography is the craft of endowing human language with a durable visual form, and thus with an independent existence."[4] Since spoken languages and music are temporal, their notational systems not only provide a visual documentation, but also create supplemental meaning through visual semantics. Kenneth Hiebert has written: "Musical notation and methods of composition can show the visual artist ways of thinking about formal relationships in another way, as encoded in notation conventions."[5]

Form, Space, and Structure

The basic unit of sound is a tone, which is equivalent to a pixel or point in a visual field. A single tone exists at a specific position within its native space, an acoustic field. Like a typographic point, a tone interacts with space in a figure/ground relationship. The position of a tone, relative to the edges of its field, creates tension and conveys meaning.

A tone contains the potential to exhibit properties and become, by extension, the equivalent of a linear or planar form. The lack of sound or a tone, at any moment of time in an acoustic space, is silence—similar to the negative space or counterform in a visual space.

As we observe the interaction of typographic elements in a visual composition, we hear a myriad of interactions in music compositions. Tones, and their extensions, interact with each other and the spaces around them. Writing about typographic rhythm, Carl Dair has stated: "The regular repetition of the same form in intervals of space is no different in essence from the regular repetition of a musical beat at intervals in time."[6]

Referring to typographic composition, Willi Kunz has remarked: "Space is visually subdivided by the tension that develops between an element and the boundaries of the space."[7] A similar effect occurs in acoustic space as the position of a tone subdivides the pitch and time dimensions, creating tension and structure. The proportional relationships of the subdivided areas, in part, determine the harmony of the composition. In both music and typography, the tension created by contrasting elements, or the intervals of space between them, provides a sense of motion.

In a discussion about vertical motion, specifically leading, Robert Bringhurst stated that "Space in typography is like time in music. It is infinitely divisible, but a few proportional intervals can be much more useful than a limitless choice of arbitrary quantities."[8] Typographic grids are visual structures, based on spatial units of measurement that describe the scales ("a modest set of distinct and related intervals"[9]) and proportions of a composition. In music, grids provide a framework for acoustic events described by proportional intervals of pitch (frequency of wave cycles) and time (patterns of pulses).

Properties of Sound

A sound or tone has four properties: amplitude, duration, pitch, and timbre. From a qualitative perspective, these properties are analogous to the formal characteristics of typographic elements.

Amplitude (magnitude of a tone's waveform, measured in decibels) describes the intensity or loudness of a tone. In typography, the size or weight of a glyph conveys amplitude. Through contrast, a relatively larger or heavier glyph creates emphasis. Extreme contrasts in amplitude create the illusion of depth or an implied advancing or receding motion relative to the audience.

Duration (interval of time, measured in pulsations or beats per minute) describes the length of time that a tone or silence exists. Intervals of time are normally represented on the horizontal axis of an acoustic field or music notation. In typography, since we usually read horizontally from left to right, the width of an individual glyph or the length of a series of glyphs (as in a word or phrase) implies duration over a period of time. Modifying the tracking value of a series of glyphs influences our perception of time and velocity of motion.

Pitch (frequency of a tone's waveform, measured in hertz or wave cycles per second) describes the relative highness or lightness (as produced by a flute) or lowness or heaviness (as produced by a tuba) of a tone. Intervals of pitch are normally represented on the vertical axis of an acoustic field or music notation. In a typographic composition, our visual perception is influenced by our sense of gravity. Corresponding to pitch, a typographic element positioned near the top of a composition seems to appear lighter (floating or ascending) than it would near the bottom (sinking or descending).

Timbre is the "color" or quality of a tone (an instrument's genome, defined by a particular set of overtones) that distinguishes one instrument from another. In 1939, the American composer, Aaron Copland, wrote. "Timbre in music is analogous to color in painting."[10] On a macro-aesthetic level, typographic timbre is the textural quality (including color) of a typeface. Timbre could also be described, on a micro-aesthetic level, as the semantic quality of a typeface—a particular combination of characteristics (i.e., serif shape) that determine its uniqueness.

Interaction of Sounds

Music is the organized interaction of multiple tones in a time-based experience. There are three fundamental aspects of music composition: rhythm, melody, and harmony. Similar visual interactions are present in the experience of reading a typographic composition.

Rhythm is a temporal pattern formed by various durations of rests (silence) and tones with different degrees of emphasis (accented or stressed beats). In a PBS program, musician Wynton Marsalis remarked, "No motion, no rhythm; no rhythm, no music."[11] Motion is essential to both music and typography, propelling the listener and reader forward through a composition. The rhythms that create motion are pervasive in typography: contrasting stroke shapes and widths; sporadic punctuation; ascenders and descenders protruding beyond the x-height; and the tremendous variety of counterforms within and between glyphs.

Melody is created by adding a second dimension, pitch, to a rhythmic sequence. Motion proceeds in both dimensions concurrently, resulting in a more complex angular or organic path. As in gestalt theory, melodic paths may be continuous or seemingly nonlinear (implied by applying the principle of closure). Typographic syntax, the spatial or temporal arrangement of glyphs into meaningful units (words, phrases, sentences, etc.), can appear to be fluid or discontinuous, reflecting the dynamics and phrasing patterns of speech.

Harmony is the simultaneous occurrence of multiple tones (vertical orientation) and the modulation of their intervals through time. The duration of a harmonic structure (chord) creates a two-dimensional planar texture, based on the density of the intervals between tones. Although motion proceeds both horizontally and vertically, like a melodic path, variations in texture can be equally apparent. Horizontal lines of type, and the vertical intervals of space (leading) between them, create a surface texture. Variations in leading, between adjacent columns of type, represent harmonic modulation in a typographic composition.

Hiebert has said, "Rhythm is certainly also a visual term. Yet when we look at visual qualities from another standpoint—the vantage point of music—we gain a fresh insight for applying rhythm to design."[12] There seem to be numerous analogies between music and typography that could provide a different frame of reference or context for students to understand both kinetic and static typography.

Notes

1. Jack Challoner, *The Visual Dictionary of Physics* (New York: DK Publishing, 1995), 21.

2. Tom Harris, "How Hearing Works," *How Stuff Works* (December 15, 2002), *www.howstuffworks.com/hearing2.htm.*

3. Phil Baines and Andrew Haslam, *Type & Typography* (New York: Watson-Guptill Publications, 2002), p. 7.

4. Robert Bringhurst, *The Elements of Typographic Style* (Vancouver: Hartley & Marks, 1997), p. 11.

5. Kenneth Hiebert, *Graphic Design Sources* (New Haven: Yale University Press, 1998), p. 93.

6. Carl Dair, *Design with Type* (Toronto: University of Toronto Press, 1993), p. 103.

7. Willi Kunz, *Typography: Macro- and Micro-Aesthetics* (Zurich: Verlag Niggli, 2000), p. 50.

8. Bringhurst, p. 36.

9. Ibid., p. 45.

10. Aaron Copland, *What to Listen for in Music* (New York: McGraw-Hill, 1939), p. 78.

11. Wynton Marsalis, "Why Toes Tap: Wynton on Rhythm," *Marsalis on Music* (New York: Sony, 1995).

12. Hiebert, p. 95.

Type Dialogues

How to See *Doyald Young*

How do you teach type design?
I teach lettering and logo design first, the basics: proportion, spacing, and optical adjustments, plus general guidelines that include the relationship of capitals to lowercase, and how to modify a letter. Drawing a letter by hand forces the student to more acutely observe its shape and the nature of a curve; how it accelerates, flattens, or turns sharply—in other words, "how to see."

Does one need to be a type designer to be a good typographer?
No, as long as the designer is familiar with basic font groups and how they may be combined, plus some historical knowledge of type, coupled with a sense of what is appropriate.

What would you say constitutes a "good typographer"?
First and foremost, the ability to communicate clearly, so the message is readable for its given application. For instance, don't put a paragraph on a billboard, or a poster, or use 7-point text in an ad targeted to senior citizens.

Is a typographer totally governed by the vicissitudes of style, or is there a more standardized aesthetic?
The way a reader perceives typography has not changed since type's beginnings, though our perception of the printed word is tempered by education—for instance, the speed in which we are taught to read. But if you mean by *style*, the unusual treatment of words within a given space, style should not impede readability—fashion be damned.

I'm offended by typographic style that forces me to rotate a piece of paper simply to read its content, or when the designer/typographer has not clearly shown me where to start reading, or when the measure is so long the words become merely bands of letters. In this case, I'm not interested in the information. It is pretentious design, not typography.

What determines whether a typeface works or not?
First, its legibility; then, its appropriate use. One word of Empire, cap and lowercase, may be set snugly and, at large size, be legible to most readers.

A paragraph of the same face set in 12-point will be difficult to read. If you mean "work" in the sense that it reflects the meaning of the text, this is often subjective, other than the obvious choice of extrabold fonts for heavy industry, or light, delicate ones for distaff readers, and squarish fonts, which suggest the mechanical, construction, or scientific—the list goes on.

As a type designer, do you feel proprietary about your work once it is out in the world?

No. They bought it. It's theirs.

How do you feel, as a typographer, about manipulating others' type designs?

First, the question should be directed to the Supreme Court. Despite my previous answer, I have no pat answer, because it is a complicated issue. Some designers are incensed when their work is tampered with. When a vendor says you can't alter something you've paid for, it suggests a bit of hubris. Why can't I change the leather color of an Eames lounger? If you alter a font for resale, the copyright laws come into effect, since the code, and not the design, is protected. The basic shapes were designed thousands of years ago.

When I design and draw a logo by hand, I am, in effect, altering an existing style, but style can't be copyrighted. If a designer chooses to alter a few letters of a font to create a logo, at what point do the revisions create an original design? Changed by 10, 20, 50, or 75 percent? Can the font industry legally prevent the designer from doing so? Who will decide what is a percentage point, using what criteria? If the x-height, even the ascenders and descenders, proportion, and weight are changed, plus the shapes of 25 percent of the letters, do the courts recognize that as an original design? The proscription has some merit, though; it prevents an enthusiast from adding serifs to Optima, an offense that should probably subject one to the peril of capital punishment.

Any designer who has ever attempted the design of a font of 256 characters knows many compromises are necessary for the font to set properly. Yet, these compromises can sometimes appear clumsy at large sizes, or, in some letter combinations, in the use of a logo. Every combination of alternate characters in an extended font does not always make happy pairings. Can the logo designer be faulted for adjusting the shapes to work better? The history of type founding has often been copycat, and down-right thievery, or of designers who attempt to improve another designer's font. Note that several foundries have Bodoni fonts, some very different than Giambattista's original. In days of metal type, reproduction type proofs were routinely altered by designers to create logos, and no one made a fuss.

Jan Tschichold went from classic to modern to classic. Do you feel this evolutionary cycle is common to typographers?

A direct answer to your question is yes, but I qualify the answer to also include designers. Note that Paul Rand, the "eminence gris," set his book, *Design and Chaos*, in Caslon. Youth strives to be innovative. The real world forces most of us to use the tried and true, and with that comes an appreciation of what the old boys have done. After I've set uncountable type styles for fifty years, I find great comfort in a paragraph of Garamond No. 3, Bembo, or Centaur; harsh critics notwithstanding, I like Baskerville. I have used Palatino for over forty years and still delight in its forms. I liken them to trustworthy, lifelong friends. The classics have a rightful, comfortable, and familiar place in design; so has the innovative. To a great extent, our clients often determine our choice of fonts. I notice that you still use Bookman.

Should typography be the "language" course in design school, or the raison d'etre of design?

I don't think you can separate the two, though some design does not rely on typography. And then, we get into semantics: what is design, and what is typography? When you arrange words, you are, in effect, designing. Too often, typography is taught as design, with insufficient emphasis on the nuts and bolts of typesetting: what tracking to use at 7 point; how tight a head-line should be; what about word spacing; column width; leading; cap and small-cap ratio; small-cap tracking; hung punctuation; the rules that govern a text column's color; etc., etc. Good typography should clarify content. The discipline is made up of minute detail, and, to be successful, must endlessly be fussed with. Once these issues are addressed, design comes center stage.

If you had to design type pedagogy, what would be the first thing students must learn?

The need to simplify.

If It's Good It Touches Me *Stefan Sagmeister*

How do you teach type design?

I never taught a pure type class, as type is always just one part of the whole of a class project. For good type, the same is true as for any other design element: It is good if it touches me. Type can do this in many ways: either by its fantastic content, its unbelievable form, its unusual execution, its incredible style, by reminding me of some important event of my past, by making me want to revisit it, or by showing me that its maker needed courage to produce it.

Does one need to be a type designer to be a good typographer?

No, not at all. People who never designed a complete typeface designed most of my favorite typographic pieces.

Is typography totally governed by the vicissitudes of style, or is there a more standardized aesthetic?

There is always the old galloping readability horse (which is also, in part, a style question—how much a reader is used to reading a certain style will determine its readability).

What determines whether a typeface works or not?

My gut.

How do you feel, as a typographer, about manipulating other's type designs?

If it's a classic font, I have no trouble messing with it in all sorts of manners; if it's a new and fairly unknown design, I'd probably want to leave it in its virgin form. We rarely use fonts that show lots of individuality of its designer. I always feel like using somebody else's work, for the same reason we seldom use stock photos.

Should typography be the "language" course in design school, or the raison d'etre of design?

Language. I know some great designers who did not have a clue about type (Tibor claimed to have never heard of Helvetica, which, I'm sure, was not true, but he surely didn't have a formal type education).

Kerning at Twenty Paces *Michael Johnson*

How do you teach type design?

Well, I don't teach it (yet), and, to be honest, I received almost no tuition in it, myself, except everything I could glean from the three books on type at my college library in the early eighties, and whatever *The Face* magazine looked like at the time. I guess if I had to teach it, I would imagine a combination of the trainspotter "how to kern at twenty paces" stuff and "anything is possible" would work best.

Does one need to know history?

You don't need the history if you have an innate ability to create something historic yourself. But that's rare. Obviously, the history could, or should, help you for the future (but I fear too much history weighs too heavily on some shoulders, and they never shake off their greatest influences).

What would you say constitutes a "good typographer"?

The ability to find the most "right" type for a project, or the ability to create something so wrong it questions all we ever thought was right. It seems to me that the designers of each decade attempt to lay down standardized aesthetics (which seem universally accepted for a short period of time); then, the next generation of designers says, "hang on a sec, why should we do what you say?" and force us all to make us look afresh at Cooper Black. Before you know it, Souvenir will be back in fashion. Heaven help us.

What determines whether a typeface works or not?

I guess it's that dull old word, *appropriateness*. When a new typeface comes out, there's always that hilarious honeymoon period when it appears on everything from club flyers to annual reports, then toothpaste posters, then the dust settles and it finds its place in the typographic canon. (Unless it's so quirky it has to suffer the fate of the Babyteeths of this world and wait thirty years for a revival).

The Luddite in me would argue, of course, that any typeface works, as long as you can read it. And, I guess, that's true—as someone once said to me, "I'm still waiting for someone to tell me why kerning's important," and I guess he's got a point, at one level.

As a type designer, do you feel proprietary about your work once it is out in the world?

The vast majority of the faces I've either designed or commissioned were for specific clients and, effectively, became their "voice," and, hence, their property. Occasionally I see uses of one of these typefaces that have strayed onto another computer, and after the initial shock (the "how dare they" moment), I often find that quite funny.

I did once do a stencil typeface for a project that Michael Bierut borrowed for a project of his own, and I have to say he used it in a much more interesting and much less hung up way than me. That felt weird. But also, kind of flattering.

How do you feel about manipulating others' designs?

Well, the odd chiseled serif or amended descender here or there, I'm fine about. For wholesale revisions, I would often go back to the designer—if they're still alive, that is. I have to say, I find complete bastardizations of fonts uncomfortable to look at. I remember showing that tool which allowed you to squish two fonts together in Fontographer at a conference once (I took Didot and Helvetica and created "Idiotica"). I fear the audience didn't get the point—someone stood up and said how great they thought it looked, and asked if you could combine three.

Jan Tschichold went from classic to modern to classic. Do you feel that this evolutionary cycle is common to typographers?

I found Tschichold's journey fascinating, but much preferred his "modern" work, and spent most of my twenties as "Mr. Modern." It's true, though, that I have renewed respect for serifs as I creak through my thirties. That may, of course, have something to do with massive boredom with the lowercase sans serif "thing" (initially driven by the spellings of URLs, I think) that seems to have dominated for way too long. Let's move on, can we?

Should typography be the "language" course in design school, or the raison d'etre of design?

Mmmm. Tough question. I think we *may* start to see great designers soon who have no real "feel" for type (because of the computers and the rise of "image making" rather than layout). But thus far, it's pretty difficult to name any great graphic designers who weren't either exceptional, or, at worst, pretty handy, with just type.

If you had to design type pedagogy, what would be the first thing that students must learn?

My greatest fear with type and type courses is that designers don't seem to think about what their typefaces mean or what their choices of typefaces and layouts are saying to people. I've had several bizarre moments recently judging student work when I've been entranced by designers' unusual use of "untrendy" typefaces, and gloried in their reappraisal of designs I thought were dead and buried. But then, when I questioned both students about their typeface choices (come on down, Avant-garde and Palatino) and listened for their postmodern rationale, my face fell flat as they both separately said the same thing: "Er, it was on the computer, so, er, I, er, used it." Pretty deflating (and more than a little depressing).

Type Is for Reading *Jeffrey Keedy*

How do you teach type design?

Quickly. I don't have the luxury of time; I teach type design as an elective course that meets once a week for three hours, over two semesters. The students are fourth-year BFAs and graduate students. We start off with calligraphy, broad nibbed pen and ink on paper, to understand the basic structure of letterforms, strokes, stress, widths, and letterform construction. Not only is it the best way to learn the anatomy and vocabulary of letterforms, but it also grounds the students' understanding of type in writing, language, and history.

By contrast, the modernist approach to typographic pedagogy (the way I was taught) is to start with the five so-called families of type, and draw the abstract "industrialized" outlines of the letterforms to familiarize the student with the modern vocabulary of type. Besides being historically shortsighted and confusing, it also reduces typography to a vocabulary of stylistic forms independent of communication and historical context.

I don't expect my students to master calligraphy (I never could), but to understand by doing the basic principles of typography that have evolved from writing. Once they have mastered a reasonable facsimile to calligraphic writing, I ask them to draw a typeface with a digital calligraphic pen tool and interpolate it into three weights. This is a purely technical exercise; the students are not concerned with "stylizing" their calligraphic font, but are learning how to draw with bézier curves and postscript. They learn the basics of digital font design, spacing, widths, x-height, etc. Then, I ask them to design a type-specimen poster with their font so they can see how well (or not) it actually works. I think it is best to teach the students *how* to design a font before they get into *why*. Once they know how, it is easier to understand why.

Next, I ask the students to design a logotype system that uses the digital type format as a generative tool by designing diverse but related graphic elements. The elements can be a logo, address, and phone number, or decorative ornaments, symbols, and illustrations that work together in numerous configurations by utilizing the spacing and kerning capabilities of fonts. It is like Neville Brody's FUSE project, using the digital font technology to make your own graphic design tool that can be used to generate numerous design possibilities. This project is a good precursor to the next project, which is designing their own original typeface.

As with the calligraphic font, they start on paper first. Once they have a good idea worked out, they go on to the computer to design a full character set (the ISO standard), complete with kerning, and they design a type specimen to show what their font can do. I also ask them to research existing typefaces that are similar in style or concept to the one they are designing to help clarify their ideas and keep them from "reinventing the wheel." As they are working on their typeface, each student also gives an oral and written report on a type designer, contemporary or historical. Thus, they are discussing the work and strategies of other type designers in the context of their own work.

My goal for the class is not to make graphic designers into type designers (although, happily, quite a few type designers have come out of the class), but to introduce the student to the discipline, history, rigor, and beauty of type design and, hopefully, inspire a lifelong admiration and interest in its development. At the very least, they will be better designers and typographers.

Does one need to be a type designer to be a good typographer?

The type designer and the typographer require similar but distinct skills and temperaments. A good musician doesn't have to make their own instrument, but they do have to make it their own. A fundamental understanding of the typeface has to be established by the typographer, or they will never be able to "play" it very well. Graphic designers tend to fall into one of three categories: illustrative, typographic, or methodical. Only a relatively small number of designers are typographers, and very few of them are type designers. The majority of typographers are not that well versed in their craft—a weak point in design education that is compensated with software.

What would you say constitutes a "good typographer"?

Someone who is literate in the fullest sense of the word and has something to say. Extra communication is essential for my definition of good typography. Appropriate, effective, or "transparent" typography is my minimal requirement of average or pedestrian typography. In spite of what designers say, it is really not that hard to do legible, readable typography, especially now that the software has improved. A bad typographer makes typography you don't want to read, in bad taste. An average typographer is someone who makes typography legible and in good taste. But a good typographer is someone who communicates a point of view with skill and imagination, and makes the type taste good.

Is the typographer totally governed by the vicissitudes of style, or is there a more standardized aesthetic?

Among design professionals, style and fashion definitely figure prominently into the critical criteria. Even what we consider traditional or classical is adjusted and reinterpreted over time. Very little in the practice of typography is as fixed as we pretend it is. Nor do the utilitarian or technical requirements of typography stabilize the practice for very long, as we in the digital age know all too well. Typography has to keep on moving, because it is attached to language, which is always in a state of flux. Predominant aesthetics, styles, and rules of typography are just there to make us feel like we know what we are doing—they will be different tomorrow. However, the idea of quality never goes out of style—that has been a standard aesthetic, or ethic, but it is a moving target.

What determines whether a typeface works or does not?

The typographer. A good typographer can make a bad typeface work, and a bad typographer can make a good typeface fail. It is up to the typographer to get the best performance out of a typeface, but if the typeface can't "sing," the typographer will have to make it "dance." Typefaces are successful only when they communicate their potential to their users.

As a type designer, do you feel proprietary about your work once it is out in the world?

No. I see it as a collaboration. I give it my best shot, try to anticipate what the typographer will need, and try to build into the design some suggestions and inspiration they can draw out of the font. Once the font is released commercially, you can only hope for the best; otherwise, keeping the font to yourself is always an option.

How do you feel, as a typographer, about manipulating others' type designs?

For me, the real challenge is to bring out aspects of the font's character that are less obvious but equally compelling, to repurpose or extend the expressive range of the typeface. For example, I would like to rethink Helvetica, but it has been squeezed dry, the typographers that still use it are just kidding themselves, or, worse yet, they like it precisely because it is empty and it won't detract attention from them. As a typographer, I don't mind sharing the attention with a type designer, but I probably tend to be *more* and *less* reverent when using other type designers' fonts.

Jan Tschichold went from classic to modern to classic. Do you feel this evolutionary cycle is common to typographers?

I don't think that particular shift from classic to modern to classic is typical, but I think any good typographer is always moving along, changing, and evolving their work to some degree. Modern, traditional, and experimental approaches have coexisted for a long time. At any given time, one may be more fashionable than another, but a good typographer works in the way that best suits their work and personal vision, whatever that may be. I think Tschichold exemplified that ethos.

Should typography be the "language" course in design school, as the lingua franca of design?

Yes. Show me a bad typographer, and I will show you a mediocre graphic designer. Although software can compensate for a lack of knowledge, sensitivity and sensibility can only be developed through disciplined practice. Typography, at this point, is the most rigorously developed area of design pedagogy, and is, therefore, the best place for a designer to develop their skill.

If you had to design type pedagogy, what would be the first thing students must learn?

Type is for reading.

Negative Space *Keith Godard*

How do you teach type design?
There are about six to ten good typefaces, and I limit the students' use
to those.

**Does one need to know the history of type to be a
good typographer?**
It helps, especially knowing about the Constructivist and Futurist movements.

What would you say constitutes a "good typographer"?
Typography: it is a discipline unto itself. It is not illustration—picture
making—but its own discipline. It is similar to jazz in the field of music,
in that it is relatively modern. What makes a good typographer is to know
the parameters of the field and what is possible and not.

**Is a typographer totally governed by the vicissitudes of style,
or is there a more standardized aesthetic?**
Style plays little in teaching typography; it is more governed by understanding the theory of abstract geometry, like two-dimensional architecture.

What determines whether a typeface works or not?
It is according to the beauty of its aesthetic form and, also, whether the
counters (the space between the characters) are of a definite form.

**How do you feel, as a typographer, about manipulating others'
type designs?**
I feel bad about it, although I did, in 1968, reduce the lengths of ascenders
and descenders of Helvetica, and I believe it improved the font for
a signage project.

**Jan Tschichold went from classic to modern to classic. Do you feel
this evolutionary cycle is common to typographers?**
No. Tschichold's cycle was against the dogmatic authoritarianism of
Germany at that time, and after the Second World War, he desired to
make classic "un-German typography." His case, I think, was an exception.

Should typography be the "language" course in design school, or the raison d'etre of design?

Yes, I think it should be the "language" course, considering it is a way of communication in all areas and media of graphic design.

If you had to design type pedagogy, what would be the first thing students must learn?

I think, grasping the fundamentals of abstract two-dimensional design. A teacher of mine once told me: in typographic layout, it is not so much where you place the type, but where you don't. The negative space (white space) is just as important as the positive space.

Attention to Detail *Nick Bell*

How do you teach type design?

Through drawing, attention to detail at a ridiculously anal level, and through repetition. Over and over again. Through testing in real situations and, of course, through reading.

Does one need to be a type designer to be a good typographer?

Absolutely not. It might even hinder you.

What would you say constitutes a "good typographer"?

The word that enters my head first is *sensitivity*.

Is a typographer totally governed by the vicissitudes of style, or is there a more standardized aesthetic?

Neo-modernists follow an aesthetic of standardized style. Both apply.

What determines whether a typeface works or does not?

Depends on how it is used. Typography can be used texturally (see Licko's Hypnopaedia), so it does not have to be legible. But for the rest, it is legibility. It doesn't have to have clarity, although, personally speaking, I would prefer it.

As a type designer, do you feel proprietary about your work once it is out in the world?

I'm not a type designer, but, as creative director of *Eye* magazine, I come up against type designers' attitudes toward the way their work is represented. The ones we have shown are of the opinion that only they know how to use their fonts "properly." And talk of the ignorance of designers. They always resist showing examples of their typefaces in use, and prefer you represent them in a format identical to their own mailings, which display their fonts as mute alphabets.

**How do you feel, as a typographer, about manipulating others'
type designs?**

I would do it if necessary, but always in such a way as not to damage the
structural integrity of the letterforms. I have no bones about changing its
character, though. I'm talking about customizing for particular projects and
clients, not for reissue.

**Jan Tschichold went from classic to modern to classic. Do you feel
this evolutionary cycle is common to typographers?**

I think that is a fair assessment. There must be exceptions, of course.
Modern can become classic with age.

**Should typography be the "language" course in design school,
or the raison d'etre of design?**

"Language" is a good way to view it—indispensable, in other words, but
not the be-all and end-all.

**If you had to design type pedagogy, what would be the first thing
students must learn?**

Drawing.

The Stroke of a Pen *Jonathan Barnbrook*

How do you teach type design?

I haven't met many people who do teach type design. Certainly, in Britain, it seems to be off the agenda, and I'm not sure why; maybe it is one of those things that very few people know how to do properly. I also think, because of the computer, type design is seen much more as part of general graphic design, meaning it is theoretically "simple" to produce a typeface easily on a computer; therefore, it does not need specialist teaching.

That is, however, not completely correct. It is still difficult to draw with correct proportion and know how to space a font properly without being taught or reading something about the subject. I think this is shown by the amount of similar typefaces that are coming out of art schools. There are some good ones, but there also are a lot of very predictable ones which are done by people who do not investigate and experiment with the con-struction of forms. The basis of all lettering is the stroke of the pen used by a hand. I am not saying you cannot deviate from this, but many of the fonts I see are the same analysis of modular forms derived from basic shapes which are simple to draw on a computer. To have a full command of typog-raphy, you should know the traditional construction, also.

On the occasions I have taught type design, such a short time was allotted that I just tried to get people interested in the subject, as I think, teaching somebody takes longer than a few weeks. It is also because many people see it as quite a cold, technical thing—that is only a small part of it; there is no point in being technically proficient if what you produce is boring. So, my main approach is to connect it with language and with the representational world; typography is as connected to the world we exist in as any creative field. Bradbury Thompson, when asked, "What do you need to be a good typographer?" said, "an interest and passion for life," and that is something I absolutely agree with.

The link with language is particularly important; it always interests me how words can be used to seduce, enrage, and control—they have amazing power. Typography is the "interface" for this. Carve some word in stone, and it has authority; print something, and words become "true." I try to bring all of that into my work and teaching. I usually start lectures off by swearing. Swearwords almost seem like words with magical powers: how you can upset people with one word, or have a phonetic sound banned, seems so strange to me. (I also use them to convince people that typography is a contemporary, living thing, and is not locked away in a dusty cupboard.)

On top of all this, I attempt to relate it to the real world. I try, above all, to make the work conceptually based. I don't know if that sounds stupid, but I want to make sure people have an idea behind the font. There are many ways to design a font—creating a revival, or just drawing letters which are beautiful—but with students, I think there should be some attempt to change the basis of letterform construction in society.

Does one need to be a type designer to be a good typographer?

Absolutely not; it is only recently that it has been an area where everybody can "have a go." I am not sure if you would even need to know how to construct letterforms if you have a respect and understanding for how type should be set. Inevitably, though, I think if you are a good typographer you would be naturally curious about the building blocks you use for your work, and that will lead to some investigation of type design.

There are direct ways in which I think it can help: appropriate use of letterforms—knowing when and why a typeface was designed, or the sociopolitical circumstances for the creation of a particular font, or the original methods that were used to construct the font and affected the way a font looks can be helpful in its usage. I suppose, though, on a less pragmatic level, I can't emphasize enough the idea of "emotional atmosphere" in typography; knowledge of the history and construction methods helps you spiritually and emotionally in your work. To me, one of the main attractions of type is the way it echoes and resonates with different things that were going on at the same time in society.

It is difficult to articulate those things directly, but I will have a go: the way some forms appear in abstract painting that affect the drawing of letterforms; the way certain philosophies indirectly affect the way the type forms are used; the popularity of certain kinds of music and the fonts that are used to publicize that music; the prevalent political ideologies that affect what typefaces are considered appropriately or not; the things the letterforms are used on (in my case, I think of decaying palaces); letterforms that have lasted long after the people who thought their power would last forever (the letterforms still reflect their important message; they are now just dust); handbills for a revolution that express an idea that is first thought of as heresy, that slowly becomes the truth; all of the letterforms on every gravestone from an unknown soldier killed in a war, to a relative whom many have cried over; the letterforms that have been used to express Christianity, which was certainly one of the first uses of printed typography. Well, the list is endless, and it all affects you when you sit down and use a letterform.

What would you say constitutes a "good typographer?"
The same things that constitute any good creative person; it is not necessary to be technically proficient. Some people would say that learning the rules of typography is boring, but I think those sorts of things are always not so exciting no matter what creative area you are working in. It is no fun learning how to do stop-frame animation if you are an animator, but it facilitates doing your work properly. However, my advice to most typographers is: get out into the world and put that into your work. Be an interesting human being, first—interact, love, and cry with other human beings—and you will have no trouble coming up with ideas.

The next thing is to "be aware of detail." Typography is all about detail, both in layout and construction of letterforms. I am so bored with students who think that being a typographer constitutes wacky display type. In fact, this has become a real problem when I am looking for people to work in my studio. Very few students take time to learn about how to set text or an address properly. I know I sound about ninety when I complain in this way, but I would say "detail" is the absolute, *absolute* fundamental thing that you must consider if you hope to be a good typographer.

The other thing I would say is read—read everything: read the text you are setting, read novels, read newspapers; it will all affect your ideas. I think literature is the one thing that has most affected my typography ideas.

Is a typographer totally governed by the vicissitudes of style, or is there a more standardized aesthetic?
Well, typography is many things; there are typefaces and ways of designing that are heavily influenced by fashion. There are ways of doing things that are considered more traditional, but, then, all areas of design are this way.

However, I would say typography is fairly unique in that technology in the mid-eighties completely changed the way it was constructed and perceived. In type design, especially, typefaces became much more fashionable and unfashionable in a short space of time. Type designers became pop stars; the sheer amount of typefaces increased with many people trying their hand at font design. This has meant that it responded much more quickly to ideas in mainstream society, which could be seen as "fashionable," because fonts were fairly simple to output; not every font has to be a "big idea." Things can be much more ephemeral.

What determines whether a typeface works or not?

Lots of different things. It depends on the context of the font—what it is being used for, what was the purpose of construction. You can look at how well a font can be drawn technically, but even this is not absolute. Much of my time in drawing type was spent unconsciously thinking about the perfect classical form. Then, when I drew a font called "Drone," I specifically went against what I thought was good proportion.

This is not a new idea. I think it was at the time of the "ugly-beautiful" debate, but it seems that nothing is absolute. You always have to be open to new perceptions, no matter where they arrive from, and, although I have complained about the amount of similar typefaces, that does not mean that somebody with no type training is going to come up with something bad. There is a phrase, "A little knowledge is a dangerous thing." In terms of type, it can mean, "Experiment can be stifled by knowing too much about the correct way to draw letterforms."

As a type designer, do you feel proprietary about your work once it is out in the world?

I feel a mixture of things; one is absolute delight that people find my font interesting or good enough to use. The other is a sense of pride that I feel, like I am adding something to the visual culture, to the world. I suppose there must be some primitive confirmation that I exist when I see the work that is out of my hands and becomes part of the currency of culture.

Another is repugnance with myself. When I go to what I consider a foreign place—a country that is completely different from my Western background—and I see my font used, I am incredibly disappointed. I wish it didn't have that effect; the place loses a little magic for me. It is like I have spoiled something in that culture. I know it is not quite as simple a matter as that, but it is sort of how I feel. I don't want designers in another country to use something like mine. (I feel my work is very English.) I want them to have a completely different viewpoint, created by their own circumstances.

I also find it really odd that those curves I drew in my studio are now, for instance, printed on a sign in the old sultans' palace in Istanbul. And, because of digital replication, they are the same curves, etc.

My attitude toward my fonts and their usage is very different from when I design a piece of printed matter. I get quite upset if people change my layouts even by a fraction; however, when I do a font, it is, from the outset part of the way it is used and what it is produced for.

I always find it interesting what people see in a typeface. Often you design it with a particular "atmosphere" in mind, and sometimes people will find something completely different in it, which is quite refreshing. They see something expressed in it that you hadn't realized was there. I will also say that, of course, there are some really bad uses of my fonts, but there will always be good and bad work in this world.

One strange way in which I do feel some responsibility is when I see a very questionable message that I don't agree with set in one of my typefaces. For instance, a few far right movements, such as Aryan Nations, whom I absolutely do not agree with, use Exocet. I think it is because you feel they are reading all of the things in a font in their own way; these things are there, but you just don't want them interpreted that way. I can see why a white power group would use Exocet, because the feeling of it is neoclassical, a particular love of Nazis. It also has crosses within it—a symbol constantly abused by people with hatred in their heart rather than compassion.

How do you feel, as a typographer, about manipulating others' type designs?

One of the original reasons I started designing fonts was because I wanted absolute control of the pages I was designing. At the time, I thought I was able to take the image and define the layout in its relation to the text. However, it seemed off limits to design the text itself (this was before the Mac really took hold). I thought if you were concerned about really representing today's aesthetics in a graphic way, you should work on the letterforms, as well. Having said that, I have no problem with working with other people's letterforms as long as I consider them good. Most of the ones I used are not contemporary fonts, but ones that are considered eternal, like Garamond. It is because they are well proportioned, beautifully drawn. It sometimes feels like a process of collage: you use various different elements, creating a composition including beautiful letterforms from a particular person drawn at a particular time, and they become another symbol of reference to an aesthetic sensibility or previous usage of the font.

Jan Tschichold went from classic to modern to classic. Do you feel this evolutionary cycle is common to typographers?

I think it is a cycle used by many creative people, not just typographers. I am thinking of artists such as Picasso, many of the futurist artists like Boccionni or Carra, and quite a few architects. I think, rather, the idea of "classic" is more tied up with humanism. I would say these people become much more human in their outlook as they get older—maybe, there is less of a desire to change the world, and more of a desire to serve it in the most appropriate way. I also think that, in terms of an underlying "current," they both have a huge element of the romantic in them and are very similar because of this. To believe you can change and make the visual language of the world more logical is a romantic idea. To believe the visual language of classicism is the most appropriate, beautiful, and highest visual representation of civilization is also a romantic idea.

If you had to design type pedagogy, what would be the first thing students must learn?

I think the absolute basics of how to use typography in relation to language. Simple things like what correct punctuation usage is. What the difference is between square and round brackets. You should know the mechanics of typography before you design the elements to be used. Another thing is to study the history of type. It is such a rich source of inspiration. The other thing is, even if you are going to be a good type designer, don't be too precious. Often, the first project I set is to design a hundred typefaces in a day. This means people work quickly, they have a bit of freedom, and they are prepared to try a few things that they consider not quite correct, as it does not really matter in the scheme of the whole project.

In contrast, I would say make sure the typefaces you make absolutely represent your philosophy. One of the other projects I set for students is to come up with a new punctuation mark for the alphabet. This brings in the conceptual side of typography and makes people think of how to express abstract thought in relation to its abstract representation in an alphabet—the absolute foundation of type design, I think.

Using and Abusing *Ed Fella*

How do you teach type design?

I really don't and never have, as such. Of course, I can crit it after it's done, but I have never formally taught it before it's done! Because I never had to, actually.

Does one need to be a type designer to be a good typographer?

No, certainly not. History abounds with great typographers who never designed type. On the other hand, it might be interesting to match typographers with type designers and take a closer look at what the differences might be.

What would you say constitutes a "good typographer"?

One who really knows what he or she is doing in relation to what you think of the result.

Is a typographer totally governed by the vicissitudes of style, or is there a more standardized aesthetic?

Partly, one should stay "current," as being part of the time one works in, and, at least, be aware of what's going on if only to go against it (which is usually the exception and, in most cases, unnecessary), but, also, keep aware of the basics necessary for decent communication. It's kind of a complex balance not easily or quickly answered.

What determines whether a typeface works or not?

The context.

As a type designer, do you feel proprietary about your work once it is out in the world?

NO.

How do you feel, as a typographer, about manipulating others' type designs?

No problem. I'm all for the using and abusing. Go ahead, put a moustache on Baskerville.

Jan Tschichold went from classic to modern to classic. Do you feel this evolutionary cycle is common to typographers?
Don't know, other than old age conservatism; didn't Churchill say something about that?

Should typography be the "language" course in design school, or the raison d'etre of design?
YES! YES! YES!

If you had to design type pedagogy, what would be the first thing students must learn?
Denote plus connote, vis-à-vis, *context*!!! I'm kind of dumb when it comes to answering these kinds of questions, but I have a beautifully lettered page that I just did, and might not necessarily use, for the cover of a student publication in Venice, Italy. It says, "Practice and preach and/or theorize and teach." That is my answer.

Syllabi and Projects

Introduction to Typography *Instructor: James Craig*

Project One: Comping Type
Purpose: Comping type is approximating the look of typesetting with pencil and paper. Before computers, this was the traditional method of appraising a design before incurring typesetting expenses. Although seldom used today, comping is an excellent way to introduce the five classic typefaces in *Designing with Type*, while providing practice in the basic skills of character counting, copyfitting, and arranging type on a page.

Project Two: Computer Typesetting
Purpose: Assuming Project One was done with pencil comps, and not directly on the computer, now is the time to check the accuracy of your copyfitting and comping by actually setting the type.

Project Three: Typestyles
Purpose: To introduce alternative typestyles and show how they affect the appearance, readability, and the length of the setting.

Project Four: Paragraph Indications
Purpose: To demonstrate a wide variety of ways to indicate paragraphs and to show how they affect the look and readability of the setting.

Project Five: Expressive Words
Purpose: To typographically enhance the meaning of a word while exploring the computer's typesetting potential.

Project Six: Visually Enhanced Quotation
Purpose: To demonstrate how a simple quotation, song, or poem can be typographically enhanced.

Project Seven: Early Letterform
Purpose: To provide a comprehensive overview of the design process, from copywriting to producing high-quality comps. Also, to develop the skills to create more than a single solution to a particular problem.

Project Eight: Double-Page Spread

Purpose: This project serves as an introduction to publication design and to the many typographic decisions that must be made regarding text type, display type, heads, subheads, captions, folios, illustrations, and their placement on a grid. This project also puts into practice lessons learned from previous projects.

Project Nine: Eight-Page Brochure

Purpose: Once again, you will be working with text type, display type, heads, subheads, captions, folios, and a grid, but for this project, you must carry a consistent design theme throughout the brochure.

Project Ten: Experimental Typography

Purpose: An exercise in free-form design to stretch the imagination.

Project Eleven: Ransom Note

Purpose: A fun exercise to prove that not all design solutions must come from the computer, and to explore the design potential in found typography.

Project Twelve: Logo

Purpose: To explore the typographic possibilities of individual letters.

Type One *Instructors: Martha Scotford and Tony Brock*

The graphic design department curriculum contains four sequential typography courses, each a fifteen-week semester long; the first three are required. The class meets twice a week for 1¾ hours at a session, in a studio where students work at their own Macintosh computer workstations.

Type One teaches basic type vocabulary and terminology, type history, beginning letterform design, beginning exploration of typographic treatment of simple texts, and introduction to typographic hierarchy, and introduces QuarkXPress software (next year, we will change to InDesign).

Type Two teaches typographic treatment of longer texts in simple sequential formats; discussion of semantics of typographic messages.

Type Three teaches typographic systems and organization of long texts and multiple pages in books and magazines; advanced grid systems.

Type Four teaches experimental typography, motion graphics, and typography for multimedia and the screen.

Type One—Course Description
- Seven projects (details below).
- Two exams on typefaces, technology, history, and terminology.
- Every week, write a short comment on found and collected typography and compile it all into a booklet.
- Assigned readings accompany projects.

Project Details

Project One: Concord and Contrast
Objectives:
- Begin to notice typography and its many forms.
- Learn terminology for letterforms.
- Learn to categorize letterforms.

Definitions:
- Concord = harmony or blending of typographic elements to give a uniform impression; color, texture, size, and proportions all have the same characteristics and work together.

• Contrast = opposite of concord; a unity of differences. To be effective it must be sharp. Dimensions of type or letterforms in which concord and contrast can be seen and used:
  • Size—height of letterform
  • Weight—overall thickness of strokes making letterform
  • Structure—nature of the strokes: uniform thickness or thick and thin combination
  • Form—capital/uppercase and lowercase letters; roman and italic, cursive, script letters; condensed and expanded letters

Exercises:

1. Look around you at all the examples of type available: newspapers, magazines, junk mail, etc. Collect many examples of large-sized (such as one inch or more) type and photocopy the useful parts. If you get stuck for certain examples, you may photocopy from typographic specimen books on the reserve shelf.

2. Use 8½ × 11-inch paper, vertical; draw with a thin pen a box 7 × 7 inches and divide this in half both ways so you have four smaller squares. Place the large box one inch from the top of the paper and centered from side to side. Photocopy this to have five sheets with boxes.

3. Using the initials of your name and using a variety of typefaces, cut out and (neatly) paste down pairs or groups of letters, all in the same line, to illustrate (only) the following:

Use two or three letters:

Sheet 1
a. concord of size
b. concord of weight
c. concord of structure
d. concord of form

Sheet 2
e. contrast of size
f. contrast of weight
g. contrast of structure
h. contrast of form

Sheet 3

i. contrast of size and weight

j. contrast of size and structure

k. contrast of size and form

l. contrast of weight and structure

Sheet 4

m. contrast of weight and form

n. contrast of structure and form

o. contrast of size, structure, and form

p. contrast of size, weight, and structure

Sheet 5

q. contrast of weight, structure, and form

r. contrast of size, weight, structure, and form

Keep ALL your found type for later use.

Project Two: Texture and Rhythm

Objectives:

• Learn the details of some typefaces better.

• Explore possibilities for texture, value, rhythm, and expression in typographic combinations.

• Explore the visual phenomenon of figure-ground visual reversals.

• Explore typographic space.

• Have fun with type.

Exercises:

• Use 8½ × 11-inch paper, vertical.

• Draw a 7 × 7-inch box (0.5-point rule) centered E-W and one inch from top edge; make this a Master Page in Quark.

• Use only black type on a white background.

For each composition:

• Use only the following type families: Garamond, Baskerville, Bodoni, Helvetica, Univers, and Futura.

• Use only ONE typeface family for each exercise (therefore, you will be working with one structure).

- Use variations in size, weight, form with a purpose (for variation, to be different, because it's pretty, etc. are not valid design purposes here); be sure you can explain each choice.
- Letters may be used in any position, but cannot overlap.
- Choose carefully which of the twenty-six letters to use; again, choose with a purpose.
- Consider the very different shapes the twenty-six letters have; choose those with straight lines or with curves, or with both, for a reason; choose caps or lowercase for a reason; know why you might use italic or extended or condensed forms.

For each situation below, using only type, create a composition that:
1. Shows a complex and even texture/pattern.
2. Shows a complex and uneven, erratic, or rhythmic texture/pattern (#2 or #3 should also show figure-ground reversal).
3. Shows three different (and discernable) values created by type.
4. Shows direction within a field of type.
5. Gives an illusion of space or depth.
6. Uses any or all of your initials to make the most beautiful thing you can (try for any other figure-ground solution).
7. Expresses something scary (no words allowed; use only analphabetic characters).
8. Expresses something funny (no words allowed).

Use at least four different fonts in your exercises. Know which fonts you have used; label them on the back. You should have at least three by the next class. Final printouts should be on bright white quality paper, laser printed (no ink-jet); this will be the standard for the semester.

Do assigned reading. Note: you may be tested later on any of the assigned reading.

Project Three: Typographic Expression
Objectives:
- To explore expressive potential of type.
- To explore effects of typeface choice on meaning.
- To explore composition in and of space.
- To explore "illustrative" potential of typography.

With assigned texts of haiku poems, and with your own "anti-haiku" texts, you are to investigate the possibilities for expression and interpretation using only typeface choice and compositions in space. You will concern yourself with activation of the space and visual interest and delight, as well as with the content of the text. You should aim to "get the most" out of the text through your typographic choices.

Space is 7 × 7-inch square; thin rule box in standard format.

Investigation means trying LOTS of ideas; the best way to evaluate your ideas is to make them visual and visible—so, create the compositions and variations you think of, and save them (with a logical labeling system).

You should do at least ten variations for each set.

Set A
• Use assigned haiku text.
• Use one sans serif typeface (Univers, Helvetica, Futura, Gill Sans) and
    any of its variations, as needed (weight, form, size).
• Present the text to express its content.

Set B
• Use same text as Set A.
• Use any typefaces you deem appropriate for expressing the context (be
    careful of using too many; consider one basic face and others, as
    needed, for accent).

Set C
• Choose another haiku from the class collection.
• Explore using directions for Set B.

Set D (optional)
• Write your own haiku that "opposes," in some way, the text from Set A.
• Present this text using directions for Set B.

Be ready to show all variations at any time to the instructor. Final submission with best three of each set; laser printed on bright white paper. Keep track of your typefaces; label on back.

Project Four: Letterform Design
Objectives:

- To explore simple letterform design.
- To understand the harmonies of form that make up distinctive typefaces.
- To master more of Illustrator software.

Exercise:
Design the letter you have been assigned (courtesy of Dr. Seuss and "On Beyond Zebra") so that it would fit into the normal weight roman alphabet of one of the following families:

Baskerville
Bodoni
Caslon
Clarendon

Process:
- Study your assigned form.
- Photocopy and enlarge the normal weight roman alphabet of your chosen typeface family.
- Mark characteristics of the family.
- Mark the idiosyncrasies of the family.
- Study what creates the harmony of form within the family.
- What parts of your letter are similar to existing forms, and what parts are new?

   1. Sketch using pencil/pen on paper your beginning ideas for the new forms; try variations.
   2. Scan the letter assigned and save using Illustrator.
   3. Create an accurate outline of the form and save the outline as your "original."
   4. Use "original" as a template for your work.
   5. Using Illustrator and manipulating bézier curves to draw your forms, create your new letterforms. Create a capital and a lower-case form for your alphabet and fill with black.
   6. Try out lots of ideas. Save each new idea/version separately so you can always go back. Use logical labeling and maintain your files.

Final submission will include:
- Original Seuss letter.
- Your scanned "original."

• Your two letterforms at one inch and three inches.
• The complete alphabet of your chosen typeface, including lowercase
  and capitals.

Your final letterforms inserted to show match should be five pages. Present
as laser prints on bright white paper. If it goes well and you want to do
optional work, create letterforms to fit into a sans serif family:

Gill Sans
Univers
Futura
Helvetica

Project Five: Hierarchy and Formats
Objectives:
• Learn and use some typographic conventions.
• Learn and use typographic hierarchy.
• Learn and use basic elements of text typography: paragraphs, justifica-
  tion, hyphenation, leading, and indents.
• Explore typographic tone.
• Explore denotation and connotation in type and typography.

Exercise:
Using mostly the same text, explore THREE of these different forms of
communication:

     1. A love letter.
     2. A manifesto.
     3. A newspaper advertisement.
     4. A scholarly text with a footnote.

How does the form and format change?
What are the parts of each form?
What are the typographic conventions that relate to each form?
What is the tone or attitude of each form?
How do you communicate the message—denotatively and connotatively—
through the form and the type?

You will be using a text from Nicholson Baker's book, *The Mezzanine*. Edit the text selection as you need to for your concepts. You may add no more than twelve words of your own, for any concept. Typeface choices relate to your form and content. Choose size of paper/visual field wisely; define with a rule if smaller than $8^{1}/_{2} \times 11$ inches. Maximum paper size is 11×17 inches. You may use different sizes for the different forms (or not). Work only in black type on white paper.

Project Six, Part One: Found Typography

Objectives:
- Discover typography in your physical environment.
- Study typography in three dimensions.
- Apply ideas about type in real space to type on a flat surface.

Exercise:
During the week of the North Carolina State Fair, visit the fairgrounds with a camera to record the typography and lettering found there. You might want to shoot both during daylight and at night. Take at least thirty-six exposures, using black-and-white film. Knowing what you will do with the photos (see below), take photos that do not need the middle tones to be "readable." Do NOT frame your photos so that only the sign/type is seen; make sure some record the surroundings.

Immediately:
Develop and scan photos. Save these "originals" and be thinking about them.

In two weeks:
Using Photoshop, posterize another set of photos and save these. "Posterize" means to remove the middle tones by limiting the levels of the grayscale; the result will be more sharply black and white. Later in the semester you will be using these photos, combined with type, in a project.

Things to look for and record:
- Interesting typefaces.
- Actual 3-D type.
- Type that creates 3-D illusion.
- Type combinations.
- Combinations and relationships that happen in space = point of view (POV).

- Scale in typography.
- Materials used for signage.
- Distortions due to POV.
- Spatial relationships.
- What YOU find intriguing about type and lettering in this
    setting.
- Discover typography in your physical environment.
- Study typography in three dimensions.
- Study 3-D typography.
- Apply ideas about type in real space to type on a flat surface.

Project Six, Part Two: Found Typography
Objectives:
- Discover typography in your physical environment.
- Study typography in three dimensions.
- Apply ideas about type in real space to type on a flat surface.

Exercise:
Using the photographs you took at the state fair, make two typographic
"reports." Both should reveal, explore, and recreate the 3-D environment.
Scan your photographs; edit out the surrounding environment, so you only
see the typography. Silhouette and/or posterize.

1. An intensified memory of the lettering and typography at the fair.
   What was it like? How did it feel? Perhaps, think of it as a dream
   or a nightmare where there was nothing but LETTERS! Use
   your fair photos as collage materials; combine digitally and/or
   physically. Final must be printed.
2. A "translation" of an actual typographic space at the fair. Use a
   photograph with lots of signs, with sharp perspective or sense of
   the space, as your spatial composition.

   Using "real" type, recreate the type in space. You may keep or
   change the typefaces, but the sense of space should be the same
   or exaggerated.

Two compositions, 11 × 17, black and white only. Vertical or horizontal,
but both in the same format.

Project Seven: Type History Booklet
Objectives:
• Rework research results.
• Look closer at typefaces.
• Learn to use Quark master pages (demo).
• Learn to use Quark style sheets (demo).
• Attention to text paragraphs, typography cues, proper punctuation, hyphenation, and typographic hierarchy.
• Create spatial sequence.
• Work with color in type.

Exercise:
• Create 8–10 panel sequence; each panel is eight inches square.
• Panels are connected side by side and folded accordion style; use tabs, and glue (demo).
• The first panel is your cover/title page, and faces out.
• Make a small paper model of your "space" before you start to understand the space and sketch ideas.
• Tell the story of your typeface and type designer. Use at least 350 words.
• Text (several sentences) must appear on at least half the panels.
• Use at least three levels of typographic hierarchy in your text (title, subtitle, text, plus?).
• Show the full cap and lowercase alphabets, including all analphabetics.
• Feature the particular characteristics of your typeface.
• At least one repeat element must appear on each panel in the same place.
• Use your typeface only (see me immediately if you don't have it, or if typeface is not a suitable text face).
• Use black and one other color, and white paper.
• Print out on white card stock and assemble.

Project: Required Reading
Project One: Dair 49–53; Carter, Day, Meggs, 25–42; Chappell 3–57.
Project Two: Bringhurst 287–298; Bringhurst 299–308; CDM 155–255 (look).
Project Three: Bringhurst 199–256; Spiekermann 35–53; CDM 43–66.
Project Four: Bringhurst 12–15, 119–142; CDM 1–24; Bringhurst 179–198.

   Test on type terms, anatomy.

Project Five: CDM 85–96.
>Test on type identification, terms.

Project Six: no readings.

Project Seven: various sources.

Weekly Type Comment

Objectives:

- To continue your exploration of type and typography around you.
- To develop your abilities to describe and discuss typographic phenomena.
- To encourage you to react to and form opinions about type and typography.

EACH WEEK on Wednesday hand in:

- One 8½ × 11-inch sheet with an example of type or typography pasted on the top and below.
- Your comments about why it interests, offends, delights, amuses, etc., you.
- Examples should come from magazines, newspapers, junk mail, books, rubbings of 3-D type, photos of signs, etc. (Be creative).
- Use a variety of sources.
- Comments are to be processed.
- Put your full name at the bottom.
- Use only one side of the sheet.
- Aesthetic/design quality of presentation will be noted.

For Type History Research

Stanley Morison—Times Roman (1931)
Bruce Rogers—Centaur (1916)
Jan Tschichold—Sabon (1964)
William Caslon—Caslon (1722)
Giambattista Bodoni—Bodoni (1780)
John Baskerville—Baskerville (1757)
Claude Garamond—Garamond (1532)
Matthew Carter—Bell Centennial (1978)
Eric Gill—Gill Sans (1928)
Adrian Frutiger—Univers (1957)

Paul Renner—Futura (1927)
Frederic Goudy—Goudy Old Style (1915)
Max Miedinger—Helvetica (1957)
Zuzana Licko—Matrix (1986)
Jonathan Barnbrook—Mason (1994)
Barry Deck—Template Gothic (1990)
Herman Zapf—Palatino (1950)
W. A. Dwiggins—Electra (1935)
Morris Benton—Century Schoolbook (1915)

Each of you will research your chosen typeface and type designer. You should find out the background of the designer (country, time period, training, professional history, etc.) and the stimulus for the specific type-face (what was it designed for, what problems did it solve, if any; other details of its creation).

For the old faces (sixteenth, seventeenth, and eighteenth century) be sure to find and research the original face (not the modern redrawings by ITC or Adobe). It is good to show both versions, however. Find full fonts (whole character sets of alphabet in several weights, numbers, analphabetic characters, ligatures, etc.) of your typeface. If you can, find a photo or portrait of the designer. If you can, find a short quote from your designer about type or typography. Write about 150 words (essential history) about each—the designer and the typeface. Have this text word processed by Monday, 9/17 class. Provide a list of sources (you must use printed publications, as well as the Web).

Books, Materials, and Supplies

Required Book
Robert Bringhurst, *The Elements of Typographic Style* (Vancouver: Hartley & Marks, 1997).

Recommended Book
Carter, Day, Meggs, *Typographic Design: Form and Communication*, New York: John Wiley and Sons

Books, Magazines, and Web Sites to Find

BOOKS
Carl Dair, *Design with Type.*
Warren Chappell and Robert Bringhurst, *A Short History of the Printed Word.*
Daniel Berkeley Updike, *Printing Types: Their History, Form and Use.*
Alexander Lawson, *Anatomy of a Typeface.*
Erik Spiekermann and E. M. Ginger, *Stop Stealing Sheep & Find Out How Type Works* (Berkeley: Adobe Press, 2003).

MAGAZINES
EYE
Emigre
Print
Visible Language

WEB SITES
www.studiomotiv.com/counterspace (anatomy, classification, history)
www.linotype.com (examples of typefaces)
www.typereview.com (links to other type sites)

Supplies:
2-inch standard ring binder
Clear plastic sheet protectors
Photocopy card
8½ × 11-inch cheap white copy paper
8½ × 11-inch bright white good paper (for finals)
T-square (at least thirty inches long; metal)
Triangle(s), metal or plastic; medium size
Haberule type scale
Tracing paper
Clear tape, dispenser
Scissors (at least 6-inch blades)
Exacto knife and blades
Plastic cutting surface
Metal ruler
Rubber cement or glue stick

Pencils (black and colored)
White eraser
Spray adhesive
Illustration board
Mac-formatted floppy disks or zip disks

QuarkXPress Exercise

This is an exercise, and following directions is important. Use one 8½ ×
11-inch page with text box of 7½ × 10 inches centered.

1. Take a favorite phrase (one line) from one of your haiku poems
   and type it on top of text box in 10-point Times Roman c&lc,
   flush left.
2. Change phrase to 60-point TR, all caps, flush left.
3. Letterspace or track longest word in phrase by +10. Use arrows or
   numbers.
4. Letterspace or track longest word in phrase by +25. Use arrows or
   numbers.
5. Letterspace or track longest word in phrase by -13. Use numbers.
6. Letterspace or track longest word in phrase by -37.5. Use numbers. Is it optically even, correct? Assess what is average space
   between letters.
7. Go back to #2 setting; look at "natural" or default spacing.
8. Take "worst" word in whole haiku in terms of letterspacing combi-
   nation(s). Adjust letters so all are optically correct—KERN properly.

Terms to Know for Test (all from Bringhurst)

sorts and characters
acute accent
aesc
ampersand
apostrophe
arithmetical signs
asterisk
"at" sign
backslash
braces
breve accent

bullet
caret
caron accent
cedilla accent
circumflex accent
colon
comma
copyright
currency symbols
dagger
dashes
degree
dieresis/umlaut
double prime
ellipsis
eszett
ethel
exclamation
figures
fist
fractions
grave accent
guillemets
hedera
inverted comma
ligatures
octothorp
parentheses
percent
period
pilcrow
prime
question mark
quotation marks
registered trademark
semicolon
solidus
square brackets

tilde
trademark
virgule

Glossary of Terms
abrupt and adnate
analphabetic
axis
baseline
bitmap
blackletter
body
body size
dingbat
dot leader
drop cap
em
en
fleuron
folio
font
gutter
italic
justify
kern
lead
old style figures
pica
point
ranging figures/lining figures
sans serif
serif
solid
swash
U&lc
weight
word space
x-height

Typefaces to Learn

Old Style
(serif, angled axis, little contrast in strokes)
*Garamond (1617)
*Caslon (1722)
*Bembo (1495)
Janson (1690)
*Palatino (1950)
*Sabon (1964)
*Centaur (1916)
*Goudy (1915)

Transitional
(serif, close to vertical axis, moderate contrast in strokes)
*Baskerville (1757)
*Times Roman (1931)
Scotch (1810)
Caledonia (1938)
*Electra (1935)
Bookman

Modern
(serif, vertical axis, strong contrast in strokes)
*Bodoni (1780)
Didot (1784)
*Walbaum (1800)

Egyptian/Slab
(slab serif, almost vertical axis, little contrast in strokes)
*Century Schoolbook (1890)
*Clarendon (1845)
Cheltenham (1896)
Lubalin Graph (1974)
Melior
*American Typewriter

Sans Serif
(no serif, no axis, uniform strokes)
*Helvetica (1957)
*Univers (1957)
*Gill Sans (1928)
*Futura (1927)
Avant Garde (1967)
*Optima
*Bell Centennial (1978)
*News Gothic (1908)
Folio
Franklin Gothic
Akzidenz Grotesk
Frutiger

Contemporary
(digital, recent)
Keedy Sans (1990)
*Matrix (1986)
*Mason (1994)
*Template Gothic (1990)
Dead History (1990)

Possibly on the test!

Test One
Terms you may need for answering questions: serif, points, sans serif, picas, old style, letterspacing, modern, kerning, transitional, x-height, linespacing, Egyptian, leading, slab serif, italic, tracking, roman, ligature, and terminal.

Identify by category name, and name one example:

1. Typefaces with thick and thin strokes and a slanted axis or stress are called _____ ex. _____.
2. Typefaces with extreme contrast between thick and thin strokes are called _____ ex. _____.
3. Typefaces with medium contrast and less slanted axis than #1 are _____ ex. _____.

4. Typefaces with heavy, squared serifs are called _____ or _____ ex. _____.

5. Typefaces without short strokes at the ends of major strokes are _____ ex. _____.

6. Letterforms that slant to the right are called _____.

7. Type is measured in (a) _____ and (b) _____. How many of each to the inch (a) _____ and (b) _____?

8. Equal space is added or subtracted between all the letters in a word or phrase; this is called _____ (old term) or (new) _____.

9. Varying amounts of space are added or subtracted between letters in one word; this is called _____ and the reason to do it is _____.

10. Space between lines of type is called (old term) _____ or (new) _____.

11. The measurement that refers to the height of letters from baseline to meanline is the _____.

12. In the examples below, label the following parts of letterforms: stem, stroke, tail, ascender, crossbar, descender, counter, serif, bowl, and leg.

T R k e S A g G

13. Name these typefaces:

the quick brown fox jumped over the lazy dog
THE QUICK BROWN FOX JUMPED OVER THE LAZY DOG

the quick brown fox jumped over the lazy dog
THE QUICK BROWN FOX JUMPED OVER THE LAZY DOG

the quick brown fox jumped over the lazy dog
THE QUICK BROWN FOX JUMPED OVER THE LAZY DOG

the quick brown fox jumped over the lazy dog
THE QUICK BROWN FOX JUMPED OVER THE LAZY DOG

the quick brown fox jumped over the lazy dog
THE QUICK BROWN FOX JUMPED OVER THE LAZY DOG

14. Name the character:

& • ... * # ß Œ £¢$
" " ¶ é {} « » ç

15. Match the term to the definition:
abrupt + adnate   bitmap   blackletter   gutter   font   dingbat
fleuron   justify   swash   u&lc   solid

_____ ornament in the shape of a leaf or flower.
_____ used to describe letterforms that are usually pointed,
condensed, pen forms; also textura, fraktur.
_____ used to describe how serifs break from or flow into the
stem of the letterform.
_____ blank space between two type columns or the margins in
the center of a book.
_____ digital representation of a letterform.
_____ letterform with extra flourish or taking up extra space.
_____ to adjust a line of type so that it is both flush left and
flush right on the measure.
_____ group of typographic symbols and pictures not related
to alphabet.
_____ lines of type set without extra leading in between.
_____ refers to upper- and lowercase.

16. What is the Quark keystroke shortcut command for hide/show guides?

17. What is OS keystroke shortcut command for COPY?

18. What is OS keystroke shortcut command for PASTE?

19. What is OS keystroke shortcut command for SELECT ALL?

20. What do you like about typography?

Test Two

Identify each of these typefaces; write letter in left margin (A–P).
Label ONE example for each category; write letter in left margin (Q–T).

A—Caslon	F—Garamond	K—Palatino	P—News Gothic
B—Bodoni	G—Sabon	L—Centaur	Q—Old Style
C—Univers	H—Times Roman	M—Futura	R—Transitional
D—Clarendon	I—Helvetica	N—Gill Sans	S—Modern
E—Am. Typewriter	J—Baskerville	O—Cent. Schoolbook	T—Egyptian/ Slab Serif

12345ABCDEFGHIJKLMNOPQRSTUVWXYZabcdefghijklmnopqrstuvw
xyz

23456ABCDEFGHIJKLMNOPQRSTUVWXYZabcdefghijklmnopqr
stuvwxyz

34567ABCDEFGHIJKLMNOPQRSTUVWXYZabcdefghijklmnopqrst
uvwxyz

45678ABCDEFGHIJKLMNOPQRSTUVWXYZabcdefghijklmnopqrstu
vwxyz

56789ABCDEFGHIJKLMNOPQRSTUVWXYZabcdefghijklmnopqrstuvwxyz

67890ABCDEFGHIJKLMNOPQRSTUVWXYZabcdefghijklmnopqrs
tuvwxyz

78901ABCDEFGHIJKLMNOPQRSTUVWXYZabcdefghijklmnopqrstu
vwxyz

89012ABCDEFGHIJKLMNOPQRSTUVWXYZabcdefghijklmnopqrstuv
wxyz

90123ABCDEFGHIJKLMNOPQRSTUVWXYZabcdefghijklmnopqrstu
vwxyz

10234ABCDEFGHIJKLMNOPQRSTUVWXYZabcdefghijklmnopqrstuvw
xyz

11234ABCDEFGHIJKLMNOPQRSTUVWXYZabcdefghijklmnopq
rstuvwxyz

12345ABCDEFGHIJKLMNOPQRSTUVWXYZabcdefghijklmnopqrstuvwxyz

13456ABCDEFGHIJKLMNOPQRSTUVWXYZabcdefghijklmnopqrstuvwxyz

14567ABCDEFGHIJKLMNOPQRSTUVWXYZabcdefghijklmnopqrstuvwxyz

15678ABCDEFGHIJKLMNOPQRSTUVWXYZabcdefghijklmno
pqrstuvwxyz

**14567ABCDEFGHIJKLMNOPQRSTUVWXYZabcdefghijklmn
opqrstuvwxyz**

16. Name these characters:

{ } / ~ fi ¶ © ß ... § *

17. Match the term with the definition; write letter in blank:
a—dot leader b—old style/text numbers c—em d—pica
e—folio f—ranging/lining figures g—justify h—word space

_____ in linear measure, a distance equal to type size; for 12-point type, the em is 12 points.
_____ row of evenly spaced periods, used to link flush-left text with flush-right number; found in tables of contents or tabular material.
_____ a typeset page number.
_____ to adjust length of the line to make flush left and flush right.
_____ fixed size in unjustified or ragged setting; variable in justified text.
_____ figures of even height.
_____ figures often with ascenders and descenders.
_____ there are six of these to an inch.

18. Describe how to achieve visual hierarchy in typography.

19. Describe how to achieve visual hierarchy in a composition.

20. List two typographic cues for a new paragraph.

21. List two conditions that would harm legibility of text.

22. What is your favorite typeface, aesthetically?

23. Which typeface do you consider the most versatile?

24. Comment on this statement from Bringhurst; agree, disagree, expound: "Typography is the craft of endowing human language with a durable visual form, and thus with an independent existence. Its heartwood is calligraphy—the dance, on a tiny stage, of the living, speaking hand— and its roots reach into living soil, thought its branches may be hung each year with new machines. So long as the root lives, typography remains a source of true delight, true knowledge, true surprise."

Final Portfolio

The portfolio will be:

- Printed on white paper, 8½ × 11 inches (unless otherwise indicated); only creative work to appear (no labels); show no work with instructor's comments.
- Spiral bound at the top; one inch from top to any part of exercise/project (go to Kinko's).
- Front and back covers of heavier paper (color optional); back cover will have a pocket inside for oversize projects.
- Some indication of "front" or "begin here" on the front cover.
- Title page with your name, course name and section, semester and year, instructor's name.

• Collected exercises and projects from the semester, presented in order (see below).

The following should be present in your final portfolio for Type One:
Project 2: Texture and Rhythm
Show best example of each exercise, in order.

Project 3: Haiku
Show best three examples; example of anti-haiku optional.

Project 4: Letterform from Suess
Show original Suess letter, your template, your designs at one inch and three inches, and your designs within both cap and lowercase alphabets.

Project 5: Hierarchy and Formats
Show best three examples; paper is your choice, but must be $8\frac{1}{2} \times 11$ (define visual space with fine rule); if larger sheet is used, show printed reduction and, also, larger one (fold only twice and put in back cover pocket).

Project 6: State Fair
Show two examples in reduction and, also, larger ones (fold only twice and put in back cover pocket).

Project 7: Type History
Trimmed, bound example placed in back cover pocket.

Type and Graphic Design *Instructor: Joseph Coates*

Objectives
Principles of letterforms, and how these principles affect the communication of ideas through graphic design.
Analysis of type style, structure, and form.
Computer applications are required for appropriate problems.

Prerequisite: Junior standing, ART 133, or consent of instructor.

We'll do a number of projects in and out of class. We'll look at:
• The aesthetic beauty and structure of letterforms.
• How a letter works (positive and negative space).
• The history of type and some classification of type.
• What are good typefaces and families of type.
• How legibility and readability work.
• Letter, word, and line spacing.
• The grid.

Project 1
To be an artist means never to avert one's eyes.—Akira Kurosawa

Objective: Letterform tracing using pencil.

Project: We'll be working in class for the next few sessions looking at letterforms and how they are structured and drawn. I'm not an expert free-hand letterer myself, nor do you have to be to be a good designer. But you do have to know everything there is to know about letters and typography and what makes good typography. To be able to truly see a letter and the type family it comes from, you have to spend some time with it. We'll be spending some time tracing our names and other words using a type specimen I'll be giving you. In doing so, we'll also learn about letterspacing and how the space between letters is just as important, if not more important than, the letters themselves.

Evaluation: Evaluation will be based on the completion of the project and project requirements; participation in class during the tracing sessions; letterform tracing quality (craftsmanship); understanding of typographic quality, and letterspacing.

You may be thinking: "But I'm already an expert in type, from when I was in high school/on the newspaper/yearbook/working as a professional at an ad agency/for a client/for a designer/while an intern/on my PC for fun. So why do I need to study more type? I know it all."

But truly dedicated and passionate designers, or those who love type, continue to explore it and manipulate it to learn about it in more detail. You need to be enveloped by and passionate about its history, design, and mysteries.

We are so accustomed to type all around us that we are oblivious to its nuances and mechanisms. These hidden qualities are what designers know and use, and what others don't realize. They just read it, it works, and they move on. Bad typography is obnoxious and hard to read and just looks bad (but most people don't know why). After you understand what good typography is, and can practice it, later, as a senior, you can do more experimental typography.

Project 2

Letters are signals . . . their function is to convey meaning. But they are more than little bits of messages. Their architecture can be examined and appreciated without reference to meaning, much the way one takes pleasure in a bridge or building without being solely preoccupied with function. . . . Familiarity with the structure of a typeface allows use of its attributes to convey information beyond the literal content of words. A passage set in a serif typeface is likely to induce in a reader's mind a somewhat different mood than would the same passage set in a sans serif face. Typefaces do have "personalities," individual characteristics that, taken together, convey subtleties not inherent in the language itself.—Malcolm Grear

Objective: Use letterform fragments to study composition, form/counter-form relationships, and patterns.

Problem: Letterforms are part of complex verbal and visual structures that have meaning in language. They also have interesting abstract qualities and beauty unto themselves.

Project:
Part 1. Look through typefaces on the computer or from a type specimen book (recommended fonts are listed below). Select a few interesting "parts"

of a few letters. Photocopy and blow up the parts. Play with the parts by cropping and turning to look for interesting forms and counterforms. The composition should have visually equal parts black and white, and balance between figure and ground. When something interesting starts to emerge, tape it down as your model.

Make three different compositions, and we'll discuss these in class. You will eventually scan the counterform parts into the computer for tracing. Your final form for part 1 of project 2 will be a 6 × 6 square on 12 × 12-inch black board with heavy vellum or paper flaps. Sign your name on the back of the board!

Part 2. Using the final abstract form you developed above and traced on the computer, you will experiment with a 4 × 4 grid on a 12 × 12 square. That is: Four 3-inch squares across and four 3-inch squares down. First, create a structured form on the grid, turning your final form within each square to form an abstract but visible pattern on the grid.

Second, overlapping letters: please create a free-form composition within the 12 × 12 square, using the sixteen letterform elements. The final form of part 2 of project 2 will be a 12 × 12 square on 12 × 12-inch bristol board with heavy vellum or paper flaps. Sign your name on the back of the board!

Evaluation: Will be based on the students' understanding, exploration, variety, and demonstration of the basic principles of composition, form/counterform, and letterform structures.

Fonts you may use: Garamond, Weiss, Futura, Gill Sans, Frutiger, Bodoni, Caslon, Baskerville, Legacy, Officina, Metro, Erbar, News Gothic, Franklin Gothic, and Syntax. Look at all versions for possibilities, from book to bold and italic. Light versions generally do not work very well for this assignment. Do not use script typefaces.

Project 3
Objective: To learn the principles of asymmetric typography applied to text.

Problem: Understanding and exercising the visual principles of typographic design, such as composition, proportion, rhythm, counterform, and gesture. You will also look at depth, scale, direction, motion, repetition, structure, detail, and anomaly. Although this particular assignment will be on paper, all of these principles can be applied to any media where typography is in use: book design, magazines, posters, corporate reports, identity design, capability brochures, television and movie titles, interface design, Web design, etc.

Project: You will be given the text of a weather report. This will be considered your pragmatic or purely informational text. You will also have to find a piece of text that is poetic in nature—such as a poem or short excerpt from literature. Do this quickly, so you can begin to work on it immediately, along with the pragmatic text. Show me the text you've chosen by next class.

Begin by reading the texts and sketching some ideas on how they might be composed. In and out of class, pencil sketch twelve thumbnail compositions per page on two to four pages, $8\frac{1}{2} \times 11$ paper, of each type of text. Then, create or pick at least eight typographic compositions of the text, using white paper cut to $10\frac{1}{2} \times 10\frac{1}{2}$ inches. Do four purely applied (or pragmatic) versions and four purely expressive (or poetic) versions for each text. A poetic weather report and a pragmatic poem! These sixteen pages will again be critiqued in class.

Although we will be dealing with some very real-world type issues, try to look more deeply into the "Zen" of typography. Your goal will be to set the type so that it looks absolutely perfect. What is perfect in design? Can you actually achieve perfection with type? Please do not distort the type in any way.

Final Form: The final form submitted will be six different compositions, each measuring $10\frac{1}{2} \times 10\frac{1}{2}$ inches, each mounted on $12\frac{1}{2} \times 12\frac{1}{2}$-inch board with a bond or velum overlay covering the entire front surface of the board. Sign your name on the back in white ink or on a label. Submit these boards in a cardboard portfolio. Plastic bags and oversized leather portfolios will not be accepted. Put your name on the portfolio, too. Your final six boards should contain three of the poem (at least one design should be a "pragmatic" typographic solution) and three of the weather report (at least one should be a "poetic" typographic solution).

Evaluation: Will be based on the students' understanding, exploration, variety, and demonstration of the basic principles of asymmetrical typography mentioned above, in addition to other techniques described in class.

Hints to success: This project is about typography—letterforms, words, phrases, sentences, paper, white space, sensitivity to the reader, and the design. It is *not* about rules, lines, dingbats, dots, color, or type spinning in circles or acting like a snake.

Think like type on a letterpress.

(Informational Text 1)
Sunday's Forecast, January 14, 2002, High 46°, Low 30°, partly sunny and cooler, northwesterly winds 10 to 15 mph, Sunrise: 7:40 A.M., Sunset: 5:08 P.M. Monday, much colder, with chance of snow showers in the evening, changing to freezing rain by midnight, High 10° Low -5°. Tuesday, temperatures expected to return to normal with clear skies. Details: 3B.

(Optional Poetic Text)
As we orbited the moon and looked back at the Earth, I could put my thumb up to the window of the spacecraft and completely hide the Earth. Everything that I have ever known is really behind my thumb. All my loved ones . . . Everything. It suddenly gave me the feeling of how insignificant we are here . . . We are really a spacecraft. We're all astronauts. There are four or five billion of us, all going through space on a spacecraft that has limited resources. So if we could all see that, and have the same impression, I think we could live and work much more closely and nicely together.—Apollo 13 astronaut Jim Lovell

Project 4
Objective: Design a poster for the university health center with binge drinking or alcohol as the theme (as discussed earlier in class with the health center director).

Problem: Images can be used but the design solution must be principally typographic, with all design elements contributing to the whole idea.

Project: Over the four weeks, begin by doing at least ten pages of pencil sketches. Number the pages. Then make and number five pages of marker sketches. Convert the most promising designs and concepts to roughs on the computer. Do at least five rough variations. Each should be as unique on its own in design and concept as possible. From those five, we'll narrow it down to two.

Final Form: Should be no larger than 17 × 22 (the shape may vary on the design needs, but no die-cuts). For example, a square poster would work, but should be no larger than 17 × 17, give or take an inch. Please experiment with a variety of the typefaces mentioned in class and those in the Bringhurst book. No handwritten styles of your own may be used.

The final comp presented for final crit and for the health center should show perfect craftsmanship and excellent presentation quality. It should be mounted and with a cover flap with your name clearly and beautifully printed on the back. Be sure to add your name in small type on the poster if it gets printed.

Evaluation: Will be based on the students understanding, exploration, variety, and demonstration of the basic principles of typography learned in the class, and without breaking any basic rules, push the boundaries of design while staying clear in the communication. Size, contrast, form/counterform, and other issues mentioned in class and in the handouts will also be the focus of evaluation.

Hints to success: This project is a typographic poster. You should not be focused only on images, illustration, or photography, except in support of or equal to the type. Type, color, geometric forms, secondary abstracted images, or lines and patterns will be the most common design elements.

Also, remember: posters present messages that should be simple and clear. It should be easy to get the main message at one glance. Watch out for colors that look good on screen but not as good in ink on paper. Use the "Pantone"-process color palette when picking colors. Pantone "coated" is a safe bet. Process is a more limited range of color. Be sure to consult with a Pantone color guide before committing to a color choice.

Books for This Class
Eric Spiekermann. *Stop Stealing Sheep*. Adobe Press
ISBN 0-672-48543-5 (but get 2nd edition, if out)
• required (on test)

Robert Bringhurst. *Elements of Typographic Style*. H & M
ISBN 0-88179-132-6
• required (on test)

Dean Phillip Lem. *Graphic Master Seven*. Dean Lem Associates
ISBN 0-914218-13-1 (student edition) or
Pocket Pal. International Paper, 1998
ISBN 0614255236
• required

Friedrich Friedl. *Typography*. Blackdog
ISBN 1-57912-023-7
• highly recommended

Books Worth Having as a Student and Designer
J.I. Rodale. *Synonym Finder*. Warner Books, 1986
ISBN 0446370290
• highly recommended

The American Heritage Dictionary (not the college edition). Houghton Mifflin
ISBN TK
• highly recommended

Philip Meggs and Rob Carter, *Typographic Specimens: The Great Typefaces*
(John Wiley & Sons, 1993).
• highly recommended (or other type specimen book)

Rob Carter, Ben Day, and Philip Meggs, *Typographic Design: Form and
Communication* (John Wiley & Sons: New York, third edition, 2002).
• highly recommended

Ray Kristof and Amy Satran, *Interactivity by Design* (Adobe Press).
ISBN 1-56830-221-5 (but get 2nd edition, if out)
• highly recommended

Fred Smeijers, *Counterpunch: Making Type in the Sixteenth Century,
Designing Typefaces Now*, Hyphen Press, London, 1996.
• recommended

Franz Zaier, *Books, Boxes, and Portfolios*
ISBN 0-8306-3483-5
• highly recommended

Michael Bierut, William Drenttel, Steven Heller, and D. K. Holland, eds. *Looking Closer: Critical Writings on Graphic Design*, vols. 1, 2, and 3 (New York: Allworth Press).
ISBN 1-880559-15-3
• highly recommended

Alan and Isabella Livingston, *The Thames and Hudson Encyclopedia of Graphic Design and Designers* (Thames and Hudson, 2003).
ISBN 0-500-20259-1
ISBN 0-8478-0944-7 (softcover)

Periodicals
Print, Graphis, Communication Arts, and *ID*
National and international publications about graphic design.
• highly recommended

Eye
An international publication about graphic design.
• recommended

Critique (back issues only)
Includes studio listings based on city.
• highly recommended, but no longer in print

How
Has many business-related articles.

New York Times or *www.nytimes.com*
National edition is basically an international paper. Probably the best English newspaper on earth, with coverage of issues on design, new media, and art.
• recommended

Also, books on QuarkXPress, InDesign, Pagemaker, Photoshop, Illustrator, and Freehand are all worth purchasing to help you solve computer problems when you are in the lab, at home, or on the job.

Web Sites

Communication Arts Magazine: *www.commarts.com/index.html*
Graphis Magazine: *www.graphis.com/*
Adobe Magazine: *www.adobe.com/publications/adobemag/main.html*
Print Magazine: *www.printmag.com/home/index.html*
ID Magazine: *www.idonline.com/*
How Magazine: *www.howdesign.com/*
Typografisch Papier: *www.typ.nl/*
American Institute of Graphic Arts (AIGA): *www.aiga.org/*
Type Directors Club: *www.tdc.org/indexfr.htm*
Font Zone: *www.fontzone.com/frameless/default.html*
Typo-L (mailing list, too): *www.lds.co.uk/preston/typo/*
A good Web resource for troubleshooting Macintosh problems is:
Ted Landau's MacFixIt page, *www.macfixit.pair.com/*
Quark Ed online, *www.quark.com/products/quarked/*

Experimental Typography *Instructor: Pablo A. Medina*

Experimental Typography is a class dedicated to the journey of finding undiscovered, inventive, nonconventional forms of typography. One can be inventive with type through concept, medium, scale, process, research, material, and presentation. The students in the class are senior level and have had an extensive education in the fundamentals of typography. They are now ready to take the rules that they've learned and reinvent them. In this class, you are not only encouraged, but expected, to think differently about typography. (Sagmeister's typography with cloth strips for Anni Kwan was an inspiration for the philosophy of the class.)

There are a series of short one- to two-week assignments that allow the students to explore numerous expressions of experimentation. A more involved, five-week assignment is given at the end of the semester. The critiques consist of each student presenting her idea and execution. After each presents her work, she receives feedback from both the rest of the class and myself. Once or twice in the semester, the class visits an outside source. (Last semester we visited the "Time Is Always Now" gallery and viewed the work of Viktor IV, an artist who used type extensively in his work.)

Assignments/Projects

Assignment 1: "Word Flyer"

Choose a favorite word and design an $8\frac{1}{2} \times 11$-inch flyer utilizing the word in a bold, readable manner. Make sure the design is in black and white. Design the flyer with a landscape (horizontal) format. When you're done designing the flyer, make twenty-five copies of the flyer onto any color paper you'd like and bring the copies to class next week.

Remember, typography is both visual and conceptual. Behind every word are many meanings and invocations. Avoid choosing words that are shallow or trite. The character of your word can be funny, serious, sad, angry, or happy—it's up to you.

After the students design and produce their flyers, the class, as a group, walks around the Parsons neighborhood (Greenwich Village) and posts the flyers in environments where the words are allowed to interact with their surroundings, like lampposts, walls, advertising postings, sidewalks, and any other ideas we come up with. These interactions are then photographed. (You can also view the images at *www.cubanica.com/eclectica*.)

Assignment 2: "New York Interpreted"

Create a piece of typographic expression relevant to the current political, social, emotional, and/or economic environment of life in New York. The content of the typography can be something you write or have written, or something you find, i.e., an article or cryptic message.

The medium of the piece is up to you. Consider type style (font, custom type, letterpress, hand-drawn type), material (i.e., paper, paint, ink, wood, metal, cloth), size, dimension (two or three dimensions), and medium (computer, silk screen, photography, etc.).

Be conscious of images and words that have been overseen and overused.

Assignment 3: "Type in Motion"

Create a time-based piece of typography in which type moves in time for at least fifteen seconds. The type can be two- or three-dimensional, and the content should be decided by you, but a conceptual connection to your idea will make the piece stronger. One example could be a typographic mobile that moves with the wind.

I will collect three tight, well-thought-out concepts, typeset on paper. Sketches are welcome as well. The following week, you must decide on one concept and bring the working constructed piece to class.

Assignment 4: "Photo Type"

Create a typographic poster that is created entirely by ONE non-manipulated photograph. An example of this could be to draw the type of the poster in salt on a table and take a photo of that composition. The poster should be 18 × 24 inches in dimension. The content of the poster is up to you.

Assignment 5: "Envelope and Letter"

Design and produce an envelope and letter and send it to every student in the class. Be aware of post office restrictions.

Assignment 6: "FINAL"

For your final project, you will choose one of the following options.

> *1.* Take a project given earlier in the semester. Expand on it and develop it.
>
> *2.* Pick one of the following projects:

• Create a photo-type documentation book. Ed Fella is a designer and illustrator well known for photographing typography. He recently published a book of his photos of typography. Create your own version of this book. It might help to focus on a theme for this project. Focusing on graffiti, or signs only using Helvetica, or spray-painted engineering type, or LCD type.

• Design a typographic experience. Affect our senses (sight, sound, smell, taste, touch, etc.) Maybe a performance, maybe a series of projections, maybe an installation. Maybe you take the entire script of a movie and do something insane with it.

> *3.* Come up with an assignment of your own.

Visual Literacy *Instructor: Audrey Bennett*

This course is for:

1. Undergraduates majoring in Electronic Media, Arts, and Communication (EMAC); Information Technology and Communication (Information Technology/Communication); Communication, with a concentration in Graphic Design: Theory, Research, Practice, or Media Design; and other disciplines in the humanities, social sciences, and sciences at RPI.

2. Graduate students working toward an M.S. in Technical Communication; Ph.D. candidates in the Department of Language, Literature, and Communication, with an interest in applied communication design.

Purpose and Goal

This course teaches students how to:

1. Communicate with text and images using the basic elements and principles of visual communication.

2. Create and/or choose appropriate graphics for relaying a message.

3. Critically analyze a layout in order to assess its aesthetic worth and effectiveness in conveying meaning.

4. Present and defend one's concepts and intentions.

Successful completion of the course depends on one's performance on:

1. Ten short-term exercises.

2. A final independent project.

3. Class participation.

Description of Course

Visual Literacy is an intermediate design studio course that explores the creation of text- and image-based graphics that communicate information to a multicultural audience. Through readings and weekly exercises, students apply visual literacy theory to the graphic design of visual layouts that serve a variety of different rhetorical purposes. This structure enables students to hone their graphic problem-solving, conceptual, and creative skills. Weekly group critiques give students an opportunity to present and defend their own solutions to a given graphic problem and to critically analyze the solutions of their peers.

Students are expected to have the technical skills necessary to complete the coursework. If any student is unfamiliar with the industry-standard design software applications for image editing,[1] layout,[2] and illustration[3] then it is strongly recommended that s/he reads: Jason Miletsky's *Digital Publishing to Go* (Upper Saddle River: Prentice Hall PTR, 2000).

Description of Classes

As a studio course situated in a computer lab, your weekly exercises are completed in the lab during class hours on Tuesday. Students may return to the lab after class hours, but before Friday's class session, to refine their work independently and prepare it for Friday's critique. During group critiques on Friday, students will give a brief presentation to their classmates and to me about each exercise. The group critiques may be conducted occasionally in small groups, with one or more graduate students leading each group discussion. Otherwise, the group critique will consist of each person presenting briefly to the entire class.

Assignments/Projects

In the course of thirteen weeks, students complete ten short-term exercises and one long-term final project. Both the exercises and the final project have a practical component (a visual design exercise) and a theoretical component (a verbal analysis). The visual/practical component is carried out according to the guidelines in *Visual Literacy: A Conceptual Approach to Graphic Problem Solving*, by Richard and Judith Wilde. The verbal/theoretical component is a written analysis of the visual component, using the vocabulary and theory they read about in *A Primer of Visual Literacy*, by Donis Dondis.

---

[1]Adobe Photoshop, or an equivalent.
[2]QuarkXPress, or an equivalent.
[3]Adobe Illustrator, or an equivalent.

Exercise 1

Practical Component: "Circle, Square, Triangle Problem," from Wilde and Wilde's book.

Theoretical Component: "The Basic Elements of Visual Communication," from Dondis's book. Use the three basic geometric shapes (circle, triangle, and square) to render theoretically grounded graphics that are recognizable by a target audience.

Exercise 2

Practical Component: "Designing with Type Problem," from Wilde and Wilde's book.

Theoretical Component: "The Basic Elements of Visual Communication," from Dondis's book. Use only typeset letters to render six theoretically grounded typographic designs.

Exercise 3

Practical Component: "Black and White Problem," from Wilde and Wilde's book.

Theoretical Component: "The Basic Elements of Visual Communication," from Dondis's book. Use negative shapes to render twelve theoretically grounded figure/ground compositions of cultural objects that are white in color.

Exercise 4

Practical Component: "Homage to André Breton," from Wilde and Wilde's book.

Theoretical Component: "Composition: The Syntactical Guidelines for Visual Literacy," from Dondis's book. Using a grid of one hundred small black dots, create a theoretically grounded composition that imitates the work of André Breton.

Exercise 5

Practical Component: "Less is More Problem," from Wilde and Wilde's book.

Theoretical Component: "The Anatomy of a Visual Message," from Dondis's book.

Using black and white only, render a theoretically grounded detailed design of a cultural object.

Exercise 6
Practical Component: "Altered Page Problem," from Wilde and Wilde's book.
Theoretical Component: "The Anatomy of a Visual Message," from
Dondis's book.
Alter an uninteresting cultural image in a theoretically grounded manner
that attracts the attention of a target audience.

Exercise 7
Practical Component: "Road Sign Problem," from Wilde and Wilde's book.
Theoretical Component: "Communication Techniques and Strategies,"
from Dondis's book. In a theoretical manner, visually translate twelve cultural objects or contexts into respective road sign graphics.

Exercise 8
Practical Component: "Jack and Jill Problem," from Wilde and Wilde's book.
Theoretical Component: "Communication Techniques and Strategies,"
from Dondis's book. In a theoretical manner, visually translate a nursery
rhyme using cultural graphics.

Exercise 9
Practical Component: "UPC Problem," from Wilde and Wilde's book.
Theoretical Component: "Communication Techniques and Strategies,"
from Dondis's book. In a theoretical manner, redesign the UPC graphic to
make a polemical or cultural statement.

Exercise 10
Practical Component: "Life and Death Problem," from Wilde and
Wilde's book.
Theoretical Component: "The Dynamics of Contrast," from Dondis's book.
Using the theory of contrast, visually translate a life-or-death circumstance
using the given graphic.

Final Project
Practical Component: "Graphic Design 101," from Wilde and Wilde's book.
Theoretical Component: "The Synthesis of Visual Style," from Dondis's book.
Using visual literacy theories of style, render a cultural object one hundred
different ways using cultural graphics that are recognizable to one or
many cultures.

Readings

The required readings for the course are:

Richard and Judith Wilde, *Visual Literacy: A Conceptual Approach to Graphic Problem Solving* (New York: Watson-Guptill Publications, 1991).

Donis A. Dondis, *A Primer of Visual Literacy* (Cambridge: The MIT Press, 1973).

Supplemental required reading includes but is not limited to:

Mark Oldach, *Creativity for Graphic Designers* (Cincinnati: North Light Books, 1995).

Steven Heller and Karen Pomeroy, *Design Literacy: Understanding Graphic Design* (New York: Allworth Press, 1997).

Description of Critique

Criteria for Critiquing Visual Communication Forms

1. Which visual literacy theory has been applied?
2. What is the intended message?
3. Who is the target audience?
4. Is it aesthetically pleasing?
5. What is the concept, and how has it been visualized?
6. Does it attract your attention and make you linger for more information?
7. Are the graphic/typographic/visual treatments appropriate for the message? The target audience?
8. Does it evoke an emotion? Which?
9. In which context could it be used more effectively? For which target audience?
10. Is it well crafted? (Assess color harmony, cropping, size, resolution, and perspective.)
11. What is the purpose of each graphic element?

CAROLINE ARCHER studied for a Ph.D. in typography and graphic communication at the University of Reading. She now works as a freelance journalist and writer, specializing in the graphic arts, and is the author of a number of books.

FRANK ARMSTRONG is a lecturer in communication design at California State University, Chico, teaching typographic information design, kinetic typography, and an online digital prepublishing course. His professional work has been published in numerous journals and books, including Rob Carter's *American Typography Today*. He has an MFA in graphic design from Yale University, and is a member of AIGA, AtypI, and IIID.

JARED ASH is an independent curator, translator, and lecturer on Russian avant-garde art and design. As curator of the Judith Rothschild Foundation from 1997 to 2002, he developed and catalogued the collection of Russian avant-garde books, periodicals, and related works that was donated to the Museum of Modern Art in 2001. He played a prominent role in preparing the collection for the MoMA exhibition, *The Russian Avant-Garde Book 1910–1934*, and the accompanying catalog. He is currently working on a translation of the memoirs, correspondence, and theoretical writings of Aleksandr Rodchenko.

TAREK ATRISSI, the founder of *www.arabictypography.com*, holds an MFA in design from the School of Visual Arts in New York, an MA in interactive multimedia from the Utrecht School of the Arts in the Netherlands, and a BA in graphic design in his homeland, Lebanon. His work has been exhibited at the Guggenheim Museum, and has been featured in numerous international design books and magazines.

JONATHAN BARNBROOK is a graphic and font designer. He lives and works in London. His previous projects include the design of the Damien Hirst monograph, *I Want To Spend . . . With Damien Hirst*, a collaboration with the anti-advertising organization and magazine, *Adbusters*, and design of the notorious typeface Manson, which was later renamed Mason. He currently runs his own radical font company, Virus.

LESLIE BECKER is chair of graphic design at the California College of the Arts, a design practitioner for thirty years, and an educator for twenty-five years. She earned her BFA in graphic design from the Cooper Union and her MA in design from the University of California at Berkeley. She has been on the San Francisco board of the AIGA, presented at AIGA and AICAD national conferences, written for *Print*, the San Francisco Design Center, *Graphis New Talent*, and *Design Book Review*, and designs everything from custom furniture and lighting to print materials.

NICK BELL is director of UNA (London) designers, a graphic design company specializing in editorial, environmental, and exhibition design, working mostly in the cultural sector for museums, art galleries, universities, and publishers. Its client list includes the British Council, the Science Museum, Imperial War Museum, Tate Britain, Phaidon Press, and the Royal Mail. In 1997, he was appointed art director of *Eye* magazine. An entire issue of *Emigre* (no. 22, 1992) was devoted to his work and teaching.

JOHN D. BERRY is an editor/typographer who works on both sides of the design/content divide. He is the former editor and publisher of *U&lc* ("Upper and lowercase") and of *U&lc Online*, and he edited the book, *Language Culture Type*, on international type design, published for ATypI by *Graphis*. He writes and consults extensively on typography, and has won numerous awards for his book designs.

TONY BROCK joined the North Carolina State University faculty in 1999, and has taught undergraduate courses focusing on montage, serial, and sequential imaging, as well as introductory and experimental typography. On the graduate level, he has taught motion and interactive design. His research interests focus on broadcast distance education, motion graphics, and ephemera. Brock's teaching and design works have been published in AIGA's *Loop*, *Typographics*, the *ACD 100 Show*, and Jan van Toorn's *Design Beyond Design*. Prior to teaching, he held several positions in design and advertising, completing work for clients including Nokia, Philips, and Whittle Communications.

STEVEN BROWER is the creative director for *Print* magazine. He teaches design at the School of Visual Arts in New York City and at Marywood University in Pennsylvania. He is the author of *Publication Design* (published by Delmar Publishing).

CHUCK BYRNE is on the graphic design faculty at San Jose State University. He has taught at the University of Cincinnati and the California College of Arts and Crafts. His design work has appeared in *Communication Arts, Idea, ID, Graphis*, and *Print*. In addition to serving as a contributing editor to *Print* magazine for over a decade, he has also written for *Eye*, the *AIGA Journal*, and *Emigre* magazines, and his articles have been included in *Looking Closer* and *Design Culture* (Allworth Press).

ART CHANTRY has been doing graphic design for thirty years. In that time, he has won hundreds of awards and been included in museum shows and exhibits ranging from Cannes to the Louvre to the Rock-and-Roll Hall of Fame. He had two 2003 exhibitions in New York, including a one-man career retrospective display at PS1/MoMA.

LAURA CHESSIN earned a BFA from Cornell University and an MFA from the Rhode Island School of Design. She maintained a design practice in Amherst, Massachusetts, for almost a decade prior to accepting her current faculty position in the communication arts and design department at Virginia Commonwealth University. Her current work includes both professional design work as well as a photo and text documentation of safe shelters for domestic violence.

JOSEPH COATES is an assistant professor at the School of Art and Art History at the University of Iowa in Iowa City.

JAMES CRAIG is the author of books on graphic design, including *Designing with Type*. He received his BFA from the Cooper Union and his MFA from Yale University. Now semiretired, he was the design director for Watson-Guptill Publications, and is a lifetime member of the New York Art Directors Club and former member of AIGA. At present, he teaches typography and design at the Cooper Union and lectures widely. His type teaching Web site is *www.designingwithtype.com*.

DENISE GONZALES CRISP has taught five levels of typography at four institutions over twelve years. She is chair of graphic design at the College of Design, at North Carolina State University. From 1997 to 2001, she was senior designer for Art Center College of Design in Pasadena, California, where she also taught as core faculty in the graduate media design program. Her studio, SuperStove! has served clients including *Artext* magazine, Southern California Institute of Architecture, and several small presses. She received an MFA from the California Institute of the Arts.

JOHANNA DRUCKER is the Robertson Professor at the University of Virginia, where she directs the media studies Program. She has published and lectured on the history of writing, typography, graphic design, book arts, visual poetry, and digital aesthetics. Her published titles include *The Alphabetic Labyrinth*, *The Visible Word*, and *The Century of Artists' Books*.

ED FELLA is an artist, educator, and graphic designer whose work has had an important influence on contemporary typography. In 1997 he received the Chrysler Award, and, in 1999, an honorary doctorate from CCS in Detroit. His work is in the National Design Museum and MoMA in New York. His book, *Edward Fella: Letters on America, Photographs and Lettering*, juxtaposes examples of his unique hand lettering with his photographs of found vernacular lettering.

GEOFFRY FRIED is chair of the design department at the Art Institute of Boston at Lesley University, where he teaches courses in graphic design and typography. He has been a designer and design educator for the past twenty years, and has taught at Boston University, Northeastern University, and the Rhode Island School of Design.

KEITH GODARD was trained at the London College of Printing and Graphic Art. He won a scholarship to the MFA program at Yale University. He is a member of Alliance Graphique Internationale, teaches design at the Fashion Institute of Technology and in the School of Visual Arts MFA Design program, and is the author of *This Way That Way*, published by Lars Muller Publications.

SHELLEY GRUENDLER is a designer and typographer working in the United States and England. She is currently completing her Ph.D. in typography and graphic communication at the University of Reading, and will soon publish a biography of Beatrice Warde.

ALLAN HALEY is director of words and letters at Agfa Monotype. Here, he is responsible for adding new designs to the Monotype and ITC typeface libraries and producing educational content for the Fonts.com and ITCFonts.com Web sites. He is the author of five books on type and graphic communication and hundreds of articles for publications such as *U&lc*, *How*, *Dynamic Graphics*, and *STEP Inside Design*.

CLAIRE HARTTEN is currently living in London pursuing postgraduate design studies, and is involved with the St. Bride Printing Library.

STEVEN HELLER is cochair of the School of Visual Arts MFA Design program, art director of the *New York Times Book Review*, and editor, author, and coauthor of ninety books on graphic design, typography, illustration, and popular art.

TERRY IRWIN is a design consultant working with businesses and schools around the country. In 1992 she cofounded the San Francisco office of MetaDesign with partners Bill Hill and Erik Spiekermann, and served as creative director for ten years. She is on the faculty of California Arts and Crafts, and has lectured at schools such as Rhode Island School of Design, Carnegie Mellon University, and North Carolina State University. She has her graduate degree from the Basel School of Design, in Switzerland.

MICHAEL JOHNSON is creative director of Johnson Banks, a design consultancy in London, and chairman of education for British Design and Art Direction (D&AD). He is the author of *Problem Solved: A Primer for Design and Communication* (Phaidon Press).

DAVID JURY has earned typographic awards from NYTC, ICOGRADA, and the International Society of Typographic Designers. He is currently the editor of *TypoGraphic*, the journal of the ISTD. He has written two books: *In Darkest England: Observing the Observers of Mass Observation 1937–1939, 1998* (boxed set, letterpress printed, limited edition) and *About Face: Reviving the Rules of Typography* (Rotovision Books, 2002). He also edited *TypoGraphic Writing: An Anthology of Writing from Thirty Years of TypoGraphic*. His articles have been published in *Eye* and *Baseline*. He is also head of graphic media at Colchester Institute in England.

JEFFREY KEEDY is a designer, writer, type designer, and educator who has been teaching in the graphic design program at the California Institute of the Arts since 1985. He was the director of the design program at CalArts between 1991 and 1995. His designs and essays have been published in *Eye, ID, Emigre, Critique, Idea, Looking Closer One, Two,* and *Four, Faces on the Edge: Type in the Digital Age, New Design: Los Angeles,* and *The Education of a Graphic Designer.*

EMILY KING is a design historian and design editor of the art magazine, *Frieze.* She edited Peter Saville's monograph, *Designed by Peter Saville,* and was on the jury of the 2003 Designer of the Year Award held at London's Design Museum.

MAX KISMAN is principal of MKDSGN, in Mill Valley, California, and founder of Holland Fonts, a small type foundry for his typefaces. Born in the Netherlands, he was a pioneer in digital technology in the mid-1980s, and is an award-winning designer and illustrator whose work includes magazines, posters, and postage stamps. He teaches graphic design and typography at the California College of the Arts and at the UC Berkeley Extension, both in San Francisco.

HUUB KOCH is a senior Web designer, with his roots in graphic design, advertising, art, photography, stage design, and writing. Since 1999, he has pondered the nature of content, the attitude of being personal, and the gentle art of creating good vibrations. The results of these reflections can be found at *www.huubkoch.nl.*

KATHERINE MC COY, a senior lecturer at Illinois Institute of Technology's Institute of Design in Chicago, cochaired the department of design at Cranbrook for twenty-four years. She is a partner at McCoy & McCoy and High Ground Tools Strategies for Design.

PABLO A. MEDINA serves on the faculty of Parsons School of Design as professor of design and typography, and has also taught at Maryland Institute College of Art. Pablo has recently launched Cubanica, an art and design studio dedicated to the exploration and interpretation of culture.

MARTIN MENDELSBERG is a typographer and graphic designer. He earned his BFA degree from Minneapolis College of Art and Design and MFA from the University of Denver. His foreign study has included Atelier 63, the Netherlands, and he was lecturer at the University of Canterbury in Christchurch, New Zealand. He is currently chair of graphic design and interactive media at Rocky Mountain College of Art and Design in Denver.

CHRIS MYERS has more than fifteen years of experience teaching at the California Institute of the Arts and the University of the Arts, where he served as chairman of the graphic design department for seven years. He currently serves on the board of trustees of the American Center for Design and is an on-site accreditation evaluator for the National Association of Schools of Art and Design. There are at least six people with the same name (and exact spelling) working today in the fields of graphic design, photography, and illustration. This one lives in Philadelphia.

HANK RICHARDSON is president of Portfolio Center in Atlanta, one of the most renowned schools for the communicating arts in America. A chronic insomniac, he spends the wee hours conjugating verbs like *charette* and preparing for his 5 A.M. classes, events famous for their heated debates and hot Krispy Kremes. He is also an AIGA fellow and a founding member of AIGA/Atlanta.

STEFAN SAGMEISTER formed the New York–based Sagmeister Inc. in 1993, and has since designed graphics and packaging for the Rolling Stones, David Byrne, Lou Reed, Aerosmith, and Pat Metheny. His work has been nominated four times for Grammys, and has won most international design awards. He teaches in the School of Visual Arts MFA Design program. His monograph, *Sagmeister, Made You Look*, was published by Booth-Clibborn Editions in 2001.

MARTHA SCOTFORD, book designer, author, and professor of graphic design at North Carolina State University, teaches design history, typography, and design studios. She is the author of articles on design and type history, the book *Cipe Pineles: A Life of Design*, published by W. W. Norton & Company in 1999, and a principal collaborator on *For the Voice: Mayakovsky and Lissitzky*, published by Artists Bookworks and the British Library in 2000. She spent early 2001 in India as a Fulbright lecturer, teaching typography and Western design history.

MICHAEL SCHMIDT is an associate professor at the University of Memphis, where he teaches undergraduate through graduate courses in graphic design. Michael volunteers his time and design services to Global Goods, a Memphis nonprofit dedicated to fair trade and fair wages for coffee growers and artists living in developing nations.

PAUL SHAW is a letter designer and graphic design historian. He has taught typography at Parsons School of Design since 1990. He is the coauthor of the monograph and catalogue accompanying the exhibition, "Blackletter: Type and National Identity."

LAURIE SZUJEWSKA is a graphic designer and typographer. Her studio, shoe yév skä design, is based in Sonoma County, California.

TEAL TRIGGS is director of postgraduate studies, faculty of art, design and music, Kingston University, London. She has written extensively on graphic design, typography, and feminism, with her most recent book titled, *The Typographic Experiment: Radical Innovation in Contemporary Type Design* (Thames & Hudson, 2003). She is a fellow of the International Society of Typographic Designers (ISTD), and a founding member of the Women's Design + Research Unit (WD+RU).

DOYALD YOUNG has been a designer, lecturer, and teacher for twenty-seven years, specializing in lettering, logo design, and typography at Art Center College of Design. He is the author of *Logotypes & Letterforms* and *Fonts & Logos, and The Art of the Letter* (Smart Papers).

254

Index

About Alphabets (Zapf), 30

Adobe Systems, 32, 153, 156–157

Adversary (Fitzgerald), 64

advertising, corporate, 64–68, 65f, 66f, 67f

aesthetics, 7, 139

Agfa Monotype Corporation, 152

Agnelli, George, 47

Alexandrine Library, 126, 133n2

algorithms, letterform, 79–81

alignment, types of, 6

Allemann, Hans, 133n4

alphabet
Arabic, 146
developing, 3
Erté's, 167
Etruscan, 3
Hebrew, 142–145
history of, 85f
sacredness of, 84–88

Amnesty International, 64–68, 65f, 66f, 67f

Anderson, Ian, 107n3

anonymity, 73, 107

Another Limited Rebellion Design, 70–71

apostrophes, 108, 109

apprenticeship
modern family, 35
traditional require-
ments for, 93

Arabic typography, 146–149

Archer, Caroline, 35–37

Arnheim, Rudolph, 33

Arts and Crafts move-
ment, 36

asymmetry, 232–234

atmosphere, creating, 97

automated errrors, 109

avant-garde movement, 134–141

Bain, Peter, 42

Baines, Phil, 44–45, 47–49, 50, 174

Barber, Benjamin, 73

Barber, Susan, 68

Barnbrook, Jonathan, 195–200

Barthes, Ronald, 167

Baskerville, John, 21, 31

beauty, of letterforms, 25, 92

Beauty: The Value of Values (Turner), 92

Becker, Joachim, 87

Behrens, Peter, 56, 62

Bell, Nick, 193–194

Biddulph, Nicholas, 44

Bielenberg, John, 27–29

Birkets, Sven, 171

Birmingham School of Printing, 35–37

blackletter typography, 13

Bliss font, 157

van Blokland, Erik, 158–159

Blumenthal, Joseph, 30

Boag, Andrew, 154

Bonsiepe, Gui, 170

Book of Creation, 85–86

book typography
author's purpose and, 107n5
class structure for, 10–12
rules of, 119–121
Russian futurist, 134–141

"The Crystal Goblet" and, 98–100

books
comprehending, 103
mass-market, 116–118
recommended, 215–216, 217–218, 235–237, 246
value of, 126–128

boustrophedon, 3

branché (plugged in, connected), 14

brand equity, 71

branding, 56–60, 62–63, 155–156

Bringhurst, Robert, 92–93, 174, 175

Brower, Steven, 116–118

Bruinsma, Max, 64

Burliuk, David, 134

Burliuk, Nikolai, 134

Caflisch, Max, 32

Cage, John, 32

calligraphy
Hebrew, 142–145
importance of, 13, 146–147
teaching, 97, 187
typography *v.,* 49, 146

capital letters
fake small, 109–110
rules for using, 8

Carnegie, Andrew, 133n1

Carolingian minuscule script, 4

Carson, David, ix

Carter, Matthew, 153–154, 156

celebrity images, 165–166

cellular phones, fonts
    on, 154–155
centering, 33, 120
Central Lettering
    Record (CLR), 44,
    48
Chantry, Art, 123–124
Chessin, Laura, 19–26
Chinese characters, ori-
    gins of, 84f
Chwast, Seymour, 121
Clarendon font, 121
ClearType, 155
clichés, 114–115
CLR. *See* Central
    Lettering Record
Cockney, 165
codex, 3
Common Ground, 64
communication,
    114–115
comping, 42–43
computers. *See* digital
    typography
concord, 206–208
Consonni auction, 158
contrast, 206–208
conventions. *See* rules
Cooper Union, 43–44
Copland, Aaron, 176
copyfitting, 43
copyrights, 63
corporate design, 56–60
    advertising for, 64–68,
    65f, 66f, 67f
    custom fonts for,
    155–156
    fighting, 70–71
craftsmanship, 95–96
Craig, James, 42–43
creativity, 104–106
Crisp, Denise Gonzales,
    17–18
critical thinking, 39–40,
    62
critiquing, 246
Crutchley, Brooke,
    107n6

"The Crystal Goblet,"
    98–100, 100nn2–5
cultural improvement,
    64, 68, 70
cuneiform, 3
curriculum guidelines,
    38–41, 130–131. *See
    also* syllabi
custom type, 155–156

Dabner, David, 43–44
Dalton Maag, 155–156
DAM. *See* Designers
    Against Monoculture
Dark Ages, 4
Davidovich, Menachem,
    143
Davies, Bur, 153
Dead Poets Society, 29
DeLillo, Don, 74n22
Derrida, Jacques, 62
Design for the World,
    70
design process, 113–114
design programs.
    See schools
Design Research
    Society, 64
Designers Against
    Monoculture
    (DAM), 70
The Designers
    Republic (TDR), 101
Dickinson, Eleanor, 29
digital typography
    benefits of, 160–164
    birth of, 112–113
    cellular phones and,
    154–155
    evolution of, 50–51
    font developments of,
    79–80, 152–159
    Hebrew, 142, 145
    integration of, 42–51
    learning curve for,
    123–124, 128
    new approaches to,
    158–159

quality and, 95–96
    shortcomings of, vii–x,
    152–153
    software companies of,
    152–156
    speed of, 94
    teaching, 160–164,
    170–171
    vocabulary for, 78
display type, 119
"The Diversity School,"
    56–60, 62–63, 71
Dixon, Catherine,
    44–46
Dowding, Geoffrey, 33
drawing
    classes, vii
    importance of, 33
    large sized fonts, 47
    subtelties of, 24
    drop shadows, 120
Druckrey, Inge, 33,
    133n4

editing, 113–114,
    162–163
*The Education of a
    Graphic Designer*, x
Egyptians, 3
Eisenman, Alvin,
    32–33
*The Elements of
    Typographic Style*
    (Bringhurst), 92–93
Ellington, Duke, 53
Émigre, 17
errrors, 108–110
Erté, 167
ethnic diversity, 59
Etruscan alphabet, 3
Experimental
    Typography, syllabus
    for, 239–241
experimenting, 33–34,
    130
expressionism, abstract,
    vii
Eye, 68, 193

fake caps, 109–110
fashion, type as, 94, 167
Fella, Ed, 201–202, 241
fine typography, 91–92
  learning, 92–94
  teaching, 95–96
  technology and, 94–95
*The Finer Points in the
  Spacing and
  Arranging of Type*
  (Dowding), 33
"First Things First
  Manifesto"
  (FTF2000), 63
Fitzgerald, Kenneth, 64
fluency, teaching, vii–x
fonts
  Adobe, 153
  Arabic, 147
  cellular phone, 154–155
  combining, 79–80
  custom, 155–156
  defined, 6
  Hebrew, 145
  international standard
    for, 153, 159n19
  large sized, 47
  Microsoft, 153–155
  new wave of, 156–157
  redesigns of, 21–22,
    181–182
  researching, 48
  selling, 155, 158
  spacial orientation of,
    31
  formality, 101–103
  formats, 212–213
  found typography,
    213–214
Fraterdeus, Peter, 68, 70
Free Trade Agreement
  of the Americas
  (FTAA), 63
FTF2000. *See* "First
  Things First
  Manifesto"
"Fudoni," 112
Fuse, 156

"FutureHistory" confer-
  ence, 58, 71–72
futurism, Russian,
  134–141

Garland, Ken, 63
genres, type, 16
German Bold Italic,
  166–167
Gill, Eric, 118, 121
Ginger, E. M., 33
Ginsburgh, Yitzchak,
  145
globalization, 56–60,
  62–63
Godard, Keith, 191–192
Goldberger, Menachem,
  142
The Grapevine, 20
graphic design
  type and, syllabus for,
    230–238
  typography *v.,* 15,
    123–124
Gray, Nicolete, 44
grayscaling, 154
Grear, Malcom, 71
Greeks, ancient, 3
The Greenwood Press, 93
Grid Systems (Müller-
  Brockmann), 33
grids, 102–103, 175. *See
  also* spacing
*The Grid: History, Use,
  and Meaning*
  (Williamson), 60
Gromala, Diane,
  172n17
"groundlessness," 71
Guertler, Andre, 97
Guro, Elena, 135
Gutenberg, Johannes,
  4, 78

haiku, 210
half-unical characters, 4
handwriting
  analysis, 89

mood and, 137–138
  resistance to, 129
  styles, 31
Haslam, Andrew, 50,
  174
headlines, rules for, 8–9
Hebrew, 142–145
hectographic composi-
  tions, 139
"He's a Keeper of the
  Fire," 132, 133n8
heterogeneity, 58–59, 72
Hiebert, Kenneth,
  133n4, 174, 177
hierarchy, 212–213
hieroglyphics, 3, 87
Hobson, Jamie, 43–44
Hofmann, Armin, 33
Hofmann, Dorotea, 33
Hofstadter, Douglas,
  79–80
Holt, Sien ten, 111
hot metal setting, 44
House Industries,
  157–158
Hyde, Matt, 47
hypnerotomachia, 87f

ICOGRADA. *See*
  International
  Council of Graphic
  Design Associations
iconography, Maori, 63
ICSID. *See*
  International
  Council of Societies
  of Industrial Design
ideology, 72–73
IFI. *See* International
  Federation of
  Interior
  Architects/Interior
  Designers
InDesign, 110
Industrial Revolution, 5
*Inside/Outside: From the
  Basics to the Practice
  of Design* (Grear), 71

INTA. *See* International Trademark Association

International Council of Graphic Design Associations (ICOGRADA), 63, 70

International Council of Societies of Industrial Design (ICSID), 70

International Federation of Interior Architects/Interior Designers (IFI), 70

International Society of Typographic Designers (ISTD), 101

International Trademark Association (INTA), 63

internet
  recommended sites on, 218, 238
  shortcomings of, 48

Introduction to Typography, syllabus for, 204–205

intuition, developing, 23–24

invisibility, of typographic structure, 98–100

ISTD. *See* International Society of Typographic Designers

Italian Renaissance, 4

Janecek, Gerald, 137

Jay, Leonard, 35–37

Jihad v. McWorld: How Globalism and Tribalism Are Reshaping the World (Barber), 73

Johnson & Wolverton, 64–68, 65f, 66f, 67f

Johnson, Michael, 184–186

Johnson, Philip, 29

Jones, Robert N., 122

Jongejans, Charles, 111

Justice, Ruth, 142

justified text, 120

Kabbala, 86f

Kamenskii, Vasilii, 134–135

Karmitz, Marim, 73

Keedy, Jeffery, 122, 163, 187–190

Kelly, Jerry, 49–50

Khlebnikov, Velimir, 136

King, Laurence, 47

Kinross, Robin, 152, 170

Kisman, Max, 111–112

Knuth, Donald, 79–81

Kress, Gunther, 170

Kruchenyhk, Aleksei, 134, 136–140

Kuipers, Abe, 111

Kunz, Willi, 175

Kurosawa, Akira, 230

Küster, Christian, 158

Lamed, 143

Language Technology, 112

leading, 121

lectures, slide, 46

van Leeuwen, Theo, 170

Lefevre, Sherry, 133n4

legibility, 7, 23, 180–181

Legible City (Shaw), 90

Leonidas, Gerry, 50

letterforms
  algorithims of, 79–81
  Arabic, 146
  arbitrary, 137–138
  beauty of, 25, 92

defining concept of, 78–90
  designing, 210–212
  Hebrew, 142–145
  history of, 83–90
  looking at, 30
  religion and, 84–88
  tracing, 230–231

lettering. *See also* drawing; handwriting
  tracing, 230–231
  typography *v.,* 124
  walks, 47

letterpresses, old, 31

"The Letter as Such," 136

Levrant de Bretteville, Shiela, 68

libraries, 126, 133nn1–2

Licko, Zuzana, ix, 63, 152

Lissitzky, El, 139–140

lithography, 136

lobbying groups, 63

localization, 58–59

London College of Printing, 43–44

Looking Closer, 63, 64

Lovell, Jim, 234

Macdonald, Nico, 155

Manuale Typographicum (Zapf), 30

Manutius, Aldus, 31

Maori iconography, 63

margin settings, 120

Margolin, Victor, 64

Marsalis, Wynton, 176

Mason, J. H., 35

mass-market books, 116–118

materials, course, 217–219

Matiushin, Mikhail, 135

Max Caflisch: Typographica Practica (Caflisch), 32

Max, Peter, 21
Mayakovsky, Vladimir, 141n14
McCoy, Kathy, 57–59, 169, 171
McLean, Ruari, 30, 93
McNickle, D'Arcy, 59–60, 74n11
Mendelsberg, Martin, 142
metafonts, 79–81
metaphor
 violin, 22–23
 wineglass, 98–100
Microsoft, 153–155
Miller, Abbott, 172n17
Minogue, Kylie, 166–167
modernism, vii, 56–60, 187
Moholy-Nagy, Laszlo, 168
Monotype, 152
Morison, Stanley, 107n5
Moussaud, 89f
movie industry, politics in, 73
Müller-Brockmann, Josef, 33, 97
music, 22–23, 103, 173–177

NAFTA. *See* North American Free Trade Agreement
narratives
 Arabic, 146–149
 genres of, 129
 Hebrew, 142–145
 importance of, 126–133
 Russian futurist, 134–141
Native Americans
 exploitation of, 59
 storytelling tradition of, 132
networks, social interactivity, 64, 68, 70

New Baskerville, 21–22
nihilism, 61
NION. *See* Not In Our Name
noise, 101, 102
North American Free Trade Agreement (NAFTA), 74n11
Not In Our Name (NION), 68, 69f
nursery rhymes, 88f

Omar, Caliph, 133n2
OpenType, 153
originality, 104–106
ornamentals, wood, 80f, 83f
orthographic reform, 138–139, 141n14

paperbacks, 116–118
patterns, 102–103
pens, reed, 3, 4
Phoenicians, 3
pluralism, 61
"Poetic Principles," 134
political activism, 64, 68, 70–72
pop culture, 103, 157–158
portfolios, creating, 228–229
postmodernism, 60–62, 68–69
The Power of the Center (Arnheim), 33
Poyner, Rick, 57
Pratt Institute, 43, 49–50
predictability, 103
"Printing Should Be Invisible," 98–100
Pritchard, Tony, 43–44
"Private Press" movement, 36
problem solving, 26

projects
 Experimental Typography, 239–241
 Introduction to Typography, 204–205
 Type 1, 206–217
 Type and Graphic Design, 230–235
 Visual Literacy, 243–245
propaganda, 73

quality, poor, 95–96, 108–111
QuarkXPress
 exercises, 219
 teaching, 48–49
quitting, 124
quotation marks, 108, 109

Rand, Paul, 27, 34, 182
Ray Gun, ix–x
readability, 102–104
readings, 215–216, 217–218, 235–237, 246
rebus, 3
redesigns, 21–22, 181–182
reed pens, 3, 4
religion, 84–88, 127–128, 142–145
Rhyme and Reason (Spiekermann), 11
rhythm, 208–209
Richardson, Hank, 27–29
Right On!, 68
Riley, Chris, 62
Rosenberg, Zvika, 145
van Rossum, Just, 158–159
rules, 101–103
 bending, 11, 33, 121–122

book text, 119–121
capital letter, 8
heading, 8–9
liberation from, 124
Russian typographers, 134–141

Sachs, Hinrich, 158
Sagmeister, Stefan, 183
Sainte-Marie, Buffy, 132, 133n8
Saltz, Ina, 51
Sanders, David, 142
Scalin, Noah, 70–71
Scher, Paula, 147
schools
  Arabic in, 148
  art phases in, vii, x
  goals of, 14–15
  typographic proficiency in, vii–x
Schulze, Jack, 47
Schwitters, Kurt, 33
Sefer Yetsirah, 85
shadows, drop, 120
Shaw, Jeffrey, 90
Shaw, Paul, 10–11
Sheehan, Jamie, 124
Signs: Lettering in the Environment, 47
Situationist International movement, 63
sizing, 120–121
"slebbing," 165–166
slide lectures, 46
Slimbach, Robert, 32, 153
sloppiness, 108–110
small caps, 109–110
social interactivity, 64, 68, 70
social justice, 25–26
software companies, 152–156
"Something Worth Leaving Behind," 132, 133n8

sound
  interaction of, 176–177
  production of, 173
  properties of, 175–176
  structure of, 174–175
spacing
  arbitrary, 137–138
  importance of, 31
  learning, 32–33
  types of, 6
Spencer, Herbert, 30
Spiekermann, Erik, 10–11, 33
stacking type, 119–120
Stauffacher, Jack, 32, 93–94
Stiff, Paul, 107n6
Stone, Sumner, 32
Stop Stealing Sheep and Find Out How Type Works (Ginger & Spiekermann), 33
Stowell, Scott, 68
student-to-student teaching, 27, 46
supplies, course, 217–219
The Surrounded (McNickle), 59
syllabi
  Experimental Typography, 239–241
  Introduction to Typography, 204–205
  Type 1, 206–229
  Type and Graphic Design, 230–238
  Visual Literacy, 242–246

Tankard, Jeremy, 156, 159
TDR. *See* The Designers Republic
teaching

aim of, 14
by apprenticeship, 35, 93
atmosphere for, 97
calligraphy, 97, 187
comping, 42–43
digital typography, 160–164, 170–171
fine typography, 95–96
fluency, vii–x
home, 35
old and new integration for, 42–51
parameters, 10–13
pedagogical, 22
personal nature of, 38
pioneers of, 35–37
QuarkXPress, 48–49
student-to-student, 27, 46
theatrical, 28–29, 46
Type 1 classes, 21–22, 38–41, 206–229
technology. *See* digital typography
Tei, Towa, 166–167
terms, 219–221
tests, Type 1, 223–228
text typography. *See* book typography
texture, 208–209
The Thames and Hudson Typography Manual of Style (McLean), 93
theatrical teaching, 28–29, 46
Thompson, Jon, 165–166
Tilson, Jake, 156
Tinkler, Marc, 72
Torah, 142–145, 144f
Tory, Geoffrey, 88
tracing, 230–231
trademarks, 63
Trap for Judges, 135–136
Turner, Frederick, 92
Twombly, Carol, 32, 153

Type 1 classes
  curriculum for, 38–41
  syllabus for, 206–229
  teaching, 21–22
  tests for, 223–228
Type and Graphic
  Design, syllabus for,
  230–238
typefaces. *See also* fonts;
  letterforms
  cultural nature of, 62–63
  custom, 155–156
  defined, vii, 5
  display, 119
  distorting, 117, 119
  experimenting with,
  33–34
  families of, 32
  as fashion, 94, 167
  genres of, 16
  inventing, 31
  perceptions of, 2
  selecting, 7, 32
  size, 120–121
  stacking, 119–120
  terminology, 5–7
  unification of, 80
  using, 7
  variations of, 6
  voice of, 28–29, 115
typewriter quotes, 108,
  109
typographers
  authors' relationship
  with, 107n5
  dialogues from,
  180–202
  graphic designers *v.*,
  123–124
  importance of, 127
  studying, 51, 216–217
  traditional, 92–94
TypoGraphic, 101

typography. *See also*
  book typography;
  digital typography;
  fine typography
  Arabic, 146–149
  calligraphy *v.,* 49, 146
  creativity in, 104–106
  evolution of, 2–5
  found, 213–214
  graphic design *v.,* 15,
  123–124
  Hebrew, 142–145
  history, 2–5, 11–12, 16,
  215, 216–217
  invisibility of, 98–100
  lettering *v.,* 124
  mechanics of, 38–39
  new styles of, ix–x
  parameters of, 10–13
  practice, 10
  purpose of, 2
  quitting, 124
  renaissance in, x
  rules of, 101–103
  Russian futurist,
  134–141
  sloppy, 108–110
  sound and, 174–177
  text, 10–12
  unlearned, 8–9

Unger, Gerard, 50–51,
  111–112
unical-style characters, 3
Unicode, 153, 159
Universal War
  (Kruchenykh), 138
Updike, John, 36
utilitarianism, 137, 139

Vandercook press, 31
VanderLans, Rudy, ix, 63
Vienne, Véronique, 63

Vinyl, 112
violins, making, 22–23
Visual Literacy, syllabus
  for, 242–246
voice, of type, 28–29, 115

Waller, Robert, 107n6
Warde, Beatrice, 91,
  98–100
Warnock, John, 153
websites, recommended,
  218, 238
Weingart, Wolfgang, 33
Williamson, Jack H.,
  60–62
window designs, 99,
  100n3
wineglasses, 98–100,
  100n2
WIPO. *See* World
  Intellectual Property
  Organization
Wollheim, Richard, 166
Wong, Jeanyee, 31
wood ornamentals, 80f,
  83f
"The Word as Such," 137
world character sets,
  153, 159n19
World Intellectual
  Property
  Organization
  (WIPO), 63
Worldbackwards, 137
Worthington, Michael,
  68
writing. *See* handwriting
Wyss, Urbanus, 82, 83f

Young, Doyald, 180–182
Yud, 143

Zapf, Hermann, 30

Books from Allworth Press

Allworth Press is an imprint of Allworth Communications, Inc. Selected titles are listed below.

American Type Design and Designers
by David Conseugra (paperback, 9 × 11, 320 pages, $35.00)

Teaching Graphic Design
edited by Steven Heller, 6 × 9, 304 pages, $19.95)

The Education of a Graphic Designer
edited by Steven Heller (paperback, 6¾ × 9⅞, 288 pages, $18.95)

The Education of an Illustrator
edited by Steven Heller and Marshall Arisman (paperback, 6¾ × 9⅞, 288 pages, $19.95)

The Education of an E-Designer
edited by Steven Heller (paperback, 6¾ × 9⅞, 352 pages, $21.95)

The Education of a Design Entrepreneur
edited by Steven Heller (paperback, 6¾ × 9⅞, 288 pages, $21.95)

Graphic Design History
edited by Steven Heller and Georgette Balance (paperback, 6¾ × 9⅞, 352 pages, $21.95)

Texts on Type
edited by Steven Heller and Philip B. Meggs (paperback, 6¾ × 9⅞, 288 pages, $19.95)

Editing by Design, Third Edition
by Jan V. White (paperback, 8½ × 11, 256 pages, $29.95)

The Elements of Graphic Design: Space, Unity, Page Architecture, and Type
by Alexander White (paperback, 6⅛ × 9¼, 160 pages, $24.95)

Citizen Designer: Perspectives on Design Responsibility
edited by Steven Heller and Véronique Vienne (paperback, 6 × 9, 272 pages, $19.95)

Inside the Business of Graphic Design: 60 Leaders Share Their Secrets of Success
by Catharine Fishel (paperback, 6 × 9, 288 pages, $19.95)

Looking Closer 4: Critical Writings on Graphic Design
edited by Michael Bierut, William Drenttel, and Steven Heller (paperback, 6¾ × 9⅞, 304 pages, $21.95)